# CANNIBAL
# SERIAL KILLERS

# CANNIBAL SERIAL KILLERS

## PROFILES OF DEPRAVED FLESH-EATING MURDERERS

**CHRISTOPHER BERRY-DEE**

with Victoria Redstall

Ulysses Press

Published in the United States by
ULYSSES PRESS
P.O. Box 3440
Berkeley, CA 94703
www.ulyssespress.com

ISBN13: 978-1-56975-902-8
Library of Congress Catalog Number: 2011922514

Printed in the United States by Bang Printing

10 9 8 7 6 5 4 3 2 1

Acquisitions: Keith Riegert
Managing Editor: Claire Chun
Editor: Richard Harris
Editorial/Production: Lauren Harrison, Judith Metzener
Cover design: what!design @ whatweb.com
Front cover photos: man © pidjoe/istockphoto.com; blood drips © melhi/istockphoto.com; blood splatter © nicolecioe/istockphoto.com; texture and scratched texture © blackred/istockphoto.com
Back cover photos: Dahmer © Associated Press/Milwaukee County Sheriff's Dept.; Chikatilo © Associated Press; Kroll © Associated Press/Herbert Knosowski

Distributed by Publishers Group West

*This book is dedicated to the love of my life,*
*Victoria Redstall,*
*the only person whom I have ever been in love with...*
*You are in my heart forever.*

# Contents

# Acknowledgments

The acknowledgments are the only part of a writer's book that no editor dare interfere with since time began.

The acknowledgments are the place in a book where the writer—namely me—wishes to express his thanks to all those who have contributed, in whatever way, to the thinking behind the thought processes, the research, the months of candlelit labor, and the support that the writer enjoys before his book is published for his reader to enjoy.

So, this is my "quality time"…where do I go from here?

With some twenty-four books published and with my loyal readers expecting the unexpected, I am going off-the-wall this time around. Dispensing with all the usual professional platitudes for a book that concerns itself with people eating people, I am going to thank those who have in so many ways made this book possible, running back to my former co-writer, Robin Odell—undoubtedly the world's leading true-crime-historian-cum-true-crime-writer who mentored me in my early days as a writer, along with Joe Gaute.

To Fraser Ashford, the producer of the twelve-part TV series *Serial Killers*, I owe a great debt of bended-knee gratitude, for it was Fraser who enabled me to interview and get into the heads of many of the most heinous serial killers in U.S. criminal history.

Then my publishers: From the old days comes W. H. Allan (London), followed in hot pursuit by Virgin Books, then Smith Gryphon, then finally to John Blake (London) and his associates, Ulysses Press (Berkeley, California). Thank you, Keith Riegert, and all of your very efficient team, along with my editor, Richard Harris, who so patiently worked this book into shape.

TwoFour Productions (Plymouth, UK) and September Films (London), and also to countless media support for work contracted to me over the past decades, thank you. And thank you, Eamonn Holmes—I am quite happy to be called at a moment's notice to profile a serial killer on morning TV, if the price is right!

On a more personal note, it now falls upon me to thank my personal friends who have listened to Christopher as he worked this book out.

In the forefront of my mind are the guys and gals at Monks Bar, High Street, Old Portsmouth, UK. Neil (owner), Arthur, Andy Dervan (with his immaculate Jaguar), and Marek Hasse (a most excellent chef), and all of the clientele… Keith and Chris with "Timmy," who made my co-author, Victoria, so welcome last time around.

On this note, I end by saying—and this will no doubt please my publishers and readers alike—had I not met Victoria Redstall, I would not have been inspired to write another word.

Thank you Victoria, once again.

# Preface

*I have been asked, did I kill? Yes, too many times for any one person to do so! It is said I have partaken of human flesh. Think back in history: You will see that man hunted man (still do in some remote parts of the world.) Think about the animal we call pig or boar. Why does it say in some books we can't eat this animal? Because it tastes just like human flesh. I have eaten flesh of man or woman...So the next time any of you sit down to eat bacon, ham or a nice juicy pot roast or pork chop, think about the taste, the flavour of eating human flesh...*
—ARTHUR JOHN SHAWCROSS,
LETTER TO CHRISTOPHER BERRY-DEE

ON A BLEAK FRIDAY IN 1994, I sat down with Arthur Shaw-cross in a small cubicle at the Sullivan Correctional Facility in New York for the last of three interviews with undoubtedly one the state's most notorious serial killers and self-confessed cannibals. It had been a laborious task, though extremely worthwhile as he had finally confessed to me on camera the murder of a young boy called Jack Blake. Due to my relationship with this killer, the Rochester Police Department were also able to close the unsolved murder case of Kimberly Logan, a deaf mute Shawcross was suspected of killing in November 1989.

For hour upon hour, I had listened as "The Monster of the Rivers"—as the media had dubbed him—related some of the most horrific acts of cannibalism in modern times. From his self-perceived exploits as a "war hero" in Vietnam, where he said he ate the body parts of young VC females (none of which is true), to the "hacking out and consuming of a woman's vagina" (which is true) in Rochester, New York, the overweight braggart that was Arthur Shawcross constantly licked his lips, as if still savoring the sweet taste of human flesh.

Throughout my last interview with Arthur, his hands fidgeted nervously. His watery, porcine eyes darted around as if someone might steal the prison lunch from in front of him.

With 250 years on his slate, "Art" was not going anywhere. Clearly still relishing his ill-gained notoriety, however, he was writing *The Cannibal's Cookbook* to be sold over the Internet. I was relieved when my TV interviews with him were finished. I would never see him again.

On November 7, 2008, Shawcross complained about a pain in his leg. He was denied the use of a wheelchair because medical staff and the duty sergeant thought that "Art" was malingering. He wasn't, for on Monday,

November 10, he was taken to the Albany Medical Center, where he had a heart attack. He died at 9:50 p.m. His body was cremated and his ashes are in the care of his daughter.

It was not until my attention was brought to one Armin Meiwes, a German cannibal who met his "willing" victim through a cannibal cult, that I gave the subject of people eating people more thought.

Meiwes took his victim back to his Rotenberg farmhouse, where he cut off his penis, which both men tried to eat while sipping claret. As his victim bled out, Meiwes videotaped the entire episode from start to finish. Then he read a *Star Trek* book before stabbing the man to death. Meiwes was said to have eaten around nine pounds of his victim when he was arrested in December 2002. He was originally convicted of manslaughter, claiming that the victim had asked to be killed and eaten, but this verdict was overturned and he was found guilty of murder after a retrial.

Nevertheless, I soon learned that there are hundreds of web sites dedicated to *anthropophagi*—literally, the consumption of humans. After burning a little more midnight oil, I learned that humanity has been eating itself—boiled, fried, sautéed, grilled, griddled, skewered on a barbecue, microwaved, stewed, braised, and roasted—since time immemorial.

# Introduction

*I believe that when man evolves a civilisation*
*higher than the mechanized but still primitive*
*one he has now, the eating of human flesh will be*
*sanctioned. For then man will have thrown off*
*all of his superstitions and irrational taboos.*
—Diego Rivera

According to archaeological evidence, at least some of our ancestors have been enjoying human meat since we lived in caves. Some anthropologists suggest that cannibalism was common in human societies before the Upper Paleolithic period, from 40,000 to 10,000 years ago. This theory, supported by paleoanthropologist Tim D. White of the University of California—Berkeley, is based on the large quantity of "butchered human bones" found in Neanderthal and other Lower and Middle Paleolithic societies. According to one historical account, Aboriginal tribes of Australia were most certainly cannibals, never failing to eat enemies killed in fights and always eating men noted for their fighting ability who died of natural causes "out of pity and consideration for the body."

It appears from the Old Stone Age fossil record and several randomly scattered cave paintings that from about three million years BC until 18,000 BC, the patriarch was the provider of much needed protein. He maintained the upper hand by keeping his woman in a manner to which she seemed ideally suited—in a cave. The man would venture out, armed with a big, sharp stick and a bag of flint tools to bring home the provisions. In his role as hunter, he enjoyed unquestioning loyalty, verging on hero worship at home. Arriving back at his cave, lathered in sweat after a strenuous day's efforts to beat the daylights out of a woolly mammoth, he could do no wrong in his woman's eyes. After she had cooked the meal, her lord and master would eat first and throw her and the kids the scraps, for which they would be suitably grateful. When four-legged creatures were off the menu, Dad expediently solved the food shortage by killing a neighbor, whom the family would eat instead.

For the readers of this book with a religious bent, it may come as a shock to learn that 2 Kings 6:25–30 refers to two mothers who decided to eat their own children; as reported in the Bible, during the siege of Samaria, these two unnamed women made a pact, an agreement which one of them honored while the other balked and did not.

Leaving Samaria aside, we may consider the second century Roman Siege of Numantia, when things got really out of hand and starvation reduced many to cannibalism. And, if we were to examine cannibalism on a large scale, one need look no further than a report scribed by Flavius Josephus, a man of some learning around Rome in 70 AD who went on the record as stating that young, human flesh was dished up by the platter full at many a Roman feast.

Living close to a large body of water does not always guarantee bountiful harvests either. Between BC 1073 and 1064, the Nile in Egypt failed to flood. The inevitable result was no irrigation, failed crops, and dying livestock. Sometime during this famine the locals started eyeing each other with dinner in mind.

In a case of "waste not, want not," Egyptian quacks came up with a bogus heal-all when they started pillaging tombs containing thousands of mummies. These they ground up and sold as medicine in what developed into a wide-scale enterprise that flourished until the late sixteenth century. The bubble burst when it was revealed that the mummies were, in fact, recently killed slaves.

Historically famous for alternative medicine, sixteenth century Chinese pharmacopoeia refers to the self-healing properties of "mellified man," otherwise known as "human mummy confection," a panacea used by the Arabians. Allegedly, elderly men approaching their sell-by date would start eating a diet consisting only of honey. The health and nutritional benefits of eating honey have been known since time immemorial as being beneficial to those suffering from anemia, asthma, baldness, fatigue and exhaustion, infertility, insect bites, paralysis, and osteoporosis. However, the honey-only diet in fact killed many of the men, who died after suffering honey's laxative properties, which caused extreme weight loss. When the person eventually expired, their honey-laden body was placed in a stone coffin and filled with honey, and it would marinade for 100 years or so. Then an enterprising medicine man came up with an idea in much the same vein the Egyptians': Why not grind up the remains, process the corpses, and sell the solution as a cure-all? It proved to be a highly lucrative venture—a honey of an idea—while it lasted.

In the fourth century, according to Moira Martingale in her book *Cannibal Killers* (London Robert Hales, 1993), week after week "hundreds, probably thousands, of guests banqueting at the court of Shi Hu, who ruled the Huns of northern China between 334 and 329 AD, savoured the delicacy of young slave girls, killed and cooked to excite their palates."

For millennia we have been eating each other during food shortages and in the name of religion, sex, and war—even consuming our deceased next of kin and captured enemies so that they may become part of us eternally.

At least until the mid-nineteenth century, indigenous groups in the Caribbean and parts of South America practiced cannibalism. Slave women were impregnated in order that their captors could eat their babies. Sometimes, still-conscious victims had their limbs removed and were made to watch while the appendages were cooked and eaten—at least according to European missionaries keen to depict the Indians as heathens and barbarians.

Thirteenth-century explorer Marco Polo and other European and Arabic traders who journeyed through Asia reported that Tibetan monks would eat condemned criminals after their executions. Apparently, however, none of the Westerners witnessed such rituals firsthand, and Polo and his publisher were not above embellishing the truth in his journal. Polo also reported that the Tibetans had tails.

*They brought the severed heads in first, on golden platters. Frozen in death, the faces of the young slave girls were still fresh and beautiful, the almond eyes lifeless. The men's mouths watered to think how sweet and tender their flesh would be when, in just a few minutes, it was served to them, the honored guests.*
—MOIRA MARTINGALE,
*CANNIBAL KILLERS*

In Africa, slaves were fattened and sold like cattle before being eaten. People-eating tribes could be instantly recognized by their teeth, which were filed to sharp points. There is suspicion that cannibalism still goes on in the Congo, Uganda, and Kenya today. In the 1960s, Emperor Jean-Bédel Bokassa of the Central African Republic was said to celebrate successful massacres by dining on the victims' children, while in the 1970s, tyrannical President Idi Amin of Uganda was rumored to eat the remains of his political enemies, though neither man was actually found guilty of these specific crimes.

Cannibalism continued into the nineteenth century in some isolated South Pacific cultures; in a few cases in insular Melanesia, indigenous flesh markets are claimed to still exist. In Fiji, human flesh was craved in preference to animal meat. Indeed, so highly prized it was that it even had a name—*puaka balava*, meaning "long pig."

Until about fifty years ago, Japanese soldiers captured in Papua New Guinea during World War II were eaten by the native people, and one modern-day anthropologist reports being told by the Korowai, one of the very few tribes still believed to eat human flesh as a cultural practice, that Japanese flesh is the tastiest of all. Another New Guinea tribe, the Fore, resorted to mortuary cannibalism, a practice that was abandoned upon learning that eating corpses caused a fatal neurodegenerative disease.

Humans have also dined on shipmates cast adrift in hostile seas under a baking sun, and victims of air crashes, to stay alive.

An early example of marine cannibalism may be found in accounts of the sinking of the *Luxborough Galley* in 1727. The trading vessel had delivered a cargo of African slaves to Spanish colonies in Latin America, when on the return trip its stores of rum caught fire and destroyed the galley. Twenty-two crewmembers escaped on an overcrowded longboat. During two weeks in the mid-Atlantic near the Bahamas, the crew drew straws to decide who should be killed and eaten first. Fortunately, murder became unnecessary when men started dying of natural causes before the need for meat became acute. The passengers first tried using pieces of human flesh as bait but could not lure either fish or birds, so at last they resorted to cannibalism.

Twelve of the men were alive when they were rescued by fishermen, but only five lived to reach port.

In 1816, surviving crew of the French ship *Medusa* resorted to cannibalism in the life raft after the ship sank sixty miles off the coast of Africa; their horrific ordeal was immortalized by artist Theodore Gericault in his painting *Raft of the Medusa*.

When British Captain Sir John Franklin made his fourth expedition attempting to transverse the Northwest Passage along the north coast of Canada in 1845, of the 129 souls who embarked, none survived. They got lost in the frozen wastes of the Arctic and were never seen again. The 1997 discovery of cut marks on human bones found on King William Island prove that the tastier parts from several of these unfortunates ended up in the stomachs of their starving compatriots. The full story of the doomed expedition remains a mystery. Captain Franklin's commemorative statue in his hometown of Spilsby, UK, bears the legend "Discoverer of the North West Passage," though no one would actually succeed in navigating the passage until 1906.

In 1884, Captain Thomas Dudley and Edwin Stephens found themselves in an awful fix when their yacht, the *Mignonette*, was shipwrecked after a storm some 1,600 miles from the Cape of Good Hope. In a boat provisioned with only two tins of turnips to sustain them, they soon cast their eyes upon Richard Parker, a seventeen-year-old cabin boy. The poor lad was ill after drinking seawater, so

Dudley killed him, and the crew shared the body among themselves. Four days later, when finally rescued, Dudley put his hands up and admitted the killing. They were all sentenced to death, but this was later commuted to six months' imprisonment.

During World War I, the U.S. merchant ship *Dumaru* was carrying a cargo of military explosives when it was struck by lightning and sank in the South Pacific. Adrift for three weeks before reaching safety in the Philippines, the surviving crew resorted to eating their shipmates who had died of exposure; their story was told by legendary journalist Lowell Thomas in his book *The Wreck of the Dumaru* (Doubleday, 1930).

The most famous incident of cannibalism involving an air disaster is the October 13, 1972, crash of Uruguayan Air Force Flight 571, carrying team members and relatives of a rugby team from Stella Maris College in Montevideo. The plane crashed on a snowpacked slope at 11,800 feet altitude in the Andes in subzero temperatures. Some of the survivors ate the bodies of deceased passengers. Of the forty-five passengers and crew on board, sixteen managed to stay alive until rescue operations commenced more than two months later. The story of the survivors was chronicled in Pier Paul Read's 1974 book *Alive: The Story of the Andes Survivors*; in a 1993 film adaptation of the book, called simply *Alive*; and in a 2008 TV documentary with the somewhat unimaginative title *Stranded: I've Come from a Plane That Crashed on the Mountains*.

As late as November 2008, a group of illegal immigrants from the Dominican Republic who were en route to Puerto Rico resorted to cannibalism when they became lost at sea for some fifteen days before being rescued by a U.S. Coast Guard patrol boat. The ignominious maritime tradition lives on.

In the United States, a group of settlers known as the Donner–Reed Party resorted to cannibalism while snowbound in the mountains over the winter of 1846–47. German-born Lewis Keseberg was with his wife and two children among a band of California-bound settlers led by an ambitious George Donner. While in the Sierra Nevada mountains near present-day Truckee, California, appalling weather conditions overwhelmed them, and the party of eighty-five men, women, and children set about building ponderosa pine lean-tos and log cabins, one for each family, in which to wait out the winter. At first, they were obliged to slaughter their animals; later they started fighting over any remaining scraps of meat. What became of George Donner is unknown, but I bet he took a ribbing whenever he went into a restaurant. At any rate, his acts of cannibalism got his name his name on the map: the Donner Pass.

While there are unconfirmed tales of earlier cannibal episodes among the Donner–Reed Party, the first confirmed incident took place between the arrivals of the second and third rescue parties in late February. In her book *Cannibal Killers*, Moira Martingale relates that the murders allegedly began when "Keseberg took a small boy to bed with him one night and presented his body to the others in the morning for butchering." Whether the boy was eaten or not is unknown; however, most of the settlers were convinced that the kid had been murdered.

Some of the travelers, including the Donners and Keseberg, were left behind after small search parties rescued the first forty-five. When the third rescue party arrived to take the Donners to safety, only a well-fed Keseberg remained alive. Close by was a simmering pot containing the liver and lungs of a human being—Mrs. Donner, to be precise! Although charged with murder, at his trial Keseberg

> She was the best I ever tasted.
>
> —LEWIS KESEBERG,
> ON EATING TAMSEN DONNER

claimed that he had resorted to cannibalism to stay alive. He was acquitted by the court for lack of evidence, where-upon he brought a civil slander lawsuit against several members of the rescue party for falsely accusing him of murder. He was eventually awarded damages of one dollar. Within a few years he was running a steakhouse.

In 1873, prospector Alferd Packer was guiding a party of five other gold-seekers from Salt Lake City into the San Juan Mountains of southwestern Colorado. Despite local Indians' warnings that fierce winter weather was on the way, the lure of gold nuggets was powerful, and Packer had no intention of letting his companions down. The party set off into the snowbound mountains in the first week of February 1874. Nevertheless, not only did he seriously let them down—he ate them, too.

On April 16, Packer arrived back in town alone. "The others abandoned me," he complained while taking a large slug of whiskey in a saloon. The other drinkers eyed Packer with suspicion. Some of the prospectors who knew the man commented that he looked fatter and healthier than when he'd left for the snowy trail. They were also puzzled as to why his packhorse was laden with money, guns, and knives that had once belonged to the missing men.

> *Stand up, Alfred Packer, you voracious, man-eating sonofabitch! There were only seven Democrats in Hinsdale County, and you ate five of them!*
>
> —JUDGE MELVILLE GERRY, PASSING SENTENCE AT ALFRED PACKER'S TRIAL

When a local Indian eventually found the bodies, four of the skulls had been crushed, apparently while the men slept. A fifth man had been shot. Four had been stripped of flesh and the other partially so.

Packer signed a confession but then escaped from jail and lived under an alias for nine years in Wyoming. When finally caught, he was charged with manslaughter and sentenced to forty years' hard labor. He was paroled after seventeen years. Legend has it that in his last years he became a vegetarian. Although Packer died at age sixty-five in obscurity and poverty, every Colorado student learns his story from state history textbooks, and he has been immortalized in dozens of songs, including C. W. McCall's "Comin' Back for More," and motion pictures such as *South Park* creator Trey Parker's movie *Cannibal! The Musical.* In 1968, the student body of the University of Colorado at Boulder officially voted to call the student union cafeteria the Alferd Packer Memorial Grill, a name that still sticks to this day. The cafeteria's slogan is "Have a Friend for Lunch."

Mountain man John Johnson, a trapper who lived in the mountains of Montana in the 1880s was a man of deep introspection who minded his own business. He was married to an Indian wife, with whom he had a child. Crow Indians killed Mrs. Johnson and her toddler while John was out in "them thar woods," and he set out for revenge.

Whenever he came across a Crow camp, he would single-handedly attack it, kill everyone he could lay his hands on, butcher their corpses, and, for some inexplicable reason, eat only their livers. He waged a one-man war with the tribe for almost twelve years. Thus he became known as "Liver-Eating Johnson," and far from being ostracized for this horrid practice, he later became a sheriff in Coulson, Montana, maintaining law and order for several years before vanishing into the mountains again. His exploits inspired the motion picture *Jeremiah Johnson*, in which he was portrayed by Robert Redford.

We have been eating each other for just about every reason a hungry psychologist or four-star chef might invent. In the following pages, I am going to take you for a tour of that dramatic theater of well-seasoned cannibalism. You may never salivate at a tasty pork chop again.

Christopher Berry-Dee
Former director of the Criminology Research
Institute UK
Editor of *The New Criminologist*

# CHAPTER 1

# A Brief History of Cannibalism— Fact and Fiction

*"For what we are about to receive, Oh Lord 'tis Thee we thank," said the cannibal as he cut off the missionary's shank.*
—E. Y. Harburg

THE WORD *CANNIBALISM* is derived from the Spanish term *caníbales,* for the West Indian Carib tribe of Native Americans who, according to explorer Christopher Columbus, supplemented their fruit and fish diet with human flesh. The Caribbean Sea is named after the Carib, who probably originated in the valley of the Orinoco River in Venezuela and are said to have swept through the islands of the Caribbean with brutal ferocity.

During the late fifteenth century, the Carib inhabited most of the islands of the Lesser Antilles and the coast of what is now Venezuela, territories from which they had expelled the more placid Arawak people. Carib men valued exploits in combat above all else. They were not organized into a hierarchical structure under a chief but fought as individual war parties and raided other tribes. It is also said that male captives were tortured and eaten, while female captives became slave-wives. Many a white Christian missionary sought to civilize the natives away from such practices for years afterward.

This missionary work was a dangerous undertaking, too. After months of hacking their way through the steamy jungle, paddling around in mosquito-infested swamps and navigating rivers alive with such nasty critters as crocodiles and piranha, armed with nothing more than a walking stick and a Bible, the priests' vocation often invited a barbarous death. It was a risky business.

But this is not perhaps the complete picture, as we will soon see. For the better part of five hundred years we may have been doing the Carib people a great disservice.

History informs us that one autumnal morning in 1492, Christopher Columbus stood on a beach on Hispaniola, trying to converse with local Taino inhabitants, listening as his almost-naked hosts informed him that the small islands to the southeast, today's Lesser Antilles, were occupied by Caniba, or Canima. According to the Taino, these Caniba were warlike eaters of human flesh who periodically raided the peaceful folk of the larger islands. According to local Taino mythology, the Caribs were associated with the underworld.

Captain Columbus recorded other hearsay about the Caniba. Despite never actually seeing one of these cannibals, on Thursday, November 4, 1492, in Cuba, he penned in his log that, "Caniba have but one eye and the faces of dogs." The subsequent colonization of the West Indies

*These people are very unskilled in arms...with 50 men they could all be subjected and made to do all that one wished.*

*—Christopher Columbus*

revealed that the islands were populated by nothing more fantastic than two-legged, two-eyed, non-tailed Native Americans

Reviewing early documents related to the island Caribs, anthropologist Robert Myers found a pattern of low-scale raiding and slave-taking throughout the Windward Islands, but there was no reliable evidence to support their reputation as cannibals. Nevertheless, for purely financial reasons, the reports of the ferocious Caniba continued to influence Spanish policy for years to come. Stories of Carib ferocity, it seems, helped to resolve a conflict between the clergy's desire to save souls and the Spanish colonists' need for slave labor.

In 1511, an edict defined Caribs as any "Indians who were hostile to Europeans, behaved violently, or consumed human flesh." Caribs, the edict most conveniently concluded, were without souls, therefore entirely suitable subjects for the slave trade.

Who were the inhabitants of the Lesser Antilles, the so-called Island Caribs? If anyone should know the answer, it would be Father Raymond Breton, a French missionary who spent years among these natives during the second quarter of the seventeenth century.

Born at Baune in 1609, Breton entered the Order of St. Dominic at the age of seventeen. In 1627, he was to be seen briskly marching up the steps of the famous priory of St. Jacques in Paris to finish his classical education in philosophy and theology.

After earning his degree, the slightly built, overtly pious Breton sailed with three other Dominicans for the French West Indies, where the party stepped ashore in 1635. He would spend nearly twenty years devoting himself to the Antilles missions, and during twelve of these he was on the Island of San Domingo, living practically alone with the Indians. Yet no one touched a hair on his almost-bald head.

The remaining eight years Breton spent visiting scores of islands, teaching and evangelizing the natives in their own tongue, becoming adept in the various Carib languages. Thus, Breton would later report with dogmatic authority that the Island Caribs, who called themselves the Kalinago, had separate men's and women's languages. He added that this dual-language system was the result of an invasion of the Lesser Antilles by Carib-speaking men from South America who took possession of the islands through raids upon their Arawak-speaking inhabitants. The Caribs, he suggested, enslaved or killed the men and married the women, and the men's language was supposedly derived from the Carib spoken by the invaders.

Efforts to identify archaeological remains reflecting the presumed Carib invasion of the Lesser Antilles have proved unsuccessful. In the 1960s, archaeologist Ripley Bullen of the University of Florida proposed a link between the Carib invasion and Suazey pottery, which appeared on islands from Martinique southward around AD 1100. Bullen's theory has been disputed by other investigators. Louis Allaire of the University of Alberta and Dutch archaeologist Arie Boomert both found similarities between ceramics in the Lesser Antilles and Guyana, but the documentation remains incomplete.

The tale reported by Breton is not without problems, and the answer to the Island Caribs' origins may lie in a different understanding of the historical and linguistic evidence. As Berend Hoff, of the University of Leiden, and the late Douglas Taylor showed, the Island Carib men's language is in fact a pidgin—a tongue lacking a full lexicon and possessing a highly simplified grammar. If their language was like most other pidgins, it more likely reflects peaceful interaction between South American Caribs and Arawaks living in the Lesser Antilles. This interpretation suggests that the Island Caribs were in fact of Arawak descent and not the successors of male invaders from the mainland. And, whatever the true extent of cannibalism among these peoples, it clearly has been exaggerated.

Notwithstanding the infamy of the Island Caribs, Breton apparently never observed a single instance of cannibalism. In the broader context of Arawak peoples in the West Indies, the Island Caribs may have been black sheep by reputation, but they were part of the same flock.

From this evidence, it is now known that cannibalism has frequently been used as a means to demonize others. For example, medieval Christian culture frequently depicted Jews as having a taste for the blood of Christian babies.

But while anthropologists approach stories of cannibalism with skepticism, there does appear to be substantiated examples of both ritualistic and survival cannibalism throughout history.

The Aztecs of Mexico are believed to have practiced cannibalism on a large scale as part of the ritual religious sacrifice of war captives and other victims. The practice is known as exocannibalism—the eating of strangers or enemies. On this primitive level, ritually eating part of the slaughtered enemy is a way of assuming the life-spirit of the departed. In a funeral ritual, this may also be done with a respected member of one's own clan, ensuring immortality. In point of fact, the Aztecs worshiped so many bloodthirsty deities that barely a week went by without some helpless infant, young man or woman, or captured prisoner being sacrificed by the priests. For the sun or moon god to bring fertility to the Aztec crops necessitated the removal of a live victim's heart, whereupon it was held aloft, still beating. The victim was then distributed to the crowd and, with heavy symbolism and seriousness rather than greed, it was cut up and eaten.

The dense population of Marquesas Islands, Polynesia, was concentrated in the narrow valleys. Warring tribes sometimes practiced cannibalism on their enemies. Historian W. D. Rubenstein writes:

> It was considered a great triumph among the Marquesan Typees (Taipi) to eat the body of a dead man. They treated their captives with great cruelty. They broke their legs to prevent them from attempting escape before being eaten, but they kept them alive so that they could brood over their impending fate...With this tribe, as with many others, the bodies of the young women were in great demand...

Other accounts tell us that all South Sea Islanders were cannibals so far as their enemies were concerned, and as every tribe was an enemy to the next, it provided for a very unstable arrangement indeed.

When the whale ship *Essex* out of Nantucket was rammed and sunk by an irate whale in 1820, the captain opted to take a small boat, into which he crammed the survivors, and sail 3,000 miles *upwind* to Chile rather than 1,400 miles *downwind* to the Marquesas because he had heard that the locals might eat him. Ironically, many of the survivors of the wrecked *Essex* resorted to cannibalism to survive.

If anyone is an authority on whales ramming ships, it is the American writer of *Moby Dick*, Herman Melville. But have we been given the Marquesan Typees bad press? Herman Melville lived happily among this most vicious of the island group's cannibal tribes, yet like Father Breton before him, not a hair on his head was touched, and his genitals remained intact throughout his stay. In his semi-autobiographical novel *Typee*, however, he reports seeing shrunken heads and having strong evidence that tribal leaders ceremonially consumed the bodies of killed warriors of a neighboring tribe after a skirmish.

Something that early travel brochures didn't enlighten us on was that in parts of Melanesia, cannibalism was still practiced in the early twentieth century for a variety of reasons, including retaliation, insulting enemies, or absorbing the dead person's qualities. One obviously overweight tribal chief, Ratu Udre Udre of Rakiraki, Fiji, is said to have consumed 872 people. To record his achievement, he constructed a pile of 872 stones. Quite understandably, news of this cannibalistic lifestyle soon filtered down to European sailors, who made every attempt to avoid going near Fijian waters, giving Fiji the name "Cannibal Isles."

It seemed that never a year went by without a traveler returning from some remote corner of the world relating a story of cannibalism; amongst them was Friar Diego de Landa, who had witnessed such acts in the Yucatán. The Purchas, from Popayan, Colombia, were apparently fond of human flesh, too. The Inuit people of Greenland killed a witch and ate a portion of her heart, reported Norwegian missionary Hans Egede.

Perhaps one of the most gruesome rituals came out of the captaincy of Sergipe, Brazil. There, the natives ate human flesh when available; perhaps more stomach-churning was the practice that if a pregnant woman miscarried, they would devour the abortive immediately.

Returning from Lake Mantumba, Congo Free State, on August 3, 1903, Roger Casement wrote to a government official called Cowper, in Lisbon, claiming that just about everyone he came across practiced cannibalism. And, with a flourish of his quill, he added that he had never seen such a "weird lot," and reported there were also dwarfs, called Batwas, living in the forest and that they ate human flesh, too.

However, the dwarfs, it seems, didn't have it all their own way. When times were hard, the larger cannibals would hunt one for their own tribal pot. "These are not fairy tales my dear Cowper," Casement reported, "but actual gruesome reality in the heart of this poor, benighted, savage land." Whether or not Mr. Cowper enjoyed his dinner that evening is not recorded in his otherwise comprehensive diary!

Legends have filtered down throughout the years concerning a strange, frightening creature named Wendigo. Generations of hunters and campers in the shadowy forests of the upper regions of Minnesota have reported encountering this monster. It is believed that the creature could only be seen if a man were very close to it because it was so finely constructed that it could only be identified via its profile. This spirit is known for its voracious appetite for human flesh; when many local villagers disappeared over the years, the Wendigo was held responsible.

The Native American Indians had their fair share of experiences with this mysterious beast, too. Different Algonquian groups across the northern United States and Canadian tribes called the creature by various names, including "Wendigo," "Witigo," "Witiko," and "Wee-Tee-Go." All translate to mean "the evil spirit that devours mankind." A German explorer translated *Wendigo* to mean "cannibal" among the tribes along the Great Lakes.

The accepted Native American vision of this being is that of a gargantuan spirit, more than fifteen feet tall. It had once been human but had slipped into the realms of the supernatural by magic. Though there are partially conflicting descriptions of these werewolflike creatures' appearance, the Wendigo is generally acknowledged as possessing a pair of huge, glowing eyes, vicious fangs, and an obscenely long tongue. Most have sallow, jaundiced skin, but others are said to be "matted with hair." They tower over men and are driven by an insatiable hunger.

The Wendigo was sometimes blamed for cannibalistic acts actually perpetrated by man, often as a means of survival—a most convenient scapegoat to deflect revulsion for man's desire to cannibalize his fellow man. A man accused of eating the flesh of another human being was said to have developed his terrible taste after being "touched by Wendigo."

In 1879, a Cree Indian named Katist-chen, or Swift Runner, claimed to have been visited by the Wendigo when he murdered and ate his mother, wife, brother, and six children during a hunting expedition. He had earlier said the family had starved to death, but neither that story nor the Wendigo defense worked, and he was found guilty of their murders. Later he confessed to a priest about the Wendigo, saying that the spirit had visited him in his cell and tortured him to make him confess. Only this way, Swift Runner said, could he banish the spirit. He was hanged, earning himself a notable place in history as the first man executed by the Royal Canadian Mounted Police.

Hindu mythology described evil demons called *asura* or *rakshasa* that dwell in the forests and practice extreme violence including devouring their own kind, and possess many evil supernatural powers. They are Hindu equivalents of "demons."

Meanwhile, Australian Aboriginals are believed to have taken part in what is seen as a more benevolent form of cannibalism—endocannibalism, the consumption of friends and relatives. The body of a dead person was ritually eaten by his relatives as a means of allowing his spirit to live on.

History also provides ample examples of cannibalism during famines and other periods of severe shortages.

In most countries, including the United States, the consumption of human flesh is not itself a crime. Instead, perpetrators are usually prosecuted for murder or, if the victim is already dead, for abuse of a corpse. Courts have recognized necessity as a defense in cases of corpse abuse but not murder.

On the mythological level, the cannibal mother is magnified to a universal principal, as in the case of the Hindu goddess Kali, "The Black One." The opening of Hell, the Zoroastrian contribution to Western mythology, is a mouth. According to Catholic dogma, bread and wine are transubstantiated into Jesus Christ's real blood and flesh, which is then distributed by the priest to the faithful.

During the Muslin-Qurays wars in the early eighth century, when the prophet Mohammad battled the established rulers of Mecca, cases of cannibalism were recorded. Following at the Battle of Uhud, in 625, it is said that after the killing of Hamzah ibn Abdu al-Muttalib, his liver was consumed by Hind bint 'Utbah, the wife of a commander of the Qurays army.

Reports of cannibalism were also recorded during the First Crusade, as crusaders fed on the bodies of their dead opponents following the Siege of Ma'arrat al-Numan.

Many instances of cannibalism by necessity were recorded during World War II. During the 872-day Siege of Leningrad, reports of cannibalism began to appear in the winter of 1941–42, after all birds, rats, and pets had been eaten by survivors. Some German soldiers trapped in the besieged city, cut off from supplies, also resorted to cannibalism.

In February 1943, roughly 100,000 German prisoners of war were sent to camps in Siberia or Central Asia. Chronically underfed by their Soviet captors, many resorted to cannibalism. Fewer than 5,000 of these prisoners survived captivity.

Transcripts of the Nuremberg Trials reveal that victims of the Holocaust reverted to cannibalism. As transports arrived daily in Dachau from Struthof, Belsen, Auschwitz, Mauthausen, and other camps, according to one eyewitness, "Many of these took ten to fourteen days on the way without water or food, and on one transport, which arrived in November 1942, I found evidence of cannibalism. The living persons had eaten the flesh from the dead bodies."

The Australian War Crimes Section of the Tokyo Tribunal, led by prosecutor William Webb, the future Judge-in-Chief, collected written reports and testimonies that documented Japanese soldiers' acts of cannibalism among their own troops, on enemy dead, and on Allied prisoners of war in parts of the Greater East Asia Co-Prosperity Sphere.

In some cases, flesh was cut from living people. An Indian POW, Lance Naik Hatam Ali, testified that in New Guinea:

> The Japanese started selecting prisoners and every day a prisoner was taken out and killed and eaten by the soldiers. I personally saw this happen and about 100 prisoners were eaten at this place by the Japanese. The remainder of us were taken to another spot 50 miles away where 10 prisoners died of sickness. At this place, the Japanese again started selecting prisoners to eat. Those selected were taken to a hut

where their flesh was cut from their bodies while they were alive and they were thrown into a ditch where they later died.

In another well-documented case, in Chichijima in February 1945, Japanese soldiers killed and consumed five American airmen. This case was investigated in 1947 in a war crimes trial. Of the thirty Japanese soldiers prosecuted, five—Major Matoba, General Tachibana, Admiral Mori, Captain Yoshi, and Dr. Teraki—were found guilty and hanged.

Cannibalism was reported by journalist Neil Davis during the South East Asian wars of the 1960s and '70s. Davis reported that Cambodian troops ritually ate portions of the slain enemy, typically the liver—the same giblet preferred by Lewis Keseberg and "Liver-Eating John" Johnson. However, he also noted that when villages were under Khmer Rouge control, and food was strictly rationed, any civilian caught participating in cannibalism was immediately executed.

Cannibalism has been documented in several more recent African conflicts, including the Second Congo War and the civil wars in Liberia and Sierra Leone. A U.N. human rights expert reported in July 2007 that sexual atrocities against Congolese women go "far beyond rape, and include sexual slavery, forced incest, and cannibalism." It was also reported that witch doctors sometimes used the body parts of children in their medicine.

In January 2008, Joshua Blahyi, a notorious thirty-seven-year-old Liberian ex-rebel and reformed warlord, confessed to participating in human sacrifices, which included killing an innocent child and plucking out its heart, dividing it into pieces for others to eat. Blahyi's cannibalism occurred during the insurgency against Liberian president Charles Taylor. Incidentally, during the same Charles Taylor's war crimes trial on March 13, 2008, Joseph Marzah, Taylor's chief of operations and head of Taylor's death squad, accused Taylor of ordering his soldiers to commit acts of cannibalism against enemies, including peacekeepers and United Nations personnel.

In West Africa, the Leopard Society, a secret society active in the mid-1990s, practiced cannibalism. Centered in Sierra Leone, Nigeria, and Cote d'Ivoire, the leopard men would dress in leopard skins and waylay travelers with sharp weapons shaped like claws and teeth. The victims' flesh would be cut from their bodies and distributed to members of the society.

Twenty-five—and still counting—albino Tanzanians have been murdered since March 2007, reportedly through witch-doctor butchery based on prevailing superstition. In 2008, Tanzania's President Kikwete publicly condemned witch doctors for killing people with albinism for their body parts, which were thought to bring good luck to the living (and a lot of bad luck to the donor).

On September 14, 2007, a man named Ozgur Denzig was captured in Ankara, the Turkish capital, after killing and eating his friend Er. After cutting slices from his victim's body, Denzig distributed the rest to stray dogs on the street. He ate some of the man's flesh raw on his way home. Denzig, who lived with his parents, arrived at the family house and placed the remaining parts of Er's body in the refrigerator without saying a word to his mother and father.

The Aghoris of northern India, a splinter sect of Hinduism, practice cannibalism in pursuit of immortality and supernatural powers by consuming the flesh of the dead floating in the Ganges River. Members of the Aghori drink from human skulls and practice cannibalism in the belief that eating human flesh confers spiritual and physical benefits such as the prevention of aging.

What does human flesh taste like? Reporter William Buehler Seabrook, allegedly in the interests of "research," obtained from a hospital intern at the Sorbonne a chunk of human meat from the body of a healthy human killed in an accident. He cooked and ate it.

Reporting the repast, he said:

> It was like good, fully developed veal, not young, but not yet beef. It was very definitely like that, and it was not like any other meat I have ever tasted. It was so nearly like good, fully developed veal that I think no person with a palate or ordinary, normal sensitiveness could distinguish from veal. It was mild, good meat with no other sharply defined or highly characteristic taste such as, for instance, goat, high game, and pork have. The steak was slightly tougher than prime veal, a little stringy, but not too tough or stringy to be agreeably edible. The roast, from which I cut a central

slice, was tender, and in color, texture, smell as well as taste, strengthened my certainty that of all the meats we habitually know, veal is the one meat to which this meat is accurately comparable.

It's almost enough to make one's mouth water. Regrettably, the veal recipes I wanted to include in this book have been removed on the urgent insistence of my publisher.

In 2002, while making a television documentary in Russia, I visited the women's prison at Sablino, about 40 miles south of Saint Petersburg. The head cook, a convicted cannibal, had murdered her abusive husband, chopped his body up in the snow and given parcels of his flesh to her unsuspecting neighbors as a Christmas treat. She has since been released.

As recently as March 23, 2009, in Irkutsk, Siberia, a female cannibal was arrested for killing a woman before cooking and eating her in front of her son, age seven. Apparently, it all started with a neighborly spat, after which Olesya Mostovschikova picked up an axe and chopped thirty-two-year-old Tatiana Romanchuk to death. She admitted to carving off parts of the victim's body and cooking them in an oven before serving dinner.

In her testimony to police, Mostovschikova calmly confessed, "I took the axe and hit her a number of times on her head. Then I cut off her ears, gouged out one eye, cut off an arm, and a hand. I took the hand, arm and eye and cooked these body parts in the oven."

Mostovschikova and another friend known only as "Julia" hid Tatiana's body in the victim's home. Incredibly, they soon returned for seconds. "Some time later, I went down to the cellar again because Julia said that was hungry," Mostovschikova claimed, adding, "We sliced off some more meat and took it upstairs to the kitchen. We fried it on the cooker and ate it." These cuts were a buttock, a breast, and a cheek.

Julia told police that she felt compelled to ask for the meat because Mostovschikova had threatened to kill and eat her too. A day later, Mostovschikova sliced up the victim's body again, putting her legs in a trash can close to her house and burying other remains in her garden.

Senior criminal investigator Vadim Shestakov said, "Locals called the police saying they saw human legs in a rubbish bin. We sent officers to the scene, and they confirmed it. We immediately checked the nearest streets, calling at fifty houses in the neighborhood. In Mostovschikova's house we found marks in the floor that looked like blood. Soon we found parts of the body in the garden."

Indeed, Mostovschikova's was not the first female Russian cannibal case in the previous six months—it was the third. In January 2009, in St. Petersburg, sixteen-year-old Karina Barduchyan was killed and eaten by twenty-one-year-old butcher Maxim Golovatskikh and his florist friend Yury, and back in September 2008, in Yaroslavl, Satanists killed and ate fifteen-year-old Olga Pukhova and sixteen-year-old Anna Gerokhova after a ritualistic murder.

Also in the former Soviet Union, on November 14, 2009, three homeless men in Perm were arrested for killing and eating portions of a twenty-five-year-old male victim. The remaining body parts were then sold to a local pie and kebab house.

Paul Durant pleaded guilty to the manslaughter of Karen Durrell after claiming to have dismembered and eaten her in Costa Blanca in January 2004. Durant sent a letter to a newspaper saying that after killing the woman, a divorced mother of two from Ilford, Essex, UK, who had just relocated to Spain, he cut her body into small parts and ate sections of the flesh.

Middle-aged Robert Maudsley was in Broadmoor Hospital for the Criminally Insane in Crowthorne, Berkshire, UK, after garrotting a man. He committed his second murder in 1977. Maudsley and another inmate took a third man hostage and locked themselves in a cell, where they tortured their victim before cutting off the top of his head. According to a guard, the dead man was found with a spoon hanging out of his head and part of his brain was missing, leading to Maudsley being dubbed "Brain-Eater" and "Hannibal the Cannibal" and by fellow prisoners. (This was soon after the nickname had been popularized by author Thomas Harris's cannibalistic Hannibal Lector novels and several films made from them—*Manhunter, Red Dragon,* and the Best Picture Oscar–winning *The Silence of the Lambs.* Maudsley was found guilty of manslaughter and sent to HM Prison Wakefield, where he killed another two prisoners and was convicted of double murder.

In February 2004, a thirty-three-year-old British man, Peter Bryan from East London, was caught after he killed and ate his friend Brian Cherry, age forty-seven, at his home in Walthamstow, East London, only hours after being let out of hospital because he was harmless. He cut off both of Cherry's arms and one of his legs and fried his brains in butter "because KFC was closed at the time," he explained. He had previously been imprisoned for bludgeoning a twenty-year-old girl to death with a claw hammer, but had been released shortly before he lost his mind. Nine weeks later, while detained in Broadmoor, Bryan throttled fellow inmate and convicted killer Richard Loudwell, sixty, after being placed in a medium-risk unit at the hospital.

More recently, Bryan revealed that he had hoped to be put in the same jail as Soham killer Ian Huntley—so he could eat him, too, and "free the spirits" of the murdered schoolgirls Holly Wells and Jessica Chapman, but he was sent to Broadmoor instead. A Broadmoor source claims Bryan is now pleased that he is in the same facility as Peter Sutcliffe, aka "The Yorkshire Ripper," who is serving twenty life sentences for murdering thirteen women and trying to kill seven more. Sutcliffe has recently changed his name to Peter Cahoon, his mother's maiden name. "I have strong urges to taste the souls of men again," the paranoid schizophrenic Bryan replied when asked if he had chosen a likely candidate for his next victim. "I've seen a couple of nature's misfits that are likely fodder in this evolutionary food chain," adding, "I want to sample

'Sutcliffe Soufflé' and 'Yorkshire Pudding,' perhaps even 'Cahoon Carbonara.'" At least Bryan has a sense of gallows humor.

Remember the rap artist Big Lurch? In 2003 he was convicted of killing his female roommate and consuming her face and lungs while her boyfriend and Lurch were smoking the horse tranquilizer PCP together.

The year 1999 witnessed the arrest of Dorangel Vargas, aka El Comegente (Spanish for "man eater"). In Venezuela, Vargas killed and ate at least ten men during a two-year period, while in Mexico City, Jose Luis Calva was arrested after police found the remains of his thirty-year-old girlfriend, Alejandra Galeana, in his apartment. The torso was found in a bedroom closet, an arm and a leg in the refrigerator, and bones in a cereal box. A hand and foot were found boiling in a pot, and human meat was being fried in lemon juice on the stove.

The same year, a court submission at the trial of perpetrators of the "Bodies in Barrels Murders" in South Australia revealed that two of the killers fried and ate part of their final victim.

If Jeffrey Dahmer is known as the most infamous serial killer in U.S. history, then Scotland can boast of having the UK's number one in the cannibal charts—Sawney Bean, who with his wife—"a woman as viciously inclined as himself," according to chronicler John Nicholson—and his numerous offspring, dwelt in a coastal cave in Bannane Head in Galloway during the sixteenth century. They lived there for some twenty-five years.

According to *The Newgate Calendar,* Alexander Bean was born in East Lothian, where his father was a ditch digger and hedge trimmer. The young Bean tried to take up the family trade, but he simply was not cut out for honest labor.

The Beans' many children and grandchildren were products of incest and lawlessness. The brood came to include eight sons, six daughters, eighteen grandsons, and fourteen granddaughters. Lacking the gumption for hard labor, the clan thrived on laying careful ambushes at night to rob and murder individuals or small groups. Any parts of the body they were unable to eat at once were pickled in brine or hung in their cave. Discarded body parts were often washed up on the nearby beach. As a side business, any clothes or valuables were sold in the Edinburgh region.

With all this happening, it seems remarkable that local villagers didn't catch on to the Beans' activities, though they knew that travelers were going missing. Eventually, several searches were launched to find the culprits. One search actually took note of the telltale cave. It was about 200 yards deep, and at high tide the entrance was blocked by water, so the searchers refused to believe anything human could live in it. Frustrated in the frenetic quest for justice, panic reigned. The townspeople lynched several innocents, but the disappearances continued. Time for Sawney Bean was running out.

One fateful night, the Beans ambushed a married couple riding from a fair on a horse. This time, however, the man was skilled in combat and deftly held off the clan with a sword and pistol. Alas, the Beans fatally mauled the wife when she fell to the ground. Before they could take the husband, a large group of fairgoers appeared on the trail, and the Beans fled.

With the Beans' existence finally revealed, it was not long before King James VI of Scotland (later James I of England) heard of the atrocities and decided to lead a man-hunt with a team of 400 men and several bloodhounds. They soon found the Beans' previously overlooked cave in Bannane Head. The soldiers were horrified to see parts of human bodies hanging up to cure or being cooked over a fire.

In 1700, the clan was captured alive and taken in chains to the Tollbooth Jail in Edinburgh, then transferred to Leith or Glasgow, where they were promptly executed without trial. The men had their genitals cut off and their hands and feet severed and were allowed to bleed to death. The women and children, after watching the men die, were burned alive.

A number of writers believe that Sawney Bean did not really exist and was merely the stuff of myth, a demonic bogeyman figure like a vampire or werewolf. Yet it is well documented that the Beans really existed, and their cave is still there if one is brave enough to venture down.

Vlad the Impaler (1431–76), who cruelly relished the murder of thousands in the bloodiest ways, is said to have provided Bram Stoker with his inspiration for *Dracula*. The sixteenth-century Hungarian Countess Elizabeth Bathory, a distant relative of Vlad's, bathed in and drank the blood of hundreds of virgin girls because she believed it would keep her youthful; it is no less reasonable to accept that Sawney Bean really did exist—not in a glittering palace but in a dark, damp cave.

During the dark, humid evening of August 20, 1979, Albert Fentress, a history teacher from Poughkeepsie Middle School in New York, invited eighteen-year-old student Paul Masters into his house, shot him, cut up his body and ate some of it, to later be dubbed "New York's own Hannibal Lecter" by the media.

Something of an oddball, Fentress was permitted to teach World War II history while wearing a Nazi military uniform and jackboots and wielding a riding crop. Apparently he was well versed in the subjects he lectured and talked about.

Fentress, an avid philatelist, treasured the finer luxuries of life. He owned a Cadillac and was always smartly dressed. He was described as a lonely yet meticulous man who kept a tidy home. In the summer months of 1979, his house was burglarized and his treasured stamp collection was stolen. The furious Fentress obtained a gun permit, resolving that he would never be robbed again.

By now, a number of local teenagers had started pestering the mild-mannered teacher. They vandalized his property before running away. Fentress kept watch for any more burglars or harassing vandals. Then, Paul Masters roamed into Fentress's backyard, and he had no business to be there at all.

Fentress was able to lure Masters into his home by offering him a beer over friendly conversation that suddenly turned into a desperate attempt for Paul Masters to save his life, which he failed to do.

After a brief struggle, Fentress subdued the young man and bound him tightly with ropes to a pole in his cellar. After sexually assaulting Masters, Fentress shot him twice in the head, then castrated him and cooked and ate his genitals.

After years of legal wrangling, the schoolteacher was found not guilty by reason of insanity. If all goes well for him, he could be released from the mental institution and be licking his stamps instead of his lips in the not too distant future.

Marcelo Costa de Andrade, who was arrested in Rio de Janeiro in December 1991, confessed to killing fourteen boys between six and thirteen years of age and drinking their blood to become young and pretty like them. This creature, who had more screws loose than a Studebaker, really existed, not in nightmares but in real life.

So did Walter Krone, a German cannibal who went to jail for seven years in 1980 for eating parts of a girl who had died in a street accident.

Mark Heggie, age twenty-three, drank the blood of his victim after trying to kill her in North London in 1992. He told detectives that he enjoyed the blood of animals, finding work in abattoirs to satisfy his craving. Now he is in a mental institution.

In 1981, Anna Zimmerman from Monchengladbach, Germany, murdered her lover and cut him into manageable, pan-sized steaks. After saving them in the freezer along with an ear and his penis, she fed him to her two children, ages six and four—as she had previously done with family pets.

# CHAPTER 2

# Stanley Dean Baker— "Uncle Fingers"

*I have a problem: I'm a cannibal.*
—STANLEY BAKER, TO CALIFORNIA HIGHWAY
PATROL OFFICERS

*I have never seen anything like it. The poor
fellow had been stabbed twenty-five times with a
sharp, pointed knife of at least five inches long.
I figure he's been in the water about a day.
He was a young fellow, probably in his early
twenties. The heart is missing!*
—MONTEREY COUNTY CORONER DAVIS,
ON THE MURDER OF JAMES SCHLOSSER

AT 3 P.M. ON SATURDAY, JULY 11, 1970, a man fishing from
the bank of the Yellowstone River in Montana snagged
a human body at the end of his line. He drove in shock
to the nearest ranch to telephone the police. Deputy Big-

elow, who was stationed at the entrance to Yellowstone National Park, responded to the call.

With the aid of a few local men, Bigelow waded into the turbulent river and dragged the body ashore. Immediately he realized this was no routine drowning: The head was missing.

Bigelow called Sheriff Don Guitoni, who drove Coroner Davis to the scene. All three men crouched over the body, which was clad only in shorts. It was that of a male. Apart from the missing head, the arms had been severed at the shoulders and the legs chopped off at the knees. The abdomen and chest were covered with stab wounds, with a particularly ugly hole in the chest.

For the sheriff it was a major headache. Normal means of identifying the corpse—the head and hands—had been removed. But why the gratuitous butchery of the rest of the body? Why cut off the legs? Why remove the heart? This all suggested some form of cult murder. There had been a rash of them recently, all connected with secret groups of devil worshippers. While the Sharon Tate case dominated the headlines, similar bizarre killings were going on all over the United States.

The mutilated torso was taken by ambulance to the morgue in Livingstone for a proper autopsy, while police teletyped details of the victim to Wyoming and other neighboring states. It was impossible to tell where the body had been dumped in the river. Although police searched the river and its banks for many miles upstream, no traces of the head or the missing limbs were found.

On Monday morning, a teletype message came chattering into Sheriff Guitoni's office. It concerned a report of a missing person, James Schlosser, age 22, from the town of Roundup, a hundred miles away.

The report stated that James had set out on Friday, July 10, to drive to Yellowstone National Park in his Opel Kadett sports car, but he had not turned up for work the next Monday. When his office colleagues telephoned James's landlady, they learned that the young social worker had not returned home.

Schlosser was described as being six feet tall and weighing about 200 pounds. This all matched the torso, so Sheriff Guitoni put out an alert for sightings of a 1969 yellow Opel Kadett with black racing stripes. An hour later the same car collided with a pickup truck on a dirt road in Monterey County, California.

On Monday, July 13, 1970, California Highway Patrol (CHP) officers responded to reports of a hit-and-run accident on a dirt road just off State Highway 1 in Pfeiffer Big Sur State Park, in the Santa Cruz Mountains south of San Francisco.

Police learned that three people had been traveling along a dirt road in a pickup truck, and they described being hit by the yellow Opel Kadett, which was on the wrong side of the road. The pickup driver was a businessman from Detroit on vacation, and while his truck suffered only a dented bumper, the Opel was totaled.

The tourist described the two men to police. One was blonde, the other dark. The blonde man was about six feet tall and powerfully built, with shoulder-length golden hair. He wore a leather waistcoat and bell-bottom trousers. His companion wore cowboy boots. Both men wore green Army field jackets. The businessman might have expected trouble, but the hippies in the Opel were friendly.

The businessman wanted to exchange driver's license and insurance details, but neither of the two men had this information, so he took the license plate number and suggested that he should drive them both the nearest pay phone so the police could be notified of the accident. Both hippies got into his truck, but when he drove into a service station in the town of Lucia, they got out and ran into nearby woods.

The businessman telephoned the police and gave them the registration number of the Opel. Almost immediately, it came back that the car was wanted in connection with a missing person and homicide.

Patrolman Randy Newton was out cruising along the Pacific Coast Highway when he got the call over his radio. He turned off onto a dirt side road, figuring that the two hippie fugitives could not have gotten far. Indeed, he was correct. He came across the men, arrested them, and when backup arrived, they were read their rights.

Now in custody, one of the hippies, Stanley Baker, readily confessed to being involved in the accident before adding, "I have a problem: I'm a cannibal." To prove his point, Baker, age twenty-three, turned his jacket pockets out and produced a gnawed human finger bone. This, he told shocked officers, he had removed from his most recent victim, someone he'd murdered in Montana.

Baker's hippie sidekick was Harry Allen Stroup, aged twenty. Some reports claim Stroup had a finger bone in his pocket, too. Both men were arrested on suspicion of homicide and taken to the Monterey police station, where Baker said that he had a compulsion to eat human flesh. He claimed to have developed a taste for it after undergoing electric shock treatment for a nervous disorder when he was seventeen. He referred to himself as Jesus. Amongst Baker's possessions were a recipe for LSD and a paperback book, *The Satanic Bible*—a handbook of devil worship with instructions on how to conduct a black mass.

Detective Dempsey Biley took over the questioning. He soon learned that his prisoners were both from Sheridan, Wyoming, and had been hitchhiking together since June 5. At one point, Baker boasted of how he had killed the owner of the Opel Kadett. He said Stroup had not been with him at the time. He and Stroup had split up when they reached Big Timber, a few miles from Livingstone, because Baker had managed to hitch a ride with James Schlosser.

When Schlosser had said that was going to Yellowstone National Park for the weekend, Baker had asked to go along, and the two men had set up camp for the night close to the Yellowstone River. Soon Schlosser was asleep—a sleep from which he would never awaken.

In the middle of the night, Baker had crept over to his companion and shot him twice in the head with a .22-caliber pistol he always carried. Then he cut the body into six parts, removing the head, arms, and legs. When he was asked what he done with the dead man's heart, Baker casually replied, "I ate it raw." He went on to say that he had cut off the dead man's fingers to have something to chew on. He dumped the remainder of the body in the river, along with the pistol, before driving off in his victim's car.

Later Baker had met up with Stroup and offered him a ride, but he insisted that Stroup had not been involved at all in the shooting or dismemberment of Mr. Schlosser.

To confirm the crime scene, Baker described the location of the camp where he had shot Schlosser to death. When officers located and searched it, they found evidence that murder had indeed taken place at that spot. The earth was spattered with dry blood, and a bloodstained hunting knife was discovered. There was also the debris one might expect to find at such a homicide scene: human bone fragments, teeth, skin, and a severed human ear.

According to his statement, Baker told police that he had been recruited by a satanic cult from a college campus in his home state of Wyoming. Rumored to be a member of the murderous Four Pi movement, Baker had sworn allegiance to the cult's master, the Grand Chignon or Head Devil, and he had committed other slayings on the cult's behalf.

With this, Baker's interrogators wanted to learn more. They were not to be left wanting.

The Process Church of the Final Judgment, a British break-away from L. Ron Hubbard's Church of Scientology, allegedly contained cells which were known variously as Four Pi, the Circle Order, and the Children, and paid homage to the Grand Master, also known as the Grand Chignon. Four Pi had a fetish for German shepherds and Dobermans. They revered them—and probably committed sex acts with the dogs before sacrificing them. They also liked to kidnap, rape, and sacrifice hitchhikers.

In 1969, while gathering material for a book on the Charles Manson case, journalist Ed Sanders encountered reports of a sinister Satanic cult alleged to practice human sacrifice in several parts of California, luring youthful members from college campuses throughout the western half of the United States. Calling itself the Four Pi or Four P movement, the cult originally boasted fifty-five members, of whom fifteen were middle-aged and the rest young men and women in their early twenties. The group's leader was said to be a wealthy middle-aged California businessman who exercised his power by compelling younger members of the cult to act as slaves and murder random targets on command. The central object of the cult was to promote "the total worship of evil."

Organized in Northern California during 1967, the Four Pi movement held its gatherings in the Santa Cruz

Mountains, close to where the hit-and-run accident had occurred. Rituals were conducted according to an astronomical timetable. But beginning in 1968, authorities in San Jose, Santa Cruz, and Los Gatos began recording discoveries of canines skinned and drained of blood without apparent motive. "Whoever is doing this is a real expert with a knife," reported the director of the Santa Cruz Animal Shelter. "The skin is cut away without even marking the flesh. The really strange thing is that these dogs have been drained of blood."

If we accept the word of a few witnesses, the missing blood was drunk by cultists during their ceremonies. So, according to reports, was human blood, obtained from sacrificial victims allegedly murdered on a dragon-festooned altar. If this a bit hard to swallow, consider that a custom-made knife, designed with six blades of varied length to penetrate a victim's stomach, is enough to make anyone's stomach churn. Each sacrifice was apparently climaxed by skewering and removing the heart, which cultists then divided up among themselves to eat. Any remaining evidence was incinerated in a portable crematorium mounted in the back of a truck.

According to other information from members of Four Pi, including Mr. Baker, the victims were mainly hitchhikers, drifters, and runaways, who would rarely be reported to police as missing. One such woman allegedly went to her death with a smile in November 1968, near

Boulder Creek, but this form of Satanic worship was a risky business. The cult was said to have mounted armed security patrols—men wielding automatic weapons and accompanied by attack-trained dogs to protect privacy.

In early 1969, the cult shifted its operations to the O'Neil Park region of the Santa Ana Mountains near Los Angeles. The move or was occasioned by a dispute between factions of the Four Pi group. One segment wanted to de-empathize satanic ritual and concentrate on kinky sex, while more traditional adherents clung to Lucifer and human sacrifice. The group apparently survived its schism and expanded nationwide. In *Ultimate Evil*, author Maury Terry cites evidence of a thousand or more members across the country by 1979. One hotbed of activity appears to have been Walden, New York, where eighty-five German shepherds and Dobermans were found skinned between October 1976 and October 1979. More were found in the Yonkers area and in Untermeyer Park.

"Son of Sam" serial killer David Berkowitz, who terrorized New York in 1967 and 1977, had a fascination for German shepherds and Dobermans. He also professed membership in the Four Pi cult, revealing inside knowledge of a California murder allegedly committed by the group. In 1979, Berkowitz smuggled a book on witchcraft out of his prison cell, with passages on Manson and the Four Pi movement underlined. One page bore a cryptic notion in the killer's own handwriting:

ARLISS [sic] Perry. Hunted, stalked, and slain.
Followed to California. Call the Santa Clara Sheriff's
office (California. Please ask the sheriff's what
happened to ARLISS [sic] PERRY.)

This was a clear reference to an unsolved homicide committed on October 13, 1974. Arlis Perry was horribly murdered in the Church at Stanford University. The body was naked from the waist down and spread eagled in a ritualistic position, with an altar candle inserted into her vagina. Her arms were folded across her chest, and between her breasts was another candle. Her jeans were so arranged across her legs that the result was a diamond pattern. She had been beaten, choked, and stabbed with an ice pick behind the ear.

Along the way, the Four Pi movement has seemingly rubbed shoulders with a number of notorious killers, feeding their sadistic fantasies. One of them was Stanley Dean Baker, who, even while in prison, organized fellow inmates into a satanic coven of his own.

Charles Manson and his "family" reportedly had contact with the Four Pi movement before the August 1969 Sharon Tate killing in Los Angeles. Ed Saunders contends that some of Manson's followers referred to him as the Grand Chingon in his presence, despite the fact that while Manson was incarcerated, the real Chingon apparently remained at large. Manson follower and co-murderer Susan Denise Atkins has described the sacrifice of dogs by the group, and searchers digging for the remains of Manson victim Shorty Shea reported finding large numbers of chicken and animal bones at the family's campsite—a peculiar form of garbage for a group of vegetarians.

Aside from participation in human and canine sacrifice, with the occasional gang rape of teenage girls, Four Pi cultists also reportedly share a fascination with Nazi racist doctrines. One alleged member named by Berkowitz was Frederick Cowan, a neofacist from Rochelle, New York, who was suspended from work after quarrelling with his Jewish boss in February 1977. Turning up at work with a small arsenal on Monday, February 14, Cowan killed five people and wounded two others before shooting himself.

Maury Terry also linked cult activity with the unsolved case of the "Westchester Dart Man," who wounded twenty-three women in Westchester and Rockland Counties between February 1975 and May 1976.

Despite the testimony of reputed Four Pi members, authorities have yet to build a case against the cult. Some witnesses have conveniently died in "accidents" or "suicides" before they could be interviewed by police. Another obstacle appears to be the use of code names, which prevents cultists from identifying one another under interrogation. The group itself relies on different names from place to place, with New York members meeting as the Children, while Alabama hosts the Children of the Light (suspected of involvement in twenty-five murders since 1987). A faction called the Black Cross is said to operate as a kind of Satanic Murder Incorporated, fielding anonymous hit teams for cultists nationwide, disposing of defectors and offering pointers on the fine art of human sacrifice.

If law enforcement spokesmen are correct, the cult is also deeply involved in white slavery, child pornography, and the international narcotics trade.

Is the Grand Chingon still at large? Maury Terry named the New York cult leader as Roy Alexander Radin, who moved to California in 1982. Radin, a theatrical producer, specialized in staging vaudeville revival shows. He was working with Robert Evans to produce *The Cotton Club* when he was shot twenty-seven times in the head in 1983. His body was dumped in Death Valley, Charles Manson's old stomping ground. A defaced Bible lay open nearby.

More recent killings suggest the coven is still alive. At the time of writing, other members of the Twenty Disciples of Hell are still at large.

Stanley Baker would not stop giving up vital information about the Four Pi movement. There had been human sacrifices, he explained, in the Santa Ana Mountains south of Los Angeles. Displaying supposed cult tattoos, Baker also confessed participation in the Monday, April 20, 1970, murder of Robert Salem, a forty-year-old lighting designer from San Francisco, perhaps because his surname was associated to the infamous Salem witchcraft trials. The victim had been stabbed twenty-seven times and nearly decapitated, his left ear severed and carried away in a crime that Baker attributed to orders from the Grand Chingon. Slogans painted on the walls in Salem's blood—including "Zodiac" and "Satan Saves"—were meant to stir up panic in an atmosphere already tense from revelations coming forth in the Manson murder trial.

Baker and Stroup were taken before a judge in California and waived extradition. They were flown back to Montana on Monday, July 20, 1970. They were arraigned before District Judge Jack Shamstrom on July 27. The pair were remanded in Park County Jail, but on August 4, Judge Shamstrom approved a motion that Baker be sent to Warm Springs State Hospital for psychiatric evaluation. Harry Stroup had remained silent throughout, apparently guilty of nothing more than having a homicidal sidekick and devil worshipper. Those short lengths of bone found on Baker were sent to a pathologist for examination and determined to be the right index finger that once belonged to James Schlosser.

Both men were sentenced to prison, where Baker continued his efforts on behalf of the cult. Full moons seemed too bring out the worst in Stanley Baker, causing him to howl like an animal. He sometimes threatened prison guards and was relieved of homemade weapons on eleven separate occasions, but administrators still saw fit to let him travel through the correctional system, teaching transactional analysis to other inmates.

Prosecutors at Baker's trial presented no motive for the killing, dismemberment, and partial cannibalism of James Michael Schlosser, but proving motive was not required, for "intent" was the issue at hand, and the intent was the satisfaction of Dean Baker's Satanic bloodlust. As we have seen from the so-called man-eating *Caníbales*, the consumption of the slain often symbolizes total conquest and contempt for the victim, who is digested and literally turned into excrement.

In his book *Cannibalism: The Last Taboo* (London: Arrow Books, 1992), author Brian Marriner suggests that "maybe Baker, the unemployed, non-conforming hippie, viewed the young Schlosser, a college graduate with a sports car, horn-rimmed glasses and expensive camping equipment, as a respectable 'square' who had prospered within the system; a system of everything he could not be and a mirror to his own failure." Marriner adds, "In that case envy would be the motive—a 'have-not' who saw himself as a social reject, lashing out violently at a respectable member of society—with the same blind ferocity as a snake striking at a stick."

This author, however, sees things somewhat differently.

To begin with, the killing of James Schlosser was purely a non-premeditated event. Both men happened to arrive at a place called Murder Crossroads, where the two lives met. One life was destroyed, and the other's life irrevocably changed forever. We call this "fate." It was a chance encounter on the road to Yellowstone.

We now know that Mr. Baker was a fully paid-up disciple of the satanic sect calling itself Four Pi. He was well informed on the cult's activities and he most certainly knew of their sacrificial rituals. By his own admissions and deeds, he enjoyed the taste of human flesh: the still-beating heart of James Schlosser. He says he ate it raw, keeping an index finger to snack on later.

If one would seek a motive for such happenstance homicide, one might focus on murder for financial gain. It is known that James Schlosser was carrying about $500 on his person when he left for his weekend trip to Yellowstone, and Stanley Baker certainly relieved him of this money, for when he was arrested, most of it was found along with the severed digit.

If Baker was hungry, why not simply shoot James Schlosser, take his money, and drive off to the nearest McDonald's to buy a decent meal? Why, the reader may ask, did Stanley Baker take on the laborious task of cutting up his victim by lamplight, when simply throwing the corpse into the Yellowstone River to be swept downstream over numerous rapids would have sufficed?

Of course, we may never know what really took place that night, in that dark clearing on the banks of the river. There was a little starlight. All was quiet. Suddenly, two gunshots rang out and James died instantly in his sleep. Then the cutting began.

Can one imagine stumbling across such a moonlit scene? There is the kneeled figure of hippie Stanley Baker, drenched in the blood of his victim. Body parts and teeth are strewn all around, while the cannibal Baker gorges on the still-warm heart of a once-living young human being. Even Stephen King could not make this one up.

Harry Stroup discharged his sentence and was released from prison in 1979, having served nine years for allegedly having one of Schlosser's finger bones in his pocket, throwing a completely different perspective on Baker's claims that Stroup was not involved with the killing of James Schlosser at all.

As for Stanley Dean Baker, he was paroled to his native Wyoming, at once requesting that his whereabouts remain confidential, and well he might! If a so-called Grand Chignon gets a handle on Stan's present whereabouts, he could end up as mincemeat too.

# CHAPTER 3

# Edward "Ed" Theodore Gein — "The Plainfield Butcher"

*Edward Gein had two faces.*
*One he showed to the neighbors.*
*The other he showed only to the dead.*
STEVEN POINTS, *DAILY JOURNAL*

THE SHADOW OF HIS monstrous mother split Ed Gein's mind forever into a Dr. Jekyll and a Mr. Hyde. Two twisted beings grew inside him—one adoring, the other hating the mother figures he saw around him. His case is, from a medical point of view, one of the most complex in criminological history. Voyeurism, fetishism, transvestism, and necrophilia all reared their ugly heads, metamorphosing into one terrifying entity—a creature so twisted that he became immortalized in the bleak annals of criminal history and dubbed by the media "the Plainfield Butcher." If ever there were a man who, through the sheer awfulness of his crimes, achieved the embodiment of a real-life Halloween ghoul, it was the late Edward Theodore Gein (pronounced "Geen").

A scrawny little guy, his pockmarked face the color of asparagus, Ed committed several horrific crimes in his time. The majority of them took place in the 1940s and '50s at his remote clapboard farmhouse in the small, rural community of Plainfield, Wisconsin.

The central region of Wisconsin in the American Midwest is so flat and featureless that even the state's official guidebook calls it "nondescript." And one might say that this is the perfect setting for a series of murders in the vein committed by Gein. In a more evocative Wisconsin phrase, it is the state's "great dead heart—bleak grassy plains scattered with lonely farmsteads and small towns devoid of life." Tumbleweed-bleak places such as Wittenberg, Rural, and Harrisville are dusty and full of scrawny dogs, closed-down movie theaters, grubby diners, and gas stations with Coke machines out front that look as though they would be grateful to get two customers a week.

With a population never exceeding eight hundred, the aptly named seed corn town of Plainfield, in Waushara County, sits between Wisconsin Rapids and Wautoma along Highway 73, truly locked into America's agricultural heartland. Raising a little livestock or growing patches of rye in the sandy, stony soil, farmers scratch for the barest of livings, eking out their existence in shacks with sagging roofs and walls that look as if they have been cannonballed or dropped from a great height. Other farms are large, scattered, and prosperous looking. Every mile or so one will pass a snug-looking farmhouse with a porch swing and a yard full of trees. Standing nearby will be a red barn with a rounded roof and a tall silo packed full of golden grain. This part of Wisconsin is the quintessential northern Midwest—54,000 square miles of rustling corn, cerulean skies, and arrow-straight roads that go on for an eternity.

As reported in the *Waushara News*, the state has a darker side: "It is a wild country that could hide violence for years and perhaps never give up its secrets." Indeed, you could drive by one of these old places set deep in the Badger State, and, with all the stored knowledge of horror movies and novels you've enjoyed, you could easily envisage a madman with a meat cleaver lurking within, happily committing atrocity after bloody atrocity, secure in the bowels of his isolated domain. And driving through these places where all strangers are eyed with grim suspicion, you might feel a cold chill creep up your spine, but you would probably not seriously consider the unpalatable possibility of it being true.

So where do the ideas for all these books and films come from? Are they simply plucked out of the ether, or are some of them actually inspired by fact? We may reflect on Norman Bates, the gaunt, retiring, archetypal mama's boy turned serial killer of young females, created in Robert Bloch's book *Psycho* and brought to the screen by Alfred Hitchcock. No coincidence, perhaps, that at the time of the Gein case, Bloch lived in the town of Weyau-wega, less than thirty miles east of Plainfield.

Or what about the hulking spectre of Leatherface, the demented, simpleton killing machine of the *Texas Chainsaw Massacre* "splatter movies," who along with his equally insane family slashed a wide-reaching swath through the annals of horror moviemaking.

We can go down the line here: William Lustig's *Maniac*, *The Silence of the Lambs*, even such gritty old gems as *Three on a Meat Hook*, *Motel Hell*, and *Deranged*. If you are a horror movie enthusiast, you will be familiar with all of these. *Bloodthirsty Butchers* and *Meat Cleaver Massacre* will not have passed you by, either.

But where did the ideas for these and countless other horror films come from in the first place? The genesis for all of them can be attributed to the sickening misdeeds of a scruffy little loner called Ed Gein.

The gory legend that has been woven around this diminutive creature over the years is truly a phenomenon. When we consider other infamous murderers, Edward Gein must surely rank very high indeed in this pantheon of homicidal bogeymen, for his was truly a grim world of cadavers, skeletons, deaths, heads, food for worms, and clay. Yet how did such a monster evolve and metamorphose from an innocent toddler into a flesh-eating monster?

ON SUNDAY, AUGUST 26, 1906, Augusta Gein—praying to the Almighty for a daughter—gave birth instead to a son in La Crosse, Wisconsin.

Augusta was a storeowner who managed the premises almost single-handedly because her husband spent most of his time and money in local bars. She called the newborn Edward. Her stern Lutheran upbringing and her marriage to drunkard George Gein, who had been orphaned at the age of five in 1879, had developed in her a loathing of men.

Augusta vowed that Edward would never be like the lustful, godless men she saw around her. As little Ed grew up, he would come to learn that crossing his tyrannical matriarch was not the wisest of moves. The fanatically religious, Bible-thumping Augusta had her alcoholic husband exactly where she wanted him: cowed and obedient. Ed and his elder brother, Henry, would also behave subordinately or face her wrath, and, after all, when it was the wrath of God himself, in the guise of Augusta Gein, bearing down upon them, they had better watch out.

In 1913, the Geins started a new life as dairy farmers. Both boys were taught early on that women—excluding Augusta, of course—could generally be written off as "painted harlots," sometimes even "whores." Small wonder that Ed turned out feeling a little confused when it came to the fairer sex.

A child who is brought up in a home where the parents yell and scream, hit each other, and hit their children will experience these outbursts as "normal." It is normal to the child because he or she has little or nothing to compare it with. This was the only world Ed knew. Later in life, children may form attachments to people who behave similarly, for although they may consciously deny it, this is what they can relate to.

Up until the age of sixteen, school was Ed's only contact with the outside world. As fast as he found a new friend, his mother would object to the lad's family. In her eyes, everyone was a threat to the moral purity of her son, so Ed withdrew from contact with other children. Those who remember him report that he was feeble and shy.

Like so many fully emerged serial killers who have suffered from this subtle form of child abuse, Ed went through childhood a lonely boy, locked in a world of his own. Such formative behavior becomes the breeding ground of fantasy. When not farming alongside his mother and father in the fields around their house, he would sometimes play with his elder brother, but mostly he just kept to himself.

Kneeling before his crazed zealot of a mother, having scripture not just quoted but screamed at him, he would often silently rejoice when allowed to retreat, to seek refuge in the secret world that waited in his bedroom.

He also professed an aversion to blood or killing—common sights in a rural community where hunting and livestock farming were a way of life. Yet he devoured horror comics and books about violence. It was the one subject that could get him talking.

In effect, his mind was splitting in two, for young Ed Gein had two worlds: the harshness of reality and the comfort of the secret fantasies into which he plunged for relief. In his bedroom, things were different from the outside world of hard, unrelenting toil and the tongue-lashings meted out by his mother. Whenever he left his room, he had the spectre of his puritanical mother to contend with.

Augusta, from a strict German immigrant family, was a fanatically religious and austere woman. She had grown to despise her feckless, drunken husband. George reacted by withdrawing into himself. Occasionally, when she goaded him beyond endurance, he would get drunk and lash out at her as Ed and his brother looked on help-lessly. After suffering from these attacks, Augusta would get down on her knees and pray for her husband's death.

Her prayers were answered in 1940, when George Gein died, a broken invalid at age sixty-six.

In the spring of 1944, the two brothers had been fight-ing a fire near their farm when they became separated. Mysteriously, Ed led a search party straight to the spot where Henry lay dead. Though there was bruising on Henry's forehead, his death was attributed to asphyxia-tion by smoke.

Shortly after her elder son's death or murder, Au-gusta Gein collapsed with a stroke. Over the next year Ed nursed her lovingly back to health, but God intervened.

She died in December 1945.

Alone at the age of thirty-nine, Gein was thrown into a world he barely understood. Within five years, he would retreat into another—a world in which the coldness, violence, and repression of his childhood would become insidiously twisted in his mind. A world centered on the mad and macabre.

Adding to his few pitiful possessions, Eddie started to collect magazines, his favorites being gory comics like *The Vault of Horror* and *Tales from the Crypt* — anything featuring rotting zombies heaving themselves out of the damp earth to visit untold horrors upon unsuspecting, scantily attired girls. Among his favorites were publications that depicted Nazi war atrocities, bloodthirsty pirates, cannibal tribes or head shrinkers. Ed would lap this stuff up as he spent hours lying on his mattress fantasizing about these wonderfully gruesome stories.

Ilsa Koche, the notorious SS death camp supervisor, was portrayed in Eddie's lurid magazines as a curvaceous blonde; suitably attired in a tight-fitting uniform and knee-high black leather boots, armed with a long whip, she particularly intrigued the impressionable youngster. What really thrilled him were the stories where the buxom "Nazi she-bitch" would upholster her fellow Nazis' furniture with human skins.

One of his favorite stories was called "The Dirty Dame of Dachau." The subtitle was, "She got her kicks from the corpses of the men she had once loved. Now I was the chosen victim for her passion."

Another of his heroines was Irma Grese, a teenage SS officer who had revelled in her task of dispatching women and children to the concentration camp gas chambers. If this was not enough to pollute his mind, he also studied closely the exploits of nineteenth-century Edinburgh grave robbers Burke and Hare, avidly cross-referencing everything with thick tomes on anatomy.

Ed was hooked. Without the restrictions placed upon him by his mother, he could now, at long last, embrace his treasured tales; gloating and devouring all his special sex-spiced sadism and pulp horror to his heart's content.

Soon he would play out his fantasies in real life.

In the '50s, Plainfield certainly was an appropriate name for the cluster of clapboard houses, decrepit storefronts and insalubrious watering holes; like much of Wisconsin at that time, Plainfield certainly did little to spice up America's heartland. One might imagine the early German immigrants passing through and laying claim to a small parcel of land, only to look around with their thumbs in the mouths, pondering on a name for their new settlement. "Fuck! It is certainly a plain field," one may have muttered. The name has stuck.

It was in this community that Ed Gein had spent his life, and as a man now in his forties and still a virgin, his existence had not exactly been akin to those of the more outgoing guys around Plainfield who had a constant stream of girls at their beck and call. Gein could only stand in the shadows and watch.

Outwardly, Gein seemed quite content. His heady fantasy world had kept him ticking along at a steady pace. However, a form of madness was now deeply entrenched in this sloppily presented, grizzled wreck of a man who would show up in town driving his battered pickup truck.

Parking it, he would then shamble off for a solitary beer at Hogan's Tavern, or to make a purchase at Worden's Hardware Store.

As a matter of fact, Eddie Gein had become somewhat of a regular fixture in both of these establishments, though he didn't show up around Hogan's so often these days, not since the proprietress, Mary Hogan, had disappeared on the bitterly cold afternoon of December 8, 1954.

The hue and cry had been raised by a local farmer named Seymour Lester, who strolled into Hogan's Tavern intending to wet his whistle. He found the place deserted. After calling for service, then for Mary, and then just some "plain ol' service again, if you please," he noticed a large splotch of coagulating blood by the door leading to Mary's private quarters behind the bar. It did not require a second glance for the message to filter through that something was wrong, so he rushed to the nearest telephone and called the police.

When County Sheriff Harold S. Thompson arrived with a number of deputies, he immediately commenced a search of Mary's bar. The place was completely empty, and there was no sign of Mary, although her car was still parked out back in its usual spot.

Closer inspection of the pool of blood, which had by now thoroughly soaked into the scratchy pine flooring, revealed some odd streaking patterns. Settling on his haunches, Thompson took a closer look. It seemed as if something weighty had been dragged through it, and indeed this was true; Mary's corpse, to be precise, freshly dispatched with a blast from a weapon. The expended .32-caliber cartridge lying nearby gave the cops a nudge in the right direction as to what kind of gun had been fired.

Leading from this blood, another sticky red trail snaked its way across the dusty floor and out of the back door, where it ceased abruptly beside a set of recently lain tire tracks that had been made by a pickup truck, in the sheriff's opinion.

Someone had bagged the fiery tavern owner as one might a deer and spirited her away. Maybe it was a robbery gone wrong, although little seemed to be missing aside from Mary herself. The cash register was untouched.

There was some speculation that the Mary Hogan had had a questionable past. Some of the locals rumored that she had been a notorious Chicago madam with organized crime connections. Another whisper was that she had even purchased her bar with some of the proceeds of her illicit forays back in the Windy City. The tough-talking, boisterous Mary Hogan, who had sprinkled her every sentence with the choicest of expletives, had made quite an impact on the conservative and, for the most part, deeply religious farming families of Plainfield, Wisconsin.

Some of the men, unbeknownst to their disapproving wives, used to enjoy the seedy aura of Hogan's Tavern and the murky reputation of the woman running the show. When Ed Gein would stop by for a beer or two after a hard day plowing the fields or repairing a barn door, he would sit alone and stare transfixed at the dark-haired Mary behind the bar.

Mary had fascinated the dour little town handyman, Ed Gein, for some time, and Mama had warned him about women like this. They were bad. So why was he so taken with her? Why were his strange inner desires stirred by this obstreperous, foul-mouthed former lady of the night? Mama would most certainly not approve. But Mama was not around anymore, so Ed could do as he chose.

Maybe Mary's Chicago past had come back to haunt her? Whatever the case, and despite the suspicion that fell on Gein, the police in Plainfield would not solve this mystery for a quite a while. Apart from her killer, nobody ever saw Mary Hogan alive again. A few years later, when the police had their hands more than full with the ghastly business up at Eddie Gein's place and America was in a state of shock, locals weren't too surprised that the vanished tavern owner's face—fondly thought of by Ed as one of his death masks—was found among the many grisly artifacts removed from his house.

With the Hogan situation unsolved, life returned to normal in Plainfield. For a while, Ed stayed clear of the town, but Worden's Hardware and Implement Store catered to his needs, so he would occasionally materialize, smiling meekly at Bernice Worden, the store owner, while twisting his peaked cap nervously in his grubby little hands as he stammered out his order.

A devout Methodist in her late fifties, Bernice was plump and made of stout stuff, having come from solid stock. Her father, Frank Canover, had been part owner of the hardware store. She had married his business partner, Leon Worden. The store was one of the oldest and most successful businesses in Plainfield. A comfortable retirement beckoned for the bespectacled, white-haired lady.

Unlike Mary Hogan, Bernice, a devout Methodist, enjoyed a spotless reputation among her fellow citizens. She had taken over the store when her husband died in 1931. In the intervening years, assisted by her son, Frank, she had built it into a thriving business to which every farmer in the area would turn at some time or another, for everything from agricultural supplies to rifle cartridges. The local newspaper archives show that she was nominated Plainfield's first Citizen of the Week. When she was not working she could be generally found with her grandchildren, whom she adored.

Bernice felt kind of sorry for Ed. She reasoned that he was such a lonely sort of a fellow—a simpleton with a plaid shirt buttoned right up to the top, bundled up in his dirty hunting jacket. She thought he looked a tad comical and harmless enough, maybe a bit weird but nothing too extraordinary. With his tousled crop of greasy hair, finely shaved away at the back and sides, and his permanently stooped posture, it appeared as if he had been in a folded-up bed all his life. Ed had also developed a facial tic somewhere along the way. Always unkempt and smelling like a dead horse, he was nonetheless unfailingly pleasant. The little chap was polite in his awkward, bashful way, and he never made trouble for anyone.

Bernice also found it difficult to believe that the unshaven little man with the drooping left eye—a condition exacerbated by a fleshy growth on the lid—had once asked her out on a date. He had suggested ice-skating. The half-joking offer unnerved her, and she related the incident to her son, Frank.

Saturday, November 16, 1957, was the start of Wisconsin's nine-day deer hunting season, and most of the town's male inhabitants were out in the surrounding woodlands. The rest of Plainfield was deserted and the shops closed, but Bernice decided to keep her place open, thinking that there would be a steady stream of visitors eager to replenish their supplies.

At 8:30 a.m., Ed Gein shuffled in clutching an empty glass jug. He wanted it filled with antifreeze. Bernice smiled at him, and he smiled back. She only became uncomfortable when Ed didn't seem to want to stop smiling, as if the laws of social etiquette had suddenly somehow gone awry between them. Come to think of it, Ed didn't appear to be making any attempt to leave the store either. "Goodbye Ed," she said, trying to keep her tone even, despite by now being a little spooked. This finally seemed to break the spell Ed had been under. Jamming his oily old cap down squarely on his head, he turned and bade his farewell to Bernice.

As he stepped out into the icy winter air, that disquieting and somewhat sinister smile was still firmly in place. Moments later, cradling an old .22-caliber hunting rifle, he returned. When Bernice's son, Frank, a deputy sheriff who had helped his mother build up the Worden family business after his father's death, pulled into the Plainfield Gas Station shortly before dusk, he was most unsettled by a tale the attendant told him.

The Worden family delivery truck had been observed pulling out from alongside the hardware store earlier that morning and later seen tooling along the highway. Mrs. Worden's presence behind the wheel was not confirmed. Rather, it seemed as though the driver was a male. Worried now, because there was no reason why his mother would leave the hardware store in the middle of a business day unless she was seriously unwell, Frank headed right on over there.

The door to the hardware store was locked. The lights were on. Frank knew in his bones that the store would prove to be deserted. The dangling light bulbs within seemed to cast an eerie glow throughout.

Frank, who had left his own key at home, rapidly went to fetch it. Upon returning, he let himself into the building, nervously calling his mother's name. He had a very bad feeling. Being a police officer, he was a naturally suspicious individual.

Moving slowly through the store, service revolver drawn, he noticed with a sickly elevated feeling in his gut that the cash register was absent, apparently yanked from its moorings on the counter. As he reached the back of the store, what he saw caused his jaw to drop. Just as at the Mary Hogan scene three years ago, a thick patch of blood lay in the shadows just beyond the glare of an overhead light. With an agonized gasp, Frank leapt for the telephone.

As granite-faced County Sheriff Art Schley traveled through fifteen miles of gathering darkness from his headquarters in Wautoma to Plainfield, he thought of Frank's call and how anxious and upset his young deputy had sounded. This could be a tough one, he thought. He had never known Frank so distraught. By the time Schley arrived at the store with another Deputy, Frank Worden was about ready to explode. "He's done something to her," he exclaimed. When asked by the sheriff to elaborate on this comment, Worden blurted, "Ed Gein."

As Frank had waited for the cavalry to arrive, he had cast his mind back to how that oddball, Eddie Gein, had been stalking his mother, from sitting parked in his old pickup truck across the street, staring intently at her through the storefront window, to coming in and regularly inquiring as to the price of items that he never actually seemed to want to purchase.

Bernice had mentioned all this to her son, but not as a cause for concern, as it was merely Ed Gein being his trademark eccentric self. Now, though, Gein's behaviors had taken on a more sinister significance. To Frank Worden's mind, Mr. Gein had some serious explaining to do in connection with his mother's disappearance.

The item that signed and sealed Frank's conviction that Ed was behind all this was a handwritten sales slip for two quarts of antifreeze dated that very day, November 16, and made out in Gein's name. Ed Gein seemed to have been very interested in antifreeze lately and now had finally gotten around to buying some on the day his mother happened to have vanished into thin air. Worden could smell a mighty rat.

An alert was quickly radioed to officers in the area to bring the little man in for questioning. Along with Sheriff Schley, Frank and his fellow deputy set off into the roaring throat of that freezing November night, headed for the Gein house.

Ed Gein's movements that bitterly cold day are remarkably well-documented and are worthy of study as they illustrate how Gein, although a bloodthirsty maniac of the highest order, was not exactly the sharpest tool in the box.

It was around 10:00 a.m. when sawmill-owner Elmo Ueeck shot a deer on Ed Gein's land. As this was illegal, Ueeck deemed it prudent to turn tail and put as much distance as possible between himself and the spot where the animal was slain.

On the road, with the quickly cooling creature lashed to the hood of his car, Ueeck noticed the pickup truck of none other than Eddie Gein himself, hurtling toward him. Sure that Eddie would be angered by the hunting escapades on his land, Ueeck squirmed in his seat as the truck passed. He was more than a little surprised when Eddie, seemingly oblivious to the huge stag attached to the front of Ueeck's car, simply gave him a cheery wave as he went by.

Ueeck would later remark on the intensity on Gein's face. "He certainly appeared to be very keen on getting home in a hurry," he told police.

When lunchtime arrived and Elmo Ueeck began to experience the first pangs of guilt for taking advantage of poor old Ed's good nature, he decided to travel back to Gein's farm to admit what he had done and offer the man a full and frank apology.

There was Ed, out in the front yard with his car up on jacks. Gein grunted a peripheral greeting to Ueeck as he busied himself with the task of changing his snow tires back to summer treads. Ueeck frowned at this spectacle. What in the hell was Eddie Gein up to with this foolishness? There were a couple of inches of snow on the ground, with more on the way. Still, it wasn't really any of his business. As he plowed ahead with his rehearsed apology for what had happened earlier that day, he found Ed to be not in the least concerned. It was fine, no problem. A deer was a deer, and Gein let him know that it was not an issue for him. Ueeck nodded gratefully at Ed's response.

As he attempted a token conversational gambit to add some levity to the exchange, Ed Gein made it clear that he had things to be getting along with, so Ueeck made his excuses and left.

Later, Ed Gein was visited by his neighbors Bob Hill and Hill's sister Darlene. Bob was a young and trusted friend of Ed's—perhaps his only real friend and certainly the only individual invited into Eddie's private lair to view all his books and porn magazines with him.

The young teen was very interested in all of Eddie's twisted reading materials, especially the stuff about the shrunken heads. Eddie had been so delighted with Bob's response to this that he had informed him of something quite special that he could show him. It turned out that Ed Gein had his own shrunken heads. He even produced one from a paper bag for Bob to see. The object was shrivelled and purple, barely identifiable as human, its features swollen and distorted. Sparse wisps of what looked like hair sprouted from the tiny cranium. Bob, a little shaken, was very impressed by how real it looked.

This particular afternoon, the Hills went to Eddie's place to ask for a lift into town so they could buy a new car battery. After they rapped on his door several times, Gein finally emerged. His movements were brisk and somewhat jerky as he drew the door shut smartly behind him and shuffled down the steps to greet them. Both noticed that Eddie's hands and the arms of his shirt were covered in blood, as was a leather apron he wore. There were even red smears across the man's cheeks.

Ed let them both know that he had just been dressing a deer but that he would be happy to lend his services to the youngsters. After stepping back inside the dark confines of his ramshackle farmhouse to sluice himself clean of all that blood, Eddie gestured for them to join him in his car.

As Ed drove, the two Hills ruminated on how strange it was that Ed had been engaged in such an activity when he had always professed to feel most queasy about butchery. Even the very sight of blood, he often claimed, made him feel faint.

When Gein returned from town sometime later with the young brother and sister in tow, it was nearly dark and extremely cold, and all were feeling positively ravenous. It was Ed's good fortune then that, Irene Hill, Bob and Darlene's mother, should invite him in for supper. It was here, in the Hill home, having just finished a steaming plate of meat and vegetables, that Ed Gein was confronted by a neighbor who had dashed in to report the disappearance of Bernice Worden.

Calmly placing his dirty dishes in the sink, Eddie opined, "It must have been someone pretty cold-blooded."

Adventurous Bob Hill excitedly suggested that Gein should drive them into town again, this time to get the lowdown on the Worden affair. Eddie grinned vapidly and happily obliged. As the pair crossed the snow-swept yard to Ed's car, they were intercepted by Officer Dan Chase and Deputy Poke Spees, both of whom were rather interested in speaking with Mr. Gein.

Having earlier been up to the old farm, the officers had found it locked and empty. The next logical step was to pay a visit to the Hill's, the most likely place for Ed to be. Standing out in the cold beside Spees's squad car, the officer asked Ed Gein what he had been doing that day. Eddie, surely not wishing to withhold anything from the law, told him. Spees asked him again, and this time Ed's story unfortunately conflicted with the yarn he had originally spun. It seemed that Eddie Gein was not what you could describe as an accomplished liar. He could barely remember what he had been saying from one moment to the next.

*How come every time somebody gets banged on the head and hauled away, you're always around?*
—IRENE HILL, TO ED GEIN

When the glaring inconsistencies in the two versions of how Ed Gein had spent his day were tossed back at him, Ed seemed almost to sag where he stood. It was as though some kind of dark guardian spirit had finally given up and left the man alone. "Somebody framed me," Gein mumbled.

"Framed you for what?" came the incredulous response.

"Well, about Mrs. Worden?"

"What about Mrs. Worden," Chase asked levelly.

"Well, she's dead ain't she?'

"Dead! How'd you know she's dead?'

"I heard it," Gein calmly retorted, hooking a thumb in the direction of the Hill's house. "They told me in there."

Ed Gein was placed under arrest on suspicion of the murder of Bernice Worden. Safely tucked into the backseat of the squad car, he cast his gaze downward. The game was up. It was only a matter of time before the cops made their discovery.

Sheriff Schley rendezvoused with Captain Lloyd Schoephoerster up at the Gein farm as soon as he got wind of Ed's arrest. Forcing the door to the kitchen extension at the rear of the property, the two men let themselves into Eddie's domain. It was the smell that hit them first, the almost overpowering stench of spoiled food and decaying matter. There was something else though, some other odor that Schley recognized from the occasional visits he paid to the county morgue. It was the smell of death. They suspected they might find a body in here someplace. There had been an awful lot of blood at Worden's hardware, after all. As they swept the beams from their flashlights across the dark room, the two policemen moved carefully so as to avoid tripping over some object or other among the unbelievable clutter. They negotiated their way through a sea of fermenting, half-eaten cans of food, filth-encrusted utensils, and miscellaneous bundles of clothing, ever mindful of the possible hazards of the mildewed sacks of grain and the jumble of rusty farming implements.

Just then, Art Schley felt something bump against his shoulder. The sudden contact startled him, and he whirled to the right with his flashlight. There, in the jittery glare, he was suddenly greeted by a sight surpassing his worst nightmares. Suspended from the rafters of Ed Gein's kitchen extension, like some twisted marionette, was what at first glance appeared to be a huge slab of meat with arms and legs. It soon became evident, though, that this was the decapitated body of a woman—a woman in her mid-to-late fifties; Bernice Worden, to be precise.

Besides having had her head sawn off directly above the shoulder blades, there was a large gaping crevice extending from the vagina to between her breasts. Bernice Worden had been completely gutted. Just as a hunter peels open the belly of a kill and removes the bloody organs from within, Eddie Gein had done the same with the former hardware store owner. Reeling with abject horror, the two hardened investigators were momentarily at a loss, unable to function. Their minds froze at this scene of savagery. "What would poor Frank Worden make of this?" they asked themselves.

Stumbling outside to escape the fetid conditions of the Gein homestead, the two men sucked breath after breath of blessed fresh air into their lungs. Standing there in the snow-blanketed yard, the two struggled to control their revulsion and maintain their professionalism. Schoephoerster made radio contact for backup.

There was no real danger. All the murdering had been done, and the man of the hour was safely in police custody, but the two cops were unable to cope with the scene alone. An air of evil pervaded the Gein place, as if Satan himself had come to visit. They did not yet know the half of it.

With help on the way, both men resolved to enter the creature's cave once more. Closer inspection of the dangling, pale-skinned corpse revealed even more abominations. In the glow of their flashlights, the corpse's skin seemed to exude a dim, waxy hue like cottage cheese. It contrasted starkly to the deep red lips of the horrendous abdominal fissure transversing Mrs. Worden's torso. Within the cavity all was slick and clean. Glistening viscera seemed to push itself out through the opening like an old teddy bear oozing its stuffing.

Bernice Worden had been hung from what looked like a gnarled tree limb. Sharpened to a wicked point at each end, it had been rammed through the sinew and gristle of one of her ankles, while the other end had been secured with chicken wire to a penetrative slash below her heel, effectively splaying her legs. Stout rope entwined each wrist, keeping her arms rigid at her sides.

It seemed that Ed had wanted plenty of room to maneuver as he sliced his way through Mrs. Worden's body.

The two men were unable to locate the woman's head anywhere in the immediate vicinity, so they reluctantly began sifting through the nauseating detritus of Ed's kitchen and beyond in the hope of retrieving it.

When they still had not found the only body part that might lend Mrs. Worden a touch of humanity amid all this depravity, it became time to start a search of some of the other rooms. Already firmly immersed in the maw of the monster, the two reluctantly continued their journey into Ed Gein's madhouse.

In the kitchen itself, they noted that the sink had been filled with sand and there was a row of ancient dentures aligned on a mantelpiece as one might arrange a collection of fine porcelain. Stacks upon stacks of true-crime magazines and comics, many warped through damp and time, spilled from boxes and cascaded from shelves. They were all over the place, scattered among all the other bizarre belongings. There was just too much here to go through for two men with flashlights, so Schley made the decision to discontinue the sickening odyssey and wait until the others had arrived.

Once the place had been well lit and there were several other deputies and investigators on the case, the search of Ed Gein's house resumed. Each discovery made the scene all the more horrendous.

Strewn about the kitchen area were a number of human skulls, some with clots of scalp and dirty hair still attached. Most of the skulls were intact, but several had been sawed in two and rendered into crude, gothic soup bowls and plates. Amid the general filth and squalor, there were what appeared to be swatches of moldering flesh and bone fragments. The stinking chaos of each room echoed throughout the house, and further indicators of Gein's raging dementia were uncovered every step of the way.

Officers were shaken to find that many of Gein's furnishings had a soft, leathery material that could only be human skin fashioned into the damp upholstery, from strips of flesh covering the seat of a chair to wastebaskets and lampshades. Stretchy tendrils of skin had been used to fashion bracelets and belts—one with female nipples grafted onto it.

Just trying to deal with the undistilled horror of a wastebasket made from flesh and bones, a tanned-skin hunting-knife sheath, and box of Quaker Oats filled with hardened globs of brain matter, Sheriff Schley muttered,

"This is just too horrible. Too horrible for words." It was not the only time he would utter these words regarding the Gein case.

When it seemed as though things could not get much worse, officers searching Gein's bedroom yelled out in shock when they found an entire wall devoted to various hanging pockets of skin. Up close they turned out to be peoples' faces. Ed had obviously carved these death masks away and mounted them on his wall like trophies.

One such mask looked very familiar to investigators. Was that Mary Hogan? Yes, it looked as though the riddle of the missing tavern owner had finally been solved. She had wound up here in Eddie Gein's charnel house, reduced to nothing more than a severed face.

Boxes were piled throughout the house, some containing innocuous items like bloated sheaves of ancient newspaper and anatomy books, yet others were a different. Opening a number of boxes, officers noted severed body parts and flesh cuttings. There were paper bags of hacked-off noses and lips. One even held a dusty old cache of shriveled vaginas. Upon opening up a bundled old suit, officers were assailed by the meaty aroma of freshly excised internal organs, heaped upon which was a ropey mass of entrails, all presently congealing in their eye-watering juices. These had once belonged to Mrs. Worden.

They found Mrs. Worden's heart stashed inside a blood-caked paper sack by the stove. And it wasn't long before the investigators came upon what they had all secretly dreaded—the dead woman's head. It had been stuffed into an old feed sack. Upon extraction, it proved to be covered in dirt and dried blood. A most unpleasant adornment consisted of two steel hooks, driven into both eardrums with a piece of twine attached. It looked like Ed had planned to hang this up somewhere around the house, maybe in his bedroom with his other demented treasures.

Rummaging along the ground floor hallway, officers came to one room that had been closed off. Thick planks of wood had been firmly nailed across the door, and, fearing that something even worse must lie within, they did not relish prying the boards away so they could gain access. But the officer's actually faced a very neatly laid out living-room.

Every piece of furniture had been arranged with care, a cluster of ornaments graced the mantel piece, and a large, centrally placed rug dominated the immacu-late room. The only thing marring it was a thick layer of dust shrouding everything. This was a room that had clearly been made off-limits many years ago. It had been Augusta Gein's special room while she was alive, and Eddie had wasted no time turning it into a shrine when she was dead.

Back in the rest of this house of horrors, even more alarming finds were occurring. The searchers grimaced in disgust as Officer Schoephoerster held aloft a crudely rendered garment made entirely from human skin. It had been cured somehow and looked as though it just might have been some kind of vest. It had come from the upper body of a woman and even boasted a pair of large, sagging breasts. There were several lengths of treated flesh that were clearly meant to be utilized as leggings. It was a hard thing, indeed, to imagine a naked Ed Gein dressed up in his woman suit, parading around his filthy den, or out in the backyard, howling at the moon, but why else would he trouble himself with such elaborate creations?

It was difficult to say with any degree of accuracy just how many dead females these body parts accounted for. When all the grisly remnants had been catalogued and packaged in plastic bags and dispatched to Goult's Funeral Home in Plainfield, it looked like around nine or ten women. The question now was: How had Eddie Gein come to have all these dead bodies in his house?

While detectives and other law enforcement officials alike were taking his farmhouse apart, Ed Gein found himself detained in the Wautoma County jail. A couple of policemen kept watch over the prisoner. As they assumed he was completely insane, they wanted to ensure that he did not commit suicide before they could question him and secure some desperately needed answers to their probing questions.

They were waiting on Sheriff Schley to return from the scene of carnage so a comprehensive interrogation of the prisoner could commence. Everyone was keen to hear an explanation as to why the little fellow had done what he had.

When all the key players were assembled, Ed Gein was questioned solidly for around twelve hours without an attorney present. The man did his level best to avoid communications with his interrogators, adopting a quiet but humble posture throughout. He did not want to inconvenience the policemen; he just didn't want to talk about it right now.

It was not until the next day, Monday, November 18, that Ed Gein finally broke his silence. In the meantime, it had been conclusively ascertained that the butchered carcass of what had once been a living, breathing Bernice Worden had been shot with a .22-caliber bullet. This bullet had plowed into the side of her head and rocketed out through the rear of her skull. This time, however, Eddie had at least had the savvy to take the spent cartridge case away with him.

Under continued pressure, Ed finally relented and, slumping back in his chair, not wanting to look his questioners in the eye, admitted that he had shot and killed Mrs. Worden in her store. He told how he had deliberately waited for an opportunity to murder her, which came when he learned that most of the male population of Plainfield would be away for the day on a mass hunting expedition.

He had found Bernice alone in the store, and after a moment's deliberation outside he had gone back in there and shot her dead. He had dragged her corpse out the back entrance to where her truck was parked and had pushed her inside, covering her over with a tarpaulin. He then slid into the driver's seat and drove the truck to a secluded pine forest which, as he planned to travel back to the location of the store to retrieve his own vehicle on foot, was within safe walking distance.

He had driven back to the forest in his sedan and loaded Bernice's bleeding body into the car. Leaving her truck abandoned among the brooding trees of the snow-swept pine forest, he made the journey back to his house, where he could have some privacy with his newly acquired plaything.

District Attorney Earl Kileen, who joined in the questioning of Ed Gein later that day, was busy relating details of Gein's confession to a mass of hungry newsmen and reporters. He speculated that some of the remains taken from Gein's house might have been that of "young people."

Back in the interview room, this time with Kileen himself posing the questions, Ed revealed how his memory of the actual killing and its gory aftermath was spotty at best, as he had apparently been "in a daze at the time."

He related as best he could how he had trussed and suspended Mrs. Worden's corpse upside down, opened her up with a sharp knife, and drained her of her blood, allowing the flow to collect in a steel bucket, which he then took out back and poured into a freshly dug hole that he subsequently covered over with earth.

When later pressed to reveal the origin of the voluminous collection of dead human artifacts recovered from his house, Gein was emphatic that the only person he had ever murdered was Bernice Worden. Despite the fact that her face had been hanging on Ed's bedroom wall, he never did admit to the killing of Mary Hogan.

His explanation of the rest of his awful totems could be put down to several years' worth of robbing graves over at Plainfield Cemetery. In a very short space of time, his nighttime visits to the graveyard had become an overwhelming addiction, and he found himself being drawn there more and more frequently.

He told how he would avidly read the local paper's obituary columns. Whenever he learned of a recent burial, he would load his digging implements, usually just a pick and shovel, into his car and cruise on over there. He seemed to take a perverse pride in relating how he had unearthed a freshly interred corpse, placed it in his car, and returned to fill the hole back in, leaving it with the illusion of being undisturbed. Though one may construe this as mere common sense for avoiding possible detection later, Ed like to describe it as his own special routine, or "apple pie order."

Regaling his mortified captors with tales of the early days of his corpse-stealing exploits, Ed told how he would sometimes become so nervous he could not go through with it. Most times, though, he did go through with it, and he had lost count of how many bodies he actually had made off with. Again, if a question became too difficult for him to answer, he sought refuge in what was quickly becoming the familiar excuse of being in one of his "dazes." When asked if he had ever sexually abused or molested any of the female cadavers once he had returned to the farmhouse, Ed was emphatic.

"Certainly not!" He found this notion abhorrent because they "smelled too bad."

Most of us might be inclined to think that the very fact that they were dead would have been enough of a deterrent.

Back to Bernice Worden, Ed was quizzed on the way she had been dressed out "just like a deer and everything." Had he dabbled in cannibalism? Was there any possibility that he had ever consumed the flesh of his bodies?

Again Ed denied these assertions. He had just messed around with the bodies. "Nothing sexual, just, well... experimental," he muttered. No, he had not consumed human flesh for any reason at all, be it sexual or just plain old hunger. He preferred apple pie à la mode, topped with ice cream. Eating people just was not his thing. Though we may wonder at the authenticity of his claims here if we are to accept that the man was, by his own admission, operating through some weird fog during these times.

Interrogators touched on Ed's childhood years in an attempt to find out what had gone wrong. Ed Gein recounted that one of his earliest memories was of a scene of violence. The event had taken place behind his parent's store back in La Crosse.

Wondering what Ma and Pa were up to in the old tin shed they had just entered, little Eddie sneaked over to dilapidated building and peered inside. What he saw instantly rooted the young boy to the spot. An intoxicating cocktail of fear, revulsion, and grim fascination flowed through him.

Inside the slaughtering shed, Ed's father George was in the process of raising a trussed pig so that his mother, clutching the biggest butcher knife Eddie had ever laid eyes on, neatly slit open its belly and with a practiced skill extracted the entrails with the blade. As Ed relived this most potent memory, he was able to conjure every last detail. He recalled the "long leather apron spattered with blood and slime" worn by Augusta Gein, the great white matriarch. In that moment she had seemed impossibly huge to Eddie, like some wild, unstoppable force, strong, powerful, and all-consuming. Ed was giddy with that special blend of fear and elation. He had fantasized about this bloody scene for many years, and it may very well have started him off on his slippery slope to cannibalism.

November 18, a cold and gloomy Monday, was the day that Edward Gein was first charged with a crime: The theft of the Worden cash register. The next day, under polygraph examination, Gein was questioned by sheriffs from Portage County regarding the disappearance of Mary Hogan. Ed still would not accept responsibility for her death. He was also interviewed by a couple of La Crosse–based detectives who wanted to talk about a missing fifteen-year-old girl named Evelyn Hartley.

Again Gein denied having anything to do with the disappearance. The next day police charged him with Hogan's murder anyway, along with that of Bernice Worden.

By this time the media was running amok. The wide-scale horror that the case engendered ensured that not just America but the whole world was coming to learn about the dark doings that had gone on at the Gein house. And, of course, with a horror story of this magnitude, there was plenty of room for hyperbole.

There were some who said that between fifty and a hundred bodies had been pulled out of Gein's murder house and that the "Plainfield Butcher," as he had quickly been dubbed, had even distributed parcels of flesh to the good folk in town. What exactly these neighbors had made of the situation upon being presented with these dubious-looking offerings went strangely unreported.

Eager reporters also took a long look at all the missing-persons cases around Wisconsin over the last ten or twenty years and started naming Ed Gein as the prime suspect. In the vast majority of these cases, such assertions were utterly without foundation, but they became a favorite tool of the press and would be echoed throughout the years whenever a sensational murder series was exposed.

> It is a wild country...country that could hide violence for years and perhaps never give up its secrets.
> —THE WAUSHARA ARGUS

From the terrible crypt in the crawlspace of John Wayne Gacy's ranch-style home in Chicago (1972–79), and across the Atlantic to the bland edifice of number 25 Cromwell Street, in Gloucester, England (1972–78), after the police discovered what Fred West had been up to, the popular media seemed to thrive on the idea of even more bodies being found up at the old Gein place.

The murderer had not killed enough. He must have murdered more. But there was no direct evidence linking Gein to the killings of anybody but Mary Hogan and Bernice Worden.

Returning to Gein's grave robbing activities, now that the murder charges had been dealt with, the police focused on a list Gein had provided as a vague guide to which tombs he had tampered with. When the cops later spoke to the sexton of Plainfield Town Cemetery they were told quite firmly that it just would not have been possible to accomplish all of Gein's alleged achievements if he were just one man acting alone.

Later, confronted with this, Gein finally conceded that there had been another man involved. Someone he tentatively named as Gus. The mysterious Gus was never located. After a number of excavations of graves at the cemetery, Gein's stories were finally substantiated. All that remained in the coffin of one vanished cadaver was a moldy burial shroud.

Hearing tell of even more human remains out there in Gein territory, as yet unaccounted for, police escorted Ed back to his farmhouse to point out a trench that he had earlier alluded to filling with the cremated remains of a number of corpses. This also proved to be true. But Ed did not know their names. Short of digging up many other graves of dead females to find out which ones were missing, they might never know the full grim toll.

Then again, on Wednesday, November 27, yet another set of remains were unearthed from a ditch, where neighbors had reported observing Gein once merrily digging away. When police visited this pit they found a skeleton, the large and slightly elongated skull of which, at first, appeared to be that of a man. There was a brief flurry of excitement when the police speculated that it might have belonged to that of a farmer who with another man, had failed to return from a hunting trip way back in 1952.

In fact there was a lot of surmising going on—mainly in press circles—as to whether Ed Gein had been taking out hunters who had strayed onto his radar while traipsing through the dense woodland around his property. However, a state pathologist was later able to divulge that forensic examination had proved conclusively that this was the skeleton of a woman—another of Eddie's decaying playthings nabbed from the town cemetery, no doubt.

In the meantime, just what was to be done with Mr. Edward Gein?

After undergoing an intense barrage of psychological testing, as ordered by the state, Ed Gein was found to be mentally unfit to stand trial. On Monday, January 6, 1958, Gein made a brief court appearance. Looking distinctly unperturbed by the whole situation, the Plainfield Butcher languished in a chair, chewing gum and looking slightly stoned, as Circuit Judge Herbert Bunde considered the evidence provided by three of the examining psychologists, then ordered him to be committed for an indefinite period of time to the Central State Hospital for the criminally insane in Waupan.

This decision on the part of the judge caused somewhat of a stir among the residents of Plainfield. Ed Gein had quite simply destroyed their town's reputation. Through his terrible deeds, he had ensured that Plainfield would forever be synonymous with murder and mayhem. The townsfolk wanted to see him go to trial and be held

*In many ways, the patient has lived a psychotic life for many years. He has substituted human parts for the companionship of human beings.*
—DR. MILTON MILLER

accountable for his wrongdoings. It would take another ten years before their collective wish would be granted.

During this time, Eddie was described variously by hospital orderlies and medical professionals alike as quiet, undemonstrative, and courteous. He was a model patient, more than capable of behaving himself when he had to. The little man took genuine pride in how good he was being for all the nice people at Central State.

One is bound to wonder what thoughts went through the mind of Ed Gein, night after night up at that hospital. Did he have nightmares? Did he feel remorse? Did he cry himself to sleep after lights-out? It seems that whatever dark force had inhabited Ed Gein during the mental disintegration he undoubtedly suffered after the death of his mother had been vanquished.

When faced with the order and enforced discipline of hospital life, there was nothing to say that Ed Gein would have been anything but a safe individual to come into contact with. The private pressures he had endured on the outside, where he had been responsible for controlling his own destiny, were now completely removed. Ed's terrible urges really did seem to have been eroded. They likely began to fade shortly after his arrest and sudden change in environment.

One windy night in March of 1958, as Ed lay asleep in his bed at Central State, his house mysteriously burned down. There were rumblings in town that some fancy entrepreneur types were negotiating to buy the property and turn it into some kind of a morbid museum. Needless to say, the locals were not impressed with this prospect. They rather wanted to try and forget the monster that had lived in their midst, and a constant stream of tourists traveling through town to visit the local House of Horrors was the last thing they needed. Although such a venture would inevitably prove to be quite a commercial boon for the businesses of Plainfield, the people around those parts just were not interested. On March 20, a plot to destroy Gein's house was put into dramatic effect, and the notorious building was burned to the ground.

Curiously, when Ed heard the news, he did not seem even remotely concerned. It was as though he had buried all of his ghosts when they had taken him away, so his old home no longer exercised any power over him. Yes, all that was behind him now, or so he said.

In May 1960, some dogs pawed their way through a trench not far from the blackened mound of rubble that had once been the Gein farm. When the dogs' owner went to see what his hounds were so excited with, he recoiled at the site of a skeletal hand protruding from the earth.

When the police arrived for another of their body finds, they observed a familiar assortment of bones, arms, legs, and a pelvis on this occasion. These would prove to be the last sets of human remains discovered on Gein farmland. It is not to say that other such caches are not in existence. The Geins after all, had a lot of land in their day, and Eddie had proved to be quite an industrious individual when it came down to his dealings with the dead.

It was not until January of 1968 that District Court Judge Robert Gollmar was informed, via a written document on behalf of Central State Hospital authorities, that it was their opinion that Ed Gein was now mentally competent to stand trial. After much ensuing legal wrangling, Gein would finally be tried for the murder of Bernice Worden.

The trial commenced on Wednesday, November 14, and it lasted just one short week. During this time the proceedings would serve as little more than a publicly accessible vehicle for determining whether Gein had been sane at the time he was killing and desecrating Bernice Worden, or if he had actually been insane and as a result unable to control his deviant impulses.

A predictable slew of psychiatrists and psychologists were paraded before the bewildered jury, most of whom were unable to fully comprehend all this mystical medical jargon anyway. The experts seemed, in their typical roundabout fashion, to be saying that all was not well in the head of Edward Gein. That much was obvious, but in the interests of legality, the question was, had he been able to appreciate the wrongfulness and the severity of his acts? That remained to be proved.

Nearly all the facets of Gein's obvious psychosis were addressed during the trial, from the grim discoveries at his house to the grave robbing and the murders. As the trial progressed, it became more and more obvious that this man had been utterly demented, and the judge ultimately found that Ed Gein could not possibly have been in his right mind while the offenses were being carried out. Although he was found guilty of murder in the case of Bernice Worden, Gein was ultimately judged not to be responsible because he was insane. Gein did not deign to reinforce his madness for anyone in court that day, perhaps by leaping from his seat and screaming incoherently or frothing at the mouth. His was a quiet insanity, and when Judge Gollmar ordered that he be returned to his home at the state hospital, he duly rose and shuffled off alongside his guard without fuss.

*Mostly, Gein liked older, more well-developed women— dead, that is.*

—JUDGE ROBERT H. GOLLMAR

Throughout the last decade, Sheriff Art Schley, had become inconsolable over the Gein case. He had been under incredible pressure for years, due as much to the constant attentions of the media as the nightmarish events he had had to deal with.

On the night Bernice Worden's body was found, he could not stop himself roughing up Gein at the County Jail.

When the Gein case had died down, Schley returned to being a simple County Sheriff. In the end it became too much for him. He died from a massive heart attack in December of 1968, only a month after testifying at Gein's trial. He was 43.

Ed Gein was transferred from the hospital in Waupan when it closed in 1978. He would spend the rest of his days at the Mendota Health Institute just outside of Madison, Wisconsin. He would die six years later on Wednesday, July 26, 1984. The cause of death was determined as respiratory failure.

Apart from a few brief exchanges with reporters in a courtroom hearing where he had been present at in 1974, no one had heard or seen anything much of Ed Gein in the intervening years. He had remained to the end a subdued yet affable and well-behaved patient. It looked as though all Ed wanted after his trial was some peace. In some measure this seems to be exactly what he attained.

When in the summer of 1984 he finally found eternal peace, the seventy-eight-year-old Plainfield Butcher was laid to rest in the same cemetery he had systematically plundered some thirty years before.

His was an unmarked grave. His mother rested in the next one over.

At an auction of Gein's property, a mystery bidder paid the exorbitant sum of $750 for his dilapidated 1949 car. The explanation for this strange purchase was revealed two months later in Seymour, Wisconsin. Visitors to the annual county fair were confronted by a tent bearing a sign: "See the car that hauled the dead from their graves… It's here—Ed Gein's crime car!" Those curious enough to pay 25 cents were treated to the sight of Gein's cleaned-up Ford with a blood-spattered dummy in the backseat.

The brainchild of one Bunny Gibbons, this traveling attraction was soon banned by the authorities, but not before Bunny Gibbons had recovered $500 on the investment.

In 1979, a year after Gein had been transferred from the now-defunct Central State Hospital to Mendota Institute, a particularly vicious killing took place in Milwaukee. An eighty-six-year-old woman, Helen Lows, was found battered to death in her bedroom. Her eyes were gouged out and slits cut in her face, which looked as if the murderer had tried to scalp her.

A few weeks later a man called Pervis Smith was arrested for the crime. In 1974 he was admitted as a mental patient to the Central State Hospital in Madison.

Smith told the police that while here was there he had often talked about murder and mutilation and the making of death masks with his best friend, "Little Eddie Gein."

But, one final question remains: Did Ed Gein actually consume human flesh? As we know, he consistently denied any suggestion of sexual activity with his luckless victims; even more so, he dismissed out of hand any notion the authorities had that he'd dined on the dead. Only Gein knows the truth, and he is now long in his grave with the sides falling in. He may have been the ultimate ghoul, his ramshackle home a human slaughterhouse all decorated and furnished with human remains, yet resorting to cannibalism was maybe a taboo too far.

Just as the cult slasher movies are guaranteed to glue our backsides into theater seats, just as many of us feed upon the blood-spattered violence portrayed on the screen, maybe we have always wanted to peep through Gein's grimy windows in the dead of night and witness the macabre happenings within. There, in the yellowy light, amidst the detritus of his domestic life, we see Gein's flickering shadow on a wall. A woman's head is boiling on the kitchen stove as other human remains silently drip blood onto the floor. And there, at his table, sits Ed, licking his lips, knife and fork in hand. With a little seasoning, maybe Bernice Worden didn't taste so bad after all.

# CHAPTER 4

# Jeffrey Lionel Dahmer—"Murder and Mutilation"

*I took the knife and the scalp part off and just peeled the flesh off the bone and kept the skull and the scalp...if I could have kept him longer, all of him, I would have.*
—JEFFREY DAHMER, ON VICTIM ANTHONY SEARS

ON MONDAY, JULY 22, 1991, Jeffrey Dahmer was arrested. He confessed to having killed and dismembered seventeen young men. Parts of many of his victims were found in his apartment and removed by the police in plastic trash bags. But it was not only Dahmer who was put on trial. Milwaukee law enforcement was accused of incompetence and prejudice against black people and homosexuals.

EMBROIDERED IN A RICH TAPESTRY of history, Milwaukee is one of the most pleasant cities in the American Midwest. With wide avenues and a fine harbor on Lake Michigan, it is a city created by the wealthy. But is also has its slum areas, and not so long ago it was ranked as the tenth most dangerous city in the United States.

One of the seedier districts of Milwaukee is tree-lined 25th Street, with a population of around 82 percent under-privileged blacks and Asians. Close to the Marquette University, it is an area of trash-covered sidewalks, boarded-up stores, gay bars, strip joints, marauding muggers, mini-skirted one-star hookers, and countless churches. Most of those who live along 25th Street inhabit cheap one-room apartments.

In a police patrol car cruising along 25th Street at 11:30 p.m., officers Robert Rauth and Rolf Mueller were looking forward to ending their shift at midnight. Although it was July, the night was cool, for the wind off Lake Michigan acts as natural air-conditioner in Milwaukee.

A cry for help made the officers brake to an abrupt halt. A slim, wiry-haired black man was running toward them. Handcuffs were dangling from his left wrist. It appeared that he had escaped from another policeman, but his relief when he saw the police car was almost hysterical, and the tale he babbled out sounded so extraordinary that the two cops had difficulty in following it. All they could gather was that a madman, "a weird dude," had been trying to kill him.

The man's story implied a homosexual encounter, which police would normally avoid, but the officers thought they ought to check this story out, so they climbed out of their car and accompanied the man, who gave his name as Tracy Edwards, to the white, two-story building called Oxford Apartments, a government-subsidized rooming house occupied almost exclusively by blacks. The door to apartment 213 was opened by a tall, nice looking thirty-one-year-old blonde man with a wispy moustache.

As the occupant of apartment 213 stood politely aside to let the officers in, he seemed perfectly calm and looked at Edwards as if he had never set eyes on him before. Both policemen thought it was a false alarm—until they smelled the unpleasant odor of decay, not unlike rotten fish, that pervaded the rooms.

When the cops asked the man, who gave his name as Jeffrey Dahmer, why he had threatened Tracy Edwards, he looked contrite and explained that he had just lost his job and had been drinking. They asked him for the key to the handcuffs. Dahmer looked nervous and tried to stall, for he knew that the key was in his bedroom along with the knife with which he had threatened Edwards. When they insisted, he refused and his calm manner vanished. He suddenly became violent and hysterical.

There was a brief struggle as the three men wrestled in the apartment. Another resident heard one of the policemen say, "The son of a bitch scratched me." Moments later, Dahmer was face down on the floor, and his rights were being read to him.

Rauth called headquarters on his radio and asked them to run a check on the prisoner. The answer came back quickly: Dahmer had a felony conviction for sexual assault on a thirteen-year-old boy.

The fact that Dahmer had a rap sheet for a sex offense now supported the story that Edwards, now able to speak calmly, went on to tell the police. The thirty-two-year-old Edwards, a recent arrival from Mississippi, had met Dahmer four hours earlier in a shopping mall on Grand Avenue. Edwards had been with friends at the time. He knew Dahmer by sight, and when the tall "dude" invited them back to his apartment for a party, they all agreed. Dahmer and Edwards had gone ahead in a taxi to buy some beer, which Edwards paid for, while the others were told to follow. What Edwards didn't know was that Dahmer had deliberately given the wrong address.

Edwards didn't like the smell in Dahmer's small apartment, nor the male pinups on the walls. His own preference was for women. But he was fascinated by an aquarium containing Siamese fighting fish. Dahmer said he liked to watch them fighting, and that the combat invariably ended with one of them dead. They sat on the settee and drank the beer, and Edwards kept glancing at the clock, wondering what had happened to his friends.

When the beer was finished, Dahmer handed him a rum and Coke. The movement of the fighting fish was oddly hypnotic, and Edwards was beginning to feel drowsy. For some reason, Dahmer kept asking him how he was feeling. But when Dahmer put his arms around him and whispered a suggestion about bed, Edwards, instantly wide awake, announced that he was leaving.

That was a mistake. Seconds later, a handcuff had been snapped around one of his wrists. He began to struggle, and Dahmer's attempt to handcuff the other wrist was unsuccessful. Then Edwards froze as Dahmer pressed a large butcher knife against his chest, above his heart, and told him that he would be killed unless he obeyed the order to undress.

Edwards saw that his only chance of survival lay in placating the attacker. Dahmer's face had changed. It looked positively demonic. As Edwards began to unbutton his shirt, trying to talk naturally, Dahmer relaxed for a while, then announced that they would move into the bedroom. Prodded by the knife, Edwards obeyed.

The smell in the room was nauseating. On the wall were more photographs. But these were not professional beefcake pinups; they were amateur shots that showed dismembered bodies and chunks of meat that looked like the joints in a butcher's shop. The unpleasant smell seemed to come from a blue plastic barrel with a black lid that stood under the window. By now, the petrified Edwards could make a good guess as to what it contained.

They sat on the bed and watched a video of *The Exorcist*. It was clear that Dahmer had a taste for the gruesome and bizarre. But now he had momentarily relaxed his importuning. Edwards began to think of escape. On a trip to the toilet, he tried to decide the best way to make a run for it. There was an electronic lock on the bedroom door, but to Edward's relief, the door had not been closed.

Then Dahmer grew tired of games. If Edwards was not going to comply, he told him, he would cut his heart out and eat it. But first he was going to strip Edwards and take some photographs. As Dahmer stood up to get the camera, the prisoner seized his opportunity. He swung his right fist in a punch that knocked Dahmer sideways, then kicked him in the stomach and ran for the door. Dahmer caught up with him there and offered to unlock the handcuff, but Edwards ignored him, wrenched open the door and fled for his life.

When Edwards had finished telling the police his story, he was ordered to stand outside in the hallway. He wanted to leave altogether but was told to wait among the growing crowd of curious neighbors. As they tried to peer into the room, they saw Dahmer lying on the floor, handcuffed. Then one of them saw a policeman open the door of the refrigerator and gasp, "Oh my God! There's a goddamn head in here!'

That was the moment Dahmer began to scream—a horrible, unearthly, animal-like scream. One of the cops rushed downstairs for shackles. When the writhing body was secure, Rauth and Mueller began their search of the apartment.

Within minutes, the officers realized they had discovered a slaughterhouse and torture chamber. The freezer compartment of the refrigerator contained meat in plastic bags, one of which looked ominously like a human heart. Another freezer contained three plastic bags, each with a severed head inside. A filing cabinet contained three skulls—some painted gray—and human bones. A box contained two more skulls and an album full of gruesome photographs. Two more skulls were found in a pan, while another contained severed hands and a male genital organ.

The stinking blue barrel proved to contain three male torsos. An electric saw stained with blood made it clear how Dahmer had dismembered his victims. There was also a large vat of murky hydrochloric acid.

The policemen again used their radio handsets to alert headquarters about their gruesome discoveries, and within minutes three homicide detectives were at the second-floor apartment. More uniformed cops arrived, and the wild-eyed Dahmer was soon led away, still shouting, shackled and handcuffed.

In the early hours of Tuesday, July 27, 1991, forensic investigators from the medical examiner's office began making a list of all the human bits and pieces in the tiny apartment. Their inventory included hands, heads, pieces of muscle, genitals, and various internal organs, as well as painted skulls and other bones. There were eleven heads and skulls in all.

More police cars pulled up in front of Oxford Apartments, and other homicide investigators poured into apartment 213. Some donned yellow protective masks.

At dawn, the blue barrel was lifted downstairs, and other body parts were removed in a series of black plastic bags.

At the medical examiner's office they began the macabre task of trying to piece together the remains. The police also began knocking on doors and questioning neighbors, crowds of whom were already awake and morbidly watching the removal of body parts. The refrigerator smelled so bad as it was being carried out that people fell back and rushed to find fresh air.

The word got around, and journalists and TV crews were the next to arrive. Before midday, the people of America had learned that Milwaukee was the scene of an outbreak of homosexual murders, but that nobody had known anything about them.

A decade earlier, it had been the neighboring city of Chicago, where a builder named John Wayne Gacy had killed thirty-three boys and hidden most of the bodies in the crawl space under his Des Plaines house. Gacy was executed by lethal injection at the Stateville Correctional Center on Tuesday, May 10, 1994.

In 1980, it had been Los Angeles, where "Freeway Killer" William Bonin was believed to have killed forty-one boys. Bonin was executed by lethal injection at San Quentin State Prison on Friday, February 23, 1996.

In 1973, it was Houston, Texas, where Dean Corll murdered twenty-nine boys. Corll was shot dead by one of his accomplices, Elmer Wayne Henley, on Wednesday, August 8, 1973.

Dahmer had not known any of his victims previously. He picked them up in an arbitrary and casual way, inviting them back to his apartment for drinks and promising to pay them if they would pose for photographs or indulge in homosexual sex. But there is no such thing as a free lunch. Tracy Edwards had been the second potential victim to escape, but the first one had not been so lucky. Dahmer had gotten him back and killed him.

Dahmer fully cooperated with the police and confessed freely to his crimes soon after his arrest. He told police that over a period of thirteen years he had murdered fewer than the other serial killers—only seventeen young men. But then, there was a major difference: Dahmer was a cannibal. The plastic bags of human meat in the freezer were intended to be eaten. He described how he had fried the biceps of one victim in vegetable oil. The threat to eat Tracy Edward's heart had been no bluff. The police discovered that Dahmer had little food in the apartment except potato chips, human meat, and a jar of mustard.

Jeffrey Lionel Dahmer was born on Saturday, May 21, 1960, in West Allis, Wisconsin, the first child of Lionel Herbert and Joyce Annette (née Flint). Lionel was still an engineering student at the time at Milwaukee's Marquette University, and the couple lived with his mother, Catherine, a schoolteacher, in West Allis, a city some seven miles west of Milwaukee. Lionel obtained a degree in electrical engineering in 1962, and four years later, a doctorate in analytical chemistry. Seven years after Jeffrey's birth, the couple had another son, whom they named David.

Lionel was a hard worker, an achiever, who had little time to pay attention to his son. Jeffrey Dahmer was later to describe him—with a touch of bitterness—as "highly controlling." He was a strong character. So was Joyce, and as the years went by, their marriage became increasingly stormy. Jeffrey became accustomed to the sight of his parents quarrelling—on at least one occasion to the point of blows. When his mother became pregnant with another child and was ill for six months, he felt neglected. Three changes of school did nothing for his sense of security. His father's work took him to Akron, Ohio, then to Doylestown, then to rural Bath Township in 1968.

The year they moved into their new home, according to Lionel Dahmer, Jeffrey was sexually assaulted by a neighbor in the woods. This, Lionel believed, was the beginning of his son's sexual problems.

He was a gentle and quiet boy, known as a melancholy loner, and he spent much of his time wandering in the woods. He showed little interest in hobbies or social interactions. He biked around his neighbor-

*When I was a little kid I was just like anybody else.*
—JEFFREY DAHMER

hood looking for dead animals, which he dissected at home, going so far as to put a dog's head on a stake. But he also liked attention and gained it from his school friends by clowning, pulling faces as if he were retarded and flapping his arms like a comic Frankenstein's monster. His sense of humor was grotesque and sometimes cruel. Inside the young Jeffrey Dahmer lay a vicious streak.

Oddly enough, although he had a high IQ, his school grades were usually low—a sign of emotional disturbance and inability to concentrate. His parents' long, messy separation and divorce left him with a feeling of having nowhere to turn to satisfy his emotional needs or express unhappiness. In a sense, Dahmer was "autistic," incapable of feeling any real connection with his fellow human beings.

After the breakup of his family when he was eighteen and his first murder, Dahmer went on to Ohio State University, hoping to major in business studies. But alcoholism had destroyed his will to work. His father visited one day to find his son's room full of empty liquor bottles. Dahmer sold his blood at a blood bank to earn money to buy booze. He even took bottles into class and got drunk as he listened to the teacher.

When $120 disappeared from the dorm, as well as a watch and a radio, Dahmer was questioned by police, but no charge was made. One fellow student saw him lying drunk in the street in Columbus and felt that nothing could save him from self-destruction. Predictably, Dahmer lasted only one term before leaving the college.

Seeing no other career opportunities, Dahmer joined the army and signed on for three years. He was posted to Baumholder in West Germany in 1979 as a medic. But he continued to drink heavily and spent much of his time wearing earphones and listening to music, totally withdrawn from the world. His fellow soldiers felt he was on the skids. Eventually, alcohol made him so inefficient that he was discharged with nine months still to serve. As he left, Dahmer told his colleagues, "Someday you'll hear of me again." They certainly did.

The first problem facing the police was to find out the identities of the men to whom the skulls, bones, and genitals belonged. Back at headquarters Dahmer was obviously relieved to be cooperating; he seemed glad that his career as a murderer was over.

It had all started, Dahmer admitted, in 1978, when he was only eighteen years old. His first victim had been a hitchhiker. It was almost ten years before he committed his next murder. But recently, the rate of killing had accelerated, as it often does with serial killers, and there had been no fewer than three murders in the last two weeks. He had attempted to kill Tracy Edwards only three days after his last murder.

Dahmer was also able to help the police establish the identities of the victims—twelve blacks, one Laotian, one Hispanic, and three whites. Some of the names he remembered; the police had to work out the others from identity cards found in Dahmer's apartment and photographs shown to parents of missing youths.

All Dahmer's confessions were sensational; but the story of one teenage victim was so appalling that it created outrage around the world.

Fourteen-year-old Laotian Konerak Sinthasomphone had met Dahmer in front of the same shopping mall where the killer was later to pick up Tracy Edwards. The boy agreed to return to Dahmer's apartment to allow him to take a couple of photographs.

Unknown to Konerak, Dahmer was the man who had enticed and sexually assaulted his elder brother, Somsack, three years earlier. Dahmer had asked the thirteen-year-old Somsack back to his apartment in September 1988 and had slipped a powerful sleeping draft into his drink then fondled him sexually. Somehow, Somsack succeeded in staggering out into the street and back home. The police were notified, and Dahmer was charged with second-degree sexual assault and sentenced to a year in a correction program that allowed him to continue to work during the day in a chocolate factory.

Now the younger brother, Konerak, found himself in the same apartment. He was also given drugged coffee and, when he was unconscious, stripped and raped. After that, Dahmer went out to buy some beer. On his way back to the apartment, Dahmer saw to his horror that his naked victim was talking to two black teenage girls, obviously begging for help. Dahmer rushed over and tried to grab the boy; the girls clung onto him. One of them succeeded in phoning the police and two squad cars arrived within minutes. Three irritable officers wanted to know what the trouble was.

When Dahmer told them that the young man was his lover, that they had merely had a quarrel, the police were inclined to believe him. He looked sober, and Konerak looked drunk. They decided to move away from the gathering crowd, and adjourned to Dahmer's apartment. There Dahmer showed them Polaroid pictures of the boy in his underwear to convince them that they were really lovers—the police had no way of knowing that the photos had been taken that evening—and told them that Konerak was 19.

Meanwhile, Konerak sat on the settee, dazed but probably relieved that his ordeal was over. His passivity was his undoing. His failure to deny what Dahmer was saying convinced the police that Dahmer must be telling the truth. They believed Dahmer and went off, leaving Konerak in the apartment. The moment the officers had left, Dahmer strangled Konerak, violated the corpse, and then took photographs as he dismembered it.

Back at District Three station house, the three policemen made their second mistake of the evening. They joked about the homosexual quarrel they had just broken up. But a tape recorder happened to be running, and when Dahmer was arrested two months later and admitted to killing the Laotian boy, the tape was located and played on radio and television.

On July 26, four days after Dahmer's arrest, the three cops—John Balcerzak, Joseph Gabrish, and Richard Portubcan—were suspended from duty with pay. (Later, administrative charges were filed against them but ultimately dismissed.) Public anger was transferred from Jeffrey Dahmer to the police department. Police Chief

Philip Arreola found himself assailed on all sides, subjected to harsh criticism from his own force for not supporting his men (in the following month, the Milwaukee Police Association passed a vote of no confidence in him) and from Milwaukee's blacks and Asians for racism.

The public outcry was not due simply to the tragic mistake made by the three policemen. It also arose because they had apparently preferred to believe Dahmer, who was white, and ignored Konerak because he was not—at least that is how Milwaukee's non-whites saw it. It had also been remarked that when Dahmer was arrested, TV cameramen had been requested not to take pictures. Someone in the crowd had shouted that if he had been black, they would have allowed the cameras down his throat.

When Dahmer appeared in court for the first time on July 25, he was dressed in his own clothes, not in the orange prison uniform. This was seen as deliberately favoring a white man. The Dahmer case caused an unpleasant build-up of racial tension in Milwaukee, and police crossed their fingers that nothing would ignite race riots. Fortunately, nothing did.

The twelve charges read out in court all concerned men who had been murdered since Dahmer had moved into Oxford Apartments in May 1960. But, according to Dahmer, his first murder had taken place thirteen years earlier in Bath Township, northeastern Ohio. At the time, his parents were in the process of a bitter and messy divorce, both alleging cruelty and neglect. Jeffrey had already learned to take refuge in alcohol.

According to Dahmer's confession, on Tuesday, June 6, 1978, he had found himself alone in the family house at 4480 Bath Road. His father had already left, and his mother and younger brother David were away visiting relatives. He had been left no money and very little food in the broken refrigerator. That evening, he explained, he decided to go out and look for some company.

It was not hard to find. A nineteen-year-old white youth, who had spent the day at a rock

*That night in Ohio, that one impulsive night. Nothing's been normal since then. It taints your whole life. After it happened, I thought that I'd just try to live as normally as possible and bury it, but things like that don't stay buried. I didn't think it would, but it does, it taints your whole life.*

—JEFFREY DAHMER, ON STEPHEN HICKS

concert, was hitchhiking home to attend his father's birthday party. When an ancient Oldsmobile driven by someone who looked about his own age pulled up, the youth climbed in. They went back to Dahmer's house, drank beer, and talked about their lives. Dahmer found he liked his new friend immensely. But when the lad looked at the clock and said that he had to go, Dahmer begged him to stay. When the youth refused, Dahmer picked up a dumbbell, struck him over the head, and strangled him. He then dragged the body to the crawl space under the house and dismembered it with a carving knife. It may sound a formidable task, but Dahmer was entirely without experience.

He wrapped up the body parts in plastic bags, but after a few days the smell began to escape. Dahmer's mother, who was due back soon, was sure to notice the sweet stench of death. So he took the plastic bags out to the woods under cover of darkness and managed to dig a shallow grave in the rock-hard soil. But even though the bags were now underground he still worried that children might come across the grave. So he dug them up again, stripped the flesh from the bones, and smashed the bones with a sledgehammer. He scattered them around the garden and the property next door. When the matriarch returned a few days later, there was nothing to reveal that her son was now a killer.

Unfortunately, Dahmer was unable to recall the name of his victim. The Milwaukee P.D. telephoned the police of Bath Township and asked them if they had a missing-person case that dated from around mid-1978. They had. On June 18, a youth named Stephen Mark Hicks had left his home in Coventry Township to go to a rock concert. Friends had driven him there, and they agreed to meet him that evening to take him home. Hicks failed to turn up at the rendezvous point, and no trace of him was ever found. The family had offered a reward for information, hired a private detective, and even consulted a psychic. Coventry Township had two photographs of Stephen Hicks on file. When shown these, Dahmer said casually, "Yes, that's him." Police went to the former Dahmer house to check his story.

In the crawl space under the property, the blood-detecting chemical Luminol caused several spots to glow in the dark. They proved to be human blood. Sprayed on a concrete block, it caused a bloody handprint to appear. The following day, more bones and three human teeth were found. Dental records eventually revealed that they had belonged to Stephen Hicks.

For nine years after killing Stephen Hicks, Dahmer kept his homicidal impulses under control. After a short stay in Florida, Dahmer had moved in with his grandmother, Catherine, in West Allis, south of Milwaukee. But he was still drinking heavily and was in trouble with the police for causing a disturbance in a bar. His family was relieved when he at last found a job at the Ambrosia Chocolate Company in Milwaukee.

Dahmer soon discovered Milwaukee's gay bars, where he became known as a monosyllabic loner. But it was not long before patrons observed that he had a more sinister habit. He would sometimes engage a fellow customer in conversation and offer him a drink. "Nothing much wrong with that," you might think, but these drinking companions often ended up in drugged comas. Yet Dahmer's intention was clearly not to commit rape. He seemed to want to try out his drugs as an experiment to see how much he had to administer and how fast they worked. But when one of his drinking friends ended up unconscious in the hospital, the owner of Club Bath told him he was barred.

On Monday, September 8, 1986, two twelve-year-old boys reported to the police that Dahmer had exposed himself to them and masturbated. Dahmer alleged that he had merely been urinating. He was sentenced to a year on probation and, with apparent sincerity, promised his probation officers, "I'll never do it again." (Judges and probation officers would later note that Dahmer had a highly convincing manner of making such promises.) The probation period ended on September 9, 1987.

A year of good behavior had done nothing to alleviate Dahmer's psychological problems; on the contrary, they had built up resentment and frustration. Six days after his probation ended, the frustration again exploded into murder.

On Tuesday, September 15, while drinking at a gay hangout called Club 219, Dahmer met twenty-four-year-old Stephen Tuomi. They decided to go to bed and adjourned to the Ambassador Hotel, where they took a room that cost $43.88 for the night.

Dahmer claimed that he could not recall much of that night, admitting that they drank themselves into a stupor. When he woke up, he stated, Tuomi was dead. Blood was coming from his mouth, and there were strangulation marks around his throat.

For Dahmer it was a terrifying situation—alone in a hotel room with a corpse and the desk clerk likely to call up at any moment to check whether the room had been vacated. Dahmer solved the problem by going out and buying a large suitcase, into which he stuffed the body. Then he got a taxi to take him back to his grandmother's house, where he had his own basement apartment, and got the driver to help him drag the heavy case indoors. There he dismembered the body and put the parts into plastic bags,

*I felt in complete shock. I just couldn't believe it happened again after all those years when I'd done nothing like this...I don't know what was going through my mind. I have no memory of it. I tried to dredge it up, but I have no memory whatsoever.*

—Jeffrey Dahmer, on Stephen Tuomi

which he put out for the garbage collector. He performed his task of disposal so efficiently that the police, unable to find the slightest sign of it, decided not to charge Dahmer with the murder.

Clearly, this second killing was a watershed in Dahmer's life. The earlier murder of Stephen Hicks might have been put behind him as a youthful aberration committed in a state of psychological stress. But the killing of Stephen Tuomi was a deliberate act, whether Dahmer was sober or not. Since Tuomi had gone to the room specifically to have sex, there could be no reason whatever to kill him unless Dahmer's needs involved more than an act of mutual intercourse.

As a result of the murder of Stephen Tuomi, Dahmer seems to have acknowledged that murder and dismemberment were necessary to satisfy his deviant sexual impulses. The fifteen murders that followed leave no possible doubt about it.

Four months later, on Thursday, January 14, 1988, Dahmer picked up a young white male prostitute named Jamie Doxtator at a bus stop outside Club 219 and asked him if he would like to earn money by posing for a video. They went back to West Allis on the bus and had sex in the basement. Then Dahmer gave the boy a drink heavily laced with a sleeping drug and strangled him when he was unconscious.

With his grandmother's garage at his disposal, getting rid of the body was easy. He told the police that he had cleaned the flesh from the bones with acid, then smashed the bones with a sledgehammer and scattered them around like those of his first victim. What he does not seem to have admitted is that the murder and dismemberment of James Doxtator was his primary purpose when he invited the youth back home.

The police interrogator looked up from his notebook to ask if there was anything distinctive about Doxtator by which he might be identified. Dahmer recalled that he had two scars near his nipples.

Two months elapsed before Dahmer killed again. On Thursday, March 24, 1988, in the Phoenix Bar, not far from Club 219, he met a twenty-three-year-old homosexual named Richard Guerrero who was virtually broke. Attracted by the graceful, slightly built Hispanic youth, Dahmer made the same proposals that he had made to his previous victim, and Guerrero, too, accompanied him back to the grandmother's house. There they had oral sex, and Guerrero was offered a drugged drink. When he was unconscious, Dahmer strangled him and then dismembered the body in the garage.

Guerrero's frantic family hired a private detective and circulated leaflets with their son's description. They also hired a psychic. They were still searching three years later when Dahmer confessed to the murder.

Dahmer's grandmother was becoming concerned about the awful smells emanating from the garage. Dahmer said it was the garbage, but it seemed to persist even when the sacks had been collected. Dahmer's father, Lionel, came to investigate and found a black, sticky residue on the garage floor. Dahmer, confronted with this evidence, said he had been using acid to strip dead animals of their flesh and fur as he had done in childhood.

In September 1988, Catherine Dahmer finally decided she could no longer put up with the stench and her grandson's drunkenness. On September 25, Dahmer moved into an apartment at 808 North 24th Street after Catherine literally threw him out.

There can be no doubt that Dahmer intended to use his newfound freedom to give full rein to his morbid sexual urges. But an unforeseen hitch occurred. Within 24 hours, the four-time murderer was in trouble with the police. On September 26, he came across Somsack Sinthasomphone, lured him back to his apartment and drugged him. As we now know, Somsack escaped by the skin of his teeth.

Nevertheless, Dahmer was charged with sexual assault and enticing a child for immoral purposes. He spent a week in jail and was then released on bail. On January 30, 1989 he was found guilty; the sentence would not be handed down until four months later.

But even the possibility of a long prison sentence could not cure Dahmer of his obsessive need to kill and dismember. When he appeared in court to be sentenced on May 23, 1989, he had already claimed his fifth victim.

Anthony Sears, a good-looking twenty-six-year-old, dreamed of becoming a male model. He was bisexual, had a girlfriend, and had just been appointed manager of a restaurant. On Friday March 25, 1989, he went drinking in a gay bar called La Cage with a friend, Jeffrey Conner, and Dahmer engaged them in conversation. By the time the bar closed, Sears had agreed to accompany Dahmer back to his grandmother's home. (Dahmer seemed to have been worried that the police were watching his own apartment.) Once there, they had sex, and Dahmer offered Sears a drink.

*I knew my grandma would be waking up and I still wanted him to stay with me so I strangled him...I brought him up to the bedroom and pretended he was still alive.*
—JEFFREY DAHMER, ON ANTHONY SPEARS

The grim routine was repeated almost without variation: strangulation, dismemberment, and disposal of the body parts in the garbage. Dahmer decided to preserve the skull as a memento. He painted it and later took it with him when he returned to Oxford Apartments.

Assistant District Attorney Gale Shelton had recognized instinctively that a man who would drug a teenage boy for sex was highly dangerous and needed to be kept out of society for a long time. She argued for a prison term of five years. She described Dahmer as evasive, manipulative, and unrepentant.

Dahmer's lawyer, Gerald Boyle, argued that the assault on Somsack Sinthasomphone was a one-time offense and would never happen again. Dahmer himself revealed considerable skills as an actor in representing himself as contrite and self-condemned. He pleaded, "I am an alcoholic and a homosexual with sexual problems."

Judge William Gardner was touched by the appeal. This clean-cut boy obviously needed psychiatric help, and there was none available in prison. So he sentenced Dahmer to five years on probation and a year in a house of corrections, where he could continue to work at the chocolate factory during the day.

Raymond Smith had been in trouble with the law since his early twenties. When he came out of prison in Illinois, he decided to live with his sister in Milwaukee and try and make a new start. Unfortunately, one of the first things he did in Milwaukee was to visit the gay Club 219, where he made the acquaintance of a tall, good-looking young white man called Jeff.

Dahmer had been in his new apartment for just over two weeks. When Dahmer offered Smith money to pose for photographs, he accepted, and they left the club. Back in room 213, Smith accepted one of his host's special cocktails and lapsed into unconsciousness.

In his confession, Dahmer described how he had strangled Smith, then removed the clothes and had oral sex with the body. Afterward, he dismembered it and disposed of the flesh. But he kept the skull and painted it gray.

Known as "the Sheik" because he wore a turban or headband, twenty-eight-year-old Eddie Smith made no secret of being a homosexual and accepted readily when Dahmer accosted him in the Phoenix Bar on Thursday, June 14, and invited him to the apartment. After oral sex, Dahmer drugged him, strangled him, and dismembered the body, which he disposed of in garbage bags.

Dahmer's career of slaughter almost came to an abrupt end on July 8, 1990. On that day he made the mistake of varying his method. He approached Ricky Beeks, a fifteen-year-old Hispanic boy, outside a gay bar and offered him $200 to pose for nude photographs. The boy returned to Dahmer's room and removed his clothes. But instead of offering the usual drugged drink, Dahmer picked up a rubber mallet and hit Beeks on the head. It failed to knock him unconscious, and the boy fought back as Dahmer tried to strangle him. Somehow Beeks succeeded in calming his attacker. And, incredibly, Dahmer allowed him to go, even calling a taxi.

The boy had pledged not to notify the police. But when he was taken to hospital for treatment he broke his promise. For a few moments Dahmer's future hung in the balance. But when the boy begged them not to allow his foster parents find out that he was homosexual, the police decided to do nothing about it.

A few weeks later, on Saturday, September 22, 1990, Dahmer picked up a twenty-two-year-old black dancer named Ernest Miller, who was home from Chicago, where he intended to start training at a dance school in the fall. They had sex in room 213, and then Dahmer offered him a drugged drink and watched him sink into oblivion.

Perhaps because he had not killed for three months, Dahmer's craving for violence and its aftermath was stronger than usual. Instead of strangling his victim, Dahmer cut his throat. He decided that he wanted to keep the skeleton, so after cutting the flesh from the bones and dissolving most of it in acid he bleached the skeleton with acid. He also kept the biceps, which he put in the freezer.

> I separated the joints, the arm joints, the leg joints, and had to do two boilings. I think I used four boxes of Soilex for each one, put in the upper portion of the body and boiled that for about two hours and then the lower portion for another two hours. The Soilex removes all the flesh, turns it into a jellylike substance and it just rinses off. Then I laid the clean bones in a light bleach solution, left them there for a day and spread them out on either newspaper or cloth and let them dry for about a week in the bedroom.
>
> — JEFFREY DAHMER, ON ERNEST MILLER

The last victim of 1990 died almost by accident. Twenty-three-year-old David Thomas had a girlfriend and a three-year-old daughter. Nevertheless, one evening in September, he accepted Dahmer's offer to return to his apartment in exchange for money. Dahmer gave him a drugged drink but then decided that Thomas was not his type after all and that he had no desire for sex. Since Thomas was now drugged and might be angry when he woke up, Dahmer killed him anyway. He filmed the dismemberment process and took photographs of the severed head. Thomas's sister later identified him by the photographs.

The first murder of 1991 was a nineteen-year-old black homosexual named Curtis Straughter whose ambition was to become a model. Dahmer picked him up in freezing, rainy weather on Tuesday, February 19. While they were engaging in oral sex in the evil-smelling apartment, Straughter began to flag as the sleeping potion took effect. Dahmer took a leather strap and strangled him, then dismembered the body and recorded the process on camera. Once again he kept the skull.

The murder of nineteen-year-old Errol Lindsey on Sunday, April 7, 1991, has a quality of déjà vu. The police report states bleakly that Dahmer met Lindsey on a street corner and offered him money to pose for photographs. Lindsey was drugged and strangled, and then Dahmer had oral sex with the body. Errol Lindsey was dismembered. Dahmer kept his skull.

Thirty-one-year-old Tony Hughes was a deaf mute who loved to dance. When Dahmer accosted him outside Club 219 on Friday, May 24, he had to make his proposition in writing—$50 for some photographs. Hughes was offered the sleeping potion, then strangled and dismembered. Dahmer had become so casual that he simply left the body lying in the bedroom for a day or so before beginning the dismemberment process. It was, after all, no riskier than having an apartment full of skulls and body parts.

Sunday, June 30, was the day of Chicago's Gay Pride Parade, and Dahmer decided to attend, taking a Greyhound bus for the ninety-mile trip. After watching the parade, he went to the police station to report that a pickpocket had taken his wallet. But he seemed to have enough money left to approach a twenty-year-old black youth he met at the bus station, another aspiring model named Matt Turner.

They traveled back to Milwaukee on the bus, then to Dahmer's apartment by cab. In his later confession, Dahmer said nothing about sex, but he admitted to drugging Turner, strangling him with a strap, then dismembering him and cutting off his head, keeping the skull.

On Friday, July 5, 1991, Dahmer was back in Chicago looking for another victim. In a gay club on Wells Street he met twenty-three-year-old Jeremiah Weinberger and invited him back to Milwaukee. Weinberger consulted a former roommate, Ted Jones, about whether he should accept. "Sure, he looks okay," said Jones. He was later to comment ruefully, "Who knows what a serial killer looks like?'

*He was exceptionally affectionate. He was nice to be with.*

—JEFFREY DAHMER, ON JEREMIAH WEINBERGER

Dahmer and Weinberger spent Saturday in the apartment having sex. Dahmer appeared to like his new acquaintance. But when, the following day, Weinberger looked at the clock and said it was time to go, Dahmer offered him a drink. Weinberger's head joined Matt Turner's in a plastic bag in the freezer.

On July 12, Dahmer was suddenly fired from his job, and his reaction was typical. The same day he picked up a twenty-three-year-old black man named Oliver Lacy, took him back to his apartment and gave him the usual drugged drink. This time, after strangling his victim, he sodomized the body.

The murder spree was almost over. Four days later, the head of the final victim joined the others in the freezer. He was twenty-five-year-old Joseph Bradehoft, an out-of-work black man who was hoping to move from Minnesota to Milwaukee with his wife and two children. He accepted Dahmer's offer of money for photographs and willingly joined in oral sex in Dahmer's apartment. Afterward he was drugged, strangled, and dismembered. His body was placed in the barrel of acid.

By then, however, Dahmer had conceived the idea of creating zombies of his victims, and attempted to do so by drilling holes into their skulls and injecting muriatic acid or boiling water into the frontal lobe area of their brains with a large syringe.

After Dahmer's arrest, his stepmother, Shari Jordan, said that, "Jeff has told me nothing more could have been done for him. He doesn't know why he did those terrible things. He told me if he'd been caught after the first murder in 1978, it would have been a blessing." She went on to say that she could not describe the nightmare it all had been. "All I will say is every parent should realize that there, but for the Grace of God, go I."

Dahmer told his parents and his stepmother not to blame themselves and that after the trial was over he would sit down with them and talk things out so that they could all have peace of mind.

Dahmer went to trial in January 1992 before Judge Laurence Gram. On the advice of his defense team, Gerald Boyle and Wendy Patrickus, he pled guilty but insane. The prosecution, led by District Attorney Michael McCann, refused to accept the insanity plea. They pointed out that if Dahmer were found guilty but insane and confined to a mental institution, he could plead for a review of his case after two years. Theoretically he might then be released. Though admittedly unlikely, it was legally possible.

*If I was killed in prison. That would be a blessing right now.*
—JEFFREY DAHMER

One of the main prosecution witnesses, psychiatrist Frederick Fosdick, testified that although Dahmer was undoubtedly suffering from a psychiatric disorder ("primarily necrophilia"), it did not prevent him from knowing the wrongness of his acts.

The jury agreed, and on a Saturday, February 15, 1992, they found Jeffrey Dahmer guilty of the fifteen murders with which he was charged. Two days later, Dahmer was sentenced to fifteen terms of life imprisonment—957 years behind bars, which meant he could never be released. Wisconsin has no death penalty.

Dahmer was never charged with the murders he admitted to committing at his grandmother's house in Ohio. These crimes would stand on the record. If tried for those he would have faced the death penalty.

Dahmer served his time at the Columbia Correctional Institution in Portage, Wisconsin, where he eventually declared himself a born-again Christian. His conversion occurred after reading evangelical literature sent to him by his father. Roy Ratcliff, a local preacher from the Churches of Christ, met with Dahmer and agreed to baptize him.

Dahmer was attacked twice in prison, the first time in July 1994. After attending a church service in the prison chapel, an inmate attempted to slash his throat with a razor blade. Dahmer escaped the incident with superficial wounds. On Monday, November 24, 1994, while on work detail in the prison gym, Dahmer and another inmate, thirty-seven-year-old Jesse Michael Anderson, were severely beaten by twenty-five-year-old Christopher

J. Scarver with a bar from a weight machine. Dahmer died of severe head trauma while on his way to hospital in an ambulance. His brain was retained for study. Anderson died two days later from his wounds.

Oxford Apartments at 924 North 25th Street has since been demolished; the site is now a vacant lot. Plans to convert the site into a memorial garden failed to materialize.

In 1994, Lionel Dahmer published *A Father's Story* and donated a portion of the proceeds to the victims and their families.

*Now is everybody happy? Now that he's been bludgeoned to death, is that good enough for everyone?*
—JOYCE FLINT, UPON HEARING OF HER SON'S MURDER

Most of the families showed support for Lionel and his second wife, Shari.

Joyce Dahmer died of cancer in 2000 at age sixty-four. Dahmer's younger brother, David, changed his surname and lives in anonymity.

Jeffrey Dahmer's estate was awarded to the families of eleven of his victims who had sued for damages. All of his possessions were destroyed.

What led him to cut up his victims? It seems to have started with his bug collection as a child—butterflies, moths, dragonflies, mantises, spiders, and beetles. He preserved them in formaldehyde. He then went on to larger creatures. Possibly he felt like a doctor—albeit a pathologist—as he stripped birds and rats of their flesh.

Perhaps turning animals into skeletons provided an outlet for his aggression and satisfied a need for self-assertion.

If this was the case, then Dahmer's explanation of his first murder—of Stephen Hicks—is untenable. He claims that, when he had been left alone in the house in Bath Township in 1978, he decided to go out and look for company, and that Hicks was murdered only when he attempted to leave. It seems far more probable, however, that Dahmer invited Hicks to the house with every intention of killing him and hacking up the body.

Dahmer's greatest pleasure so far had been dissecting animals, but he had probably daydreamed of dissecting a human being. Now he was alone in the house, and he knew he would be alone for days. There were woods nearby, so disposal of the body would be easy. Without the stimulus of rage and self-pity, murder might have remained in the realms of fantasy. But resentment, loneliness, and opportunity combined to turn it into reality.

Dahmer's confession says nothing about having sexual intercourse with the corpse, but his later record makes it highly unlikely that he simply dissected Hicks and disposed of the body.

The death of Stephen Hicks must have had a crystallizing effect on Dahmer's sexual inclinations. He was no longer a misunderstood loner; he was a killer, potentially an outcast from society. Did he wake up the next morning wishing it had all been a nightmare? If so, he had the means of forgetfulness ready at hand—alcohol. Dahmer had been a heavy drinker since his mid-teens. As with

Dennis Nilsen (another heavy drinker), alcohol combined with homosexuality and a morbid obsession with death, leading inevitably to necrophilia.

If he not turned to alcohol, Dahmer may have become an "achiever" like his father. But in his late twenties he was still a dropout, a nobody working at a labouring job in a chocolate factory. He had been virtually alone in the world for more than a decade. Alcoholism, insecurity, lack of self-esteem, and an overwhelming craving to rape and mutilate, combined to turn him into one of America's worst serial killers to escape the death penalty.

*I couldn't find any meaning in my life when I was out there. I'm sure as hell not going to find it in here [prison]. This is the grand finale of a life poorly spent and the end result is just overwhelmingly depressing...it's just a sick, pathetic, wretched, miserable life story, that's all it is. How it can help anyone, I've no idea.*
— JEFFREY DAHMER

In His Own Words: Excerpts from Dahmer's Confession

I think in some way I wanted it to end, even if it meant my own destruction.

... To relieve the minds of the parents... I mean, it's a small, very small thing, but I don't know what else I could do. At least I can do that... because I created this horror and it only makes sense that I do everything to put an end to it, a complete end to it.

It's just a nightmare, let's put it that way. It's been a nightmare for a long time, even before I was caught ... for years now, obviously my mind has been filled with gruesome, horrible thoughts and ideas ... a nightmare.

I don't even know if I have the capacity for normal emotions or not because I haven't cried for a long time. You just stifle them for so long that maybe you lose them, partially at least. I don't know.

I don't know why it started. I don't have any definite answers on that myself. If I knew the true, real reasons why all this started, before it ever did, I wouldn't probably have done any of it.

I'd rather be talking about anything else in the world right now [other than Stephen Hicks].

At about eleven o'clock at night, when everyone was gone and the store was locked up from the outside, I went out and undressed the mannequin and I had a big sleeping bag cover. I put it in that, zipped it up and carried it out of the store, which was a pretty dangerous thing to do. I never thought of them maybe having security cameras or being locked in the store, but I walked out with it and took it back home. I ended up getting a taxi and brought it back and kept it with me a couple of weeks. I just went through various sexual fantasies with it, pretending it was a real person, pretending that I was having sex with it, masturbating, and undressing it.

## On his childhood:

One thing I know for sure. It was a definite compulsion because I couldn't quit. I tried, but after the Ambassador, I couldn't quit. It would be nice if someone could give the answer on a silver platter as to why I did all this and what caused it, because I can't come up with an answer.

Am I just an extremely evil person or is it some kind of satanic influence, or what? I have no idea. I have no idea at all. Do you? Is it possible to be influenced by spirit beings? I know that sounds like an easy way to cop out and say that I couldn't help myself, but from all that the Bible says, there are forces that have a direct or indirect influence on people's behavior. The Bible calls him Satan. I suppose it's possible because it sure seems like some of the thoughts aren't my own, they just come blasting into my head... These thoughts are very powerful, very destructive, and they do not leave. They're not the kind of thoughts that you can just shake your head and they're gone. They do not leave.

After the fear and terror of what I'd done had left, which took about a month or two, I started it all over again. From then on it was a craving, a hunger; I don't know how to describe it, a compulsion!

On his parent's marriage:

I decided I wasn't ever going to get married because I never wanted to go through anything like that.

On his aquarium:

It was nice, with African cichlids and tiger barbs in it and live plants, it was a beautifully kept fish tank, very clean ... I used to like to just sit there and watch them swim around, basically. I used to enjoy the planning and the set-up, the filtration, read about how to keep the nitrate and ammonia down to safe levels and just the whole spectrum of fish-keeping interested me ... I once saw some puffer fish in the store. It's a round fish, and the only ones I ever saw with both eyes in front, like a person's eyes, and they would come right up to the front of the glass and their eyes would be crystal blue, like a person's, real cute… It's a fun hobby. I really enjoyed that fish tank. It's something I really miss.

On his crimes:

I didn't want to keep killing people and have nothing left except the skull… This is going to sound bad, but … should I say it? … I took the drill while he was asleep…

Yes, I do have remorse, but I'm not even sure myself whether it is as profound as it should be. I've always wondered myself why I don't feel more remorse.

If I'd been thinking rationally I would have stopped. I wasn't thinking rationally because it just increased and increased. It was almost like I wanted to get to a point where it was out of my control and there was no return. I mean, I was very careful for years and years, you know. Very careful, very careful about making sure that nothing incriminating remained, but these last few months, they just went nuts… It just seemed like it went into a frenzy this last month. Everything really came crashing down. The whole thing started falling down around my head… That was the last week I was going to be in that apartment building. I was going to have to move out and find somewhere to put all my possessions. Should I get a chest and put what I wanted to keep in that, and get rid of the rest? Or should I put an end to this, try to stop this and find a better direction for my life? That's what was going through my mind that last week.

Something, stronger than my conscious will made it happen. I think some higher power got good and fed-up with my activity and decided to put an end to it. I don't really think there were any coincidences. The way it ended and whether the close calls were warning to me or what, I don't know. If they were, I sure didn't heed them... If I hadn't been caught or lost my job, I'd still be doing it, I'm quite sure of that. I went on doing it and doing it and doing it, in spite of my anxiety and the lack of lasting satisfaction... How arrogant and stupid of me to think that I could do something like this and just go about my life normally as if nothing ever happened. They say you reap what you sow, well, it's true, you do, eventually ... I've always wondered, from the time that I committed that first horrid mistake, sin, with Hicks, whether this was sort of predestined and there was no way I could have changed it. I wonder just how much predestination controls a person's life and just how much control they have over themselves.

I was completely swept along with my own compulsion. I don't know how else to put it. It didn't satisfy me completely so maybe I was thinking another one will. Maybe this one will and the numbers started growing and growing and just got out of control, as you can see.

It's just like a big chunk of me has been ripped out and I'm not quite whole. I don't think I'm overdramatizing it, and I'm certainly deserving of it, but the way I feel now, it's just like you're talking to someone who is terminally ill and facing death. Death would be preferable to what I am facing. I just feel like imploding upon myself, you know? I just want to go somewhere and disappear.

When you've done the types of things I've done, it's easier not to reflect on yourself. When I start thinking about how it's affecting the families of the people, and my family and everything, it doesn't do me any good. It just gets me very upset.

I should have gone to college and gone into real estate and got myself an aquarium, that's what I should have done.

I still have guilt. I will probably never get rid of that, but yes, I'm free of the compulsion and the driving need to do it… I don't think I'm capable of creating anything. I think the only thing I'm capable of is destroying … I'm sick and tired of being destructive. What worth is life if you can't be helpful to someone?

This is the grand finale of a life poorly spent and the end result is just overwhelmingly depressing . . . a sick pathetic, miserable life story, that's all it is.

*In 1970, Stanley Dean Baker, left, and Harry Allen Stroup were arrested for the murder of James Schlosser, whose flesh Baker admitted to enjoying. He ate the young man's still-beating heart raw, and kept an index finger to snack on later. Baker also confessed to his involvement with the Four Pi movement, a cult whose objective was to promote "the total worship of evil."*

*Upon his arrest in Plainfield, Wisconsin, in November 1957, Edward Gein was escorted to the Central State Hospital for the Criminally Insane. When police first entered Gein's home, they found his last victim's body hanging like meat in a butcher's shop, as well as furniture fashioned from human skin and "masks" made from the faces of the dead.*

*Joachim Kroll admitted to murdering twelve people. He particularly relished the taste of his victims' buttocks.*

*Although sentenced to life in prison, Ed "the Co-Ed Killer" Kemper, could be released as early as 2012.*

*Issei Sagawa's murder and consumption of a young Dutch woman created a media sensation. Sagawa, a free man, detailed the brutal crime in a best-selling memoir and on the Japanese talk show circuit.*

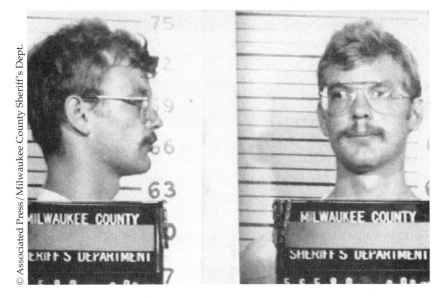

*Top: On July 12, 1991, the date of his final murder, Jeffrey Dahmer was arrested in Milwaukee, Wisconsin. Bottom: Dahmer was found guilty of killing fifteen young men, although he confessed to having slain and dismembered seventeen.*

*Andrei Chikatilo, "The Rostov Ripper," held a reign of terror across southeastern Russia from the late 1970s to the early 1990s. While experts declared him a sado-sexual psychopath, he was found legally competent to stand trial. During the court proceedings, he was kept in a specially designed iron cage to protect him from the hysterical families of his fifty-three victims.*

# CHAPTER 5

# Hamilton Howard "Albert" Fish—"The Brooklyn Vampire"

*And I will cause them to eat the flesh of their sons and the flesh of their daughters, and they shall, eat every one, the flesh of his friend in the siege and straightness, wherewith their enemies, and they seek their lives, shall straighten them.*
—JEREMIAH 19:9 (ALBERT FISH'S FAVORITE SCRIPTURAL PASSAGE)

HAMILTON HOWARD "ALBERT" FISH was born on Thursday, May 19, 1870, in Washington, D.C. After Walter, Annie, and Edwin, he was the last of the surviving Fish children, and one could reasonably argue that Hamilton was genetically flawed from conception.

Moving swiftly through the mental and physical deficiencies of the Fish clan, we find that Hamilton's uncle suffered from religious mania and died in a state mental hospital. A paternal aunt was completely crazy. A brother was feebleminded and died of hydrocephalus. Another brother suffered from chronic alcoholism. A half-brother also died in a state asylum, while his sister, Annie, also had "some sort of mental affliction."

The patriarch, Captain Randall Fish, a thirty-second-degree Mason, was born in 1795. Living on B Street NE, between Second and Third Avenue (just a stone's throw from the now Titanic Memorial) his wife was forty-three years younger than Randall, and by all accounts she was "very queer"—a borderline schizophrenic who was said to hear and see things. A Potomac River boat captain for most of his life, Randall ended up as a fertilizer manufacturer. On October 15, 1875, aged eighty, he died of a heart attack at the Sixth Street Station of the Pennsylvania Railroad in 1875. He had remarkably brought Hamilton into the world at age seventy-five.

Yet not all of the Fishes were nuts. One relative—how far removed we do not know—was none other than Hamilton Fish (1808–93), an American statesman who served as the sixteenth Governor of New York and U.S. Secretary of State under Ulysses S. Grant.

Without the support of her husband, Mrs. Fish was forced to fend for herself, and this necessitated dumping Hamilton into St. John's Orphanage in Washington. There he was often stripped naked, whipped, and beaten in front of other boys by the staff to the degree that eventually he came to enjoy the physical pain, which would often cause erections for which he was teased and called "Ham and Eggs." Later, he would change his name to that of his dead brother Albert. The nickname dissociated him from the abuse he had suffered at St. John's.

By 1880, it seems that Mrs. Fish had pulled herself together and was able to remove Albert from St. John's. In 1882, at age twelve, he started his first sexual relationship with a telegraph boy who was a good bit older. This youth soon introduced Albert to urophagia (drinking urine) and coprophagia (the consuming of feces). Fish then started frequenting public baths on weekends so he could watch other boys undress. It is also of interest to note that he was profligate and compulsively wrote obscene letters to women found from classified ads and marriage agencies.

> I was there [St. John's Orphanage] till I was nearly nine and that's where I got started wrong. We were unmercifully whipped. I saw boys doing many things they should not have done.
>
> —ALBERT FISH, PRIOR TO HIS EXECUTION

In 1890, Albert Fish turned up in New York City to become a male prostitute. It was around this time he starting raping young boys. Somehow he managed—probably with the help of his mother—to scrape together enough funds to rent an apartment at 76 West 101st Street. He invited his mother to move in, and it was here that he met his future twenty-one-year-old wife—it was a coupling arranged by Mrs. Fish in 1896, which brought about six children: Albert, Anna, Gertrude, Eugene, John, and Henry Fish.

Throughout 1898, he worked as a house painter. "I was a good painter, interiors or anything," Fish later explained. Yet, still he continued to molest young boys, probably the reason his wife eventually left him. Fish would later recount an incident in which a male lover took him to the waxworks museum, where Fish was so fascinated by a bisection of a penis he soon developed a morbid interest in castration. Indeed, during a relationship with a mentally retarded man, Fish attempted to castrate him after tying him up, but the man's screaming scared Fish, who fled after leaving him a $10 bill. Afterward, Fish increased the frequency of his visits to brothels where he could be whipped and beaten, then, in 1903, at age thirty-three, he was arrested for embezzlement and sentenced to incarceration in Sing Sing.

In January 1917, Fish's wife left him for John Straube, a handyman who boarded with the family. Following this rejection, Fish began to hear voices. For example, he once wrapped himself up in a carpet, explaining that he was following the instructions of John the Apostle. Around that time, he began to indulge in self-harm. He would embed needles into his groin, which he would normally remove afterward, but soon he began to embed them so deep they were impossible to take out. Later x-rays revealed that Fish had at least twenty-nine needles lodged in his pelvic region.

*After our six children were born, my wife left me. She took all the furniture and didn't even leave a mattress for the children to sleep on.*
—ALBERT FISH, TO DR. WERTHAM

He also took to bashing himself over the head with a nail-studded paddle, all of which pointed directly to him having a borderline personality, the least of his developing mental problems.

It is confirmed that one of Fish's earliest victims, if not the first, was one Thomas Bedden, whom he attacked in 1910 in Wilmington, Delaware.

In 1919, he stabbed a mentally retarded youth in Georgetown, Washington, D.C.

On Friday, July 11, 1924, eight-year-old Beatrice Kiel was playing on her parents' Staten Island farm. Fish, now aged fifty-four, offered her money to come and help him look for rhubarb in the neighboring fields. Fortunately, the child's mother spotted her daughter wandering off with the unkempt stranger so she chased him away. But he returned to the Kiels' barn, where he endeavoured to sleep the night before being discovered by Hans Kiel, who smartly ordered him off his property.

On Tuesday, July 15, 1924, Francis was playing on the front stoop of his home in the Charlton Woods section of Staten Island while his mother sat close by nursing her infant daughter. Her eyes were taken by a scruffy, elderly, gaunt man shuffling along the street, and she noted that he had gray hair and a moustache. Clenching and unclenching his fists, he looked like a vagrant, she thought, and paid him little more notice after he tipped his hat to her and wandered off.

Later that afternoon, the same man was spotted again. He was paying particular interest in Francis, who was now playing ball with four other boys. The witness watched as the man called over to Francis. Moments later, almost in the blink of an eye, the man and Francis had disappeared from sight.

When the boy failed to turn up for dinner, his father, a police officer, organized a search. Francis's body was later found in nearby woods under some branches. He had been sexually assaulted and strangled with his own suspenders.

Albert Fish admitted this murder after he was sentenced to death in 1936.

In 1925, Fish's mental condition deteriorated further. He started to experience delusions and hallucinations that God had commanded him to torture and castrate little boys. He was later diagnosed as having a religious psychosis.

Aged five, Emma Richardson was murdered by Fish on Sunday, October 3, 1926.

On a wintry Friday, February 11, 1927, it was far too cold to venture outside. Four-year-old Billy Gaffney was playing in the hallway of his family's apartment in Brooklyn. His playmates were Billy Beaton, age three, and Beaton's twelve-year-old brother, who was babysitting his sleeping baby sister. When the older boy went back into his own apartment after he heard the baby cry, the two other kids disappeared. Billy Beaton was soon found on the roof of the apartment building by his desperate father, but Billy Gaffney had vanished. When asked what had happened to Billy Gaffney, the younger Beaton said "the bogeyman took him."

At first, the police assumed that Billy Gaffney had simply wandered off, so a squad of officers searched nearby factory buildings and vacant lots. They even dragged the Gowanus Canal, just a few blocks away, but Billy, it seemed, had vanished into thin air.

Initially, a man named Peter Kudzinowski was the prime suspect. He had killed three children, and he was suspected in the murder of a fourth. Kudzinowski would be executed in the electric chair at Trenton State Prison, New Jersey. But he did not murder Billy Gaffney.

Then Joseph Meehan, a motorman on a Brooklyn trolley bus, saw a picture of Fish in a newspaper and identified him as the old man he saw on February 11 trying to quiet a little boy sitting with him. The child was not wearing a jacket and was crying for his mother when the man dragged him on and off the vehicle. The younger Beaton described the "bogeyman" as elderly with a slim build. Police matched the description of the child to Billy Gaffney. The boy's body was never found.

Mrs. Gaffney later visited Fish in prison, and he confessed as follows:

I brought him to the Riker Avenue dumps. There is
a house that stands alone, not far from where I took
him. I took the boy there. Stripped him naked and tied
his hands and feet and gagged him with a piece of
dirty rag I picked out of the dump. Then I burned his
clothes. Threw his shoes in the dump. Then I walked
back and took the trolley to 59th Street at 2 a.m. and
walked from there home. Next day about 2 p.m., I
took tools, a good heavy cat-of-nine-tails. Home made.
Short handle. Cut one of my belts in half, slit these
halves in six strips about 8 inches long. I whipped his
bare behind till the blood ran from his legs. I cut off his
ears—nose—slit his mouth from ear-to-ear. Gouged
out his eyes. He was dead then. I stuck the knife in his
belly and held my mouth to his body and drank his
blood. I picked up four old potato sacks and gathered
a pile of stones. Then I cut him up. I had a grip with
me. I put his nose, ears and a few slices of his belly
in the grip. Then I cut him through the middle of his
body. Just below the belly button. Then through his
legs about 2 inches below his behind. I put this in
my grip with a lot of paper. I cut off the head—feet—
arms—hands and the legs below the knee. This I put
in sacks and weighed with stones, tied the ends and
threw them into the pools of slimy water you will see
all along the road going to North Beach. I came home
with my meat. I had the front of his body I liked best.
His monkey and pee wees and a nice little fat behind
to roast in the oven and eat. I made a stew out of his
ears—nose—pieces of his face and belly. I put onions,

carrots, turnips, celery, salt and pepper. It was good. Then I split the cheeks of his behind open, cut off his monkey and pee wees and washed them first. I put strips of bacon on each cheek of his behind and put them in the oven. Then I picked 4 onions and when the meat had roasted about ¼ hour, I poured a pint of water over it for gravy and put in the onions. At frequent intervals I basted his behind with a wooden spoon. So the meat would be nice and juicy. In about 2 hours, it was nice and brown, cooked through. I never ate any roast turkey that tasted half as good as his sweet little behind did. I ate every bit of the meat in about four days. His little monkey was as sweet as a nut, but his pee wees I could not chew. I threw them down the toilet.

Albert Fish is also suspected of murdering Yetta Abramowitz, aged twelve, in 1927; Mary Ellen O'Conner, aged sixteen, on Monday, February 15, 1932; and Benjamin Collings, aged seventeen, on Thursday, December 15, 1932.

On Thursday, February 6, 1930, Albert Fish married Estella Wilcox in Waterloo, New York. They divorced a week later. In May of that same year, sixty-year-old Fish was arrested for sending an obscene letter to a woman who answered one of his phoney advertisements for a maid. He was charged with a misdemeanor and sent to the Bellevue Psychiatric Hospital between 1930 and 1931 for observation and evaluation.

Perhaps the most notorious of Fish's murders is that of ten-year-old Grace Budd.

On Friday, May 25, 1928, Grace's older brother, Ed Budd, placed a classified ad in the Sunday edition of the *New York World* that read:

> Young man, 18, wishes position in country. Edward
> Budd, 406 West 15th Street.

Fish immediately zeroed in on the advertisement and, on Monday, May 28, he presented himself to the Budd family in Manhattan. He introduced himself as one Frank Howard, a farmer from Farmingdale, Long Island. He was interested in hiring Edward, he said, but unfortunately Ed wasn't at home.

A mountain of a woman, Delia Budd told her five-year-old daughter Beatrice to get her brother, who was at a friend's apartment. The old man beamed and pressed a nickel into the little girl's hand. While they waited for Edward, Delia had a chance look the visitor over. He had a kindly face, framed by gray and accented by a large, droopy gray moustache. He explained to Mrs. Budd that he had earned his living for decades as an interior decorator in the city before retiring to a farm he had bought with his savings. He had six children that he had raised by himself since his wife had abandoned them all a decade earlier.

With the help of his children, five farmhands and a Swedish cook, Mr. Howard explained how he had made the farm into a successful business with several hundred chickens and half a dozen dairy cows. Of course, Mrs. Budd, being a trustworthy person, had no idea that a farm containing such little stock would only take two people to run. But, now that one of his "farmhands" intended to move on, Mr. Howard needed someone to replace him.

At that moment, Edward came in, and Mr. Howard remarked at the boy's size and strength. Edward assured Howard that he was a hard worker, and the old man offered him fifteen dollars a week, which Edward accepted. Howard even agreed to also hire Willie, Edward's closest friend.

Saturday, June 2, was supposed to be the big day the boys would go to work, but Howard failed to pick them up. Instead they received a handwritten note saying that their new employer had been delayed but would call on Sunday morning.

On his second visit, which took place around 11 a.m. on Sunday, June 3, Mr. Howard brought gifts of strawberries and fresh, creamy pot cheese. "These products come direct from my farm," he told them. Delia persuaded the old man to stay for lunch, and for the first time her husband, Albert Budd, a porter for the Equitable Life Assurance Society, had an opportunity to speak to the "farmer."

It was the kind of talk that would make most fathers happy. The kindly, polite old gentleman rapturously described his twenty acres of farmland, his friendly crew of farmhands, and a simple, hearty country life. Mr. Budd knew it was what his son wanted. It seemed almost too good to be true. He wasn't was overly impressed with the way the old man looked in his rumpled blue suit, but he was a credible and gentile sort.

Just as they sat down at the table, in walked Gracie, humming a song. She had huge brown eyes, and her dark brown hair contrasted with her milky skin and pink lips. She had come straight from church wearing a white confirmation dress, her white silk stockings, and a string of pearls that made her look much older than her ten years.

Mr. Howard couldn't keep his eyes off her. "Let's see how good a counter you are," he said as he handed over a wad of bills for Gracie to count. "Ninety-two dollars and fifty cents," Gracie responded within seconds, while the Budds remained speechless at the huge amount of money in front of them. "What a bright little girl," Howard praised, giving her fifty cents to buy some candy for herself and her sister Beatrice.

Mr. Howard, aka Albert Fish, said that he would come back later in the evening to collect Edward and Willie. First, however, he had to go to a birthday party that his sister was throwing for one of her children. He gave the boys two dollars to go to the movies.

It was at this point that Howard invited Gracie to the party, promising to take good care of her and make sure she was back home by nine that evening. Delia had her doubts and asked where the party was to be held. "She lives at an apartment house at Columbus and 137th Street," the man replied. For his part, Albert Budd was convinced that it would be okay. "Let the poor kid go," he told his wife. "She don't see much good times." Then, watching from a window, Delia saw her precious daughter, all dressed up in her best coat and a gray hat with streamers, walk hand-in-hand with Mr. Howard down the street and out of sight.

Nine o'clock came and went. Every minute dragged by as father and mother anxiously awaited their daughter's return. They couldn't sleep, and the next morning Edward was sent down to the police station to report Gracie as missing.

Police Lieutenant Samuel Dribben soon learned that the children's party address given by "Mr. Howard" was false. In fact, there was no Frank Howard. There was no "as described farm" in Farmingdale, either. On June 7, 1,000 fliers were sent to police stations throughout the country, but a dedicated squad of over twenty detectives found no trace of the missing child. However, a few clues did surface. Mailed in East Harlem, the original hand-written message sent to the Budds on Saturday, June 2, showed that it had been written by someone of "refine-ment and education," this already being patently obvious to Mr. and Mrs. Budd, who had entertained the man in their very home. The second clue came about from the pot cheese brought by their visitor. Police located the vendor's handcart in East Harlem, too.

Six years later, in November 1934, an anonymous letter delivered in an envelope that had a small hexagonal emblem with the letters N.Y.P.C.B.A (New York Private Chauffeur's Benevolent Association) was sent to Grace's parents. It was this letter that ultimately led to Fish's arrest. Mrs. Budd was illiterate and could not read the letter herself, so she had her eldest son read it. The boy was so shocked that he refused to reveal the content to his mother. Instead, he rushed out and gave it straight to the police. It is quoted below, complete with Fish's misspellings and grammatical errors:

My Dear Mrs. Budd,

In 1894 a friend of mine shipped as a deck hand on the Steamer Tacoma, Capt. John Davis. They sailed from San Francisco for Hong Kong, China. On arriving there he and two others went ashore and got drunk. When they returned the boat was gone. At that time there was famine in China. Meat of any kind was from $1–3 per pound. So great was the suffering among the very poor that all children under 12 were sold for food in order to keep others from starving. A boy or girl under 14 was not safe in the street. You could go in any shop and ask for steak—chops—or stew meat. Part of the naked body of a boy or girl would be brought out and just what you wanted cut from it. A boy or girl's behind which is the sweetest part of the body and sold as veal cutlet brought the highest price. John staid [sic] there so long he acquired a taste for human flesh. On his return to N.Y. he stole two boys, one 7 and one 11. Took them to his home stripped them naked tied them in a closet. Then burned everything they had. Several times every day and night he spanked them—tortured them—to make their meat good and tender. First he killed the 11 year old boy, because he had the fattest ass and of course the most meat on it. Every part of his body was cooked and eaten except the head—bones and guts. He was roasted in the oven (all of his ass), boiled, broiled, fried and stewed. The little boy was next, went the same way. At that time, I was living at 409 W 100 St, near—right side. He told me so often how good human flesh was I made up my mind to taste it. On Sunday June the 3, 1928 I called on you at 406 W 15 St. Bought you pot cheese—strawberries. We had lunch. Grace sat on my lap and kissed me. I made up my mind to eat her. On the pretense [sic] of taking her to a party. You said yes she could go. I took her to any empty house in Westchester (Wisteria Cottage) I had already picked out. When we got there, I told her to remain outside. She picked wildflowers. I went upstairs and stripped all my clothes off. I knew if I did not I would get blood on them. When all was ready I went to the window and called her. Then I hid in a closet until she was in the room. When she saw me all naked she began to cry and tried to run down the stairs. I grabbed her and she said she would tell her mamma. First I stripped her naked. How she did kick—bite and scratch. I choked her to death, then cut her in small pieces so I could take my meat to my rooms. Cook it and eat it. How sweet and tender her little ass was roasted in the oven. It took me 9 days to eat her entire body. I did not fuck her tho [sic] I could have had I wished. She died a virgin.

During the course of tracing this headed stationary, police interviewed the association's janitor, who admitted that he had taken some 200 sheets home. However, he had left it at his rooming house at 200 East 52nd Street when he moved out. The landlady of the lodgings said that one Albert Fish had checked out of the same room just a few days earlier, explaining that his son, who worked with the

Civilian Conservation Corps in North Carolina, sent him money regularly and had sent a check to the address. He asked her to hold it for him.

William F. King was the lead investigator in the case. He waited outside until his man returned. Fish agreed to be interviewed but then brandished a razor blade. King disarmed him with those immortal words "I've got you now," and conveyed him to the police headquarters. Fish made no attempt to deny the Grace Budd murder, saying that he had meant to go to the house to kill Edward Budd, Grace's brother. Fish said that, "it never even entered my head to rape the girl." However, later he admitted to his attorney that he did have two involuntary ejaculations, an admission which was used at trial to make the claim that the kidnapping was sexually motivated and thus avoid the even more unpalatable subject of cannibalism.

Not surprisingly, Fish was no stranger to police, for his rap sheet stretched way back to 1903, when he was jailed for grand larceny. Since then he had been arrested six times for various petty offenses such as sending obscene letters and petty theft. Half of those arrests occurred around the time of Grace's abduction and murder. Each time, the charges were dismissed. Fish, it transpired, had been in mental institutions more than once.

In his confession, Fish explained how he and Grace had stopped at a newsstand to pick up his bundle of "tools" before taking a train to the Bronx, then on to Worthington in Westchester. For the little girl, this callous pervert had only bought a one-way ticket, while he had a return. This was only the second train ride in her life, and Fish explained that she was very excited with the treat. At Worthington Station, Fish said that he was so over-whelmed that his plan was coming true that he left his package of tools on the train. Grace noticed the mistake and reminded him before the train departed.

Then the monster turned to a detective: "I'm still worried about my children," he sniffed. "You'd think they'd come to visit their old dad in jail, but they haven't."

The trial of Albert Fish for the premeditated murder of Grace Budd began on Monday, March 11, 1935, in White Plains, New York, with Judge Frederick P. Close presiding. Chief Assistant D.A. Elbert F. Gallagher appeared for the state, while James Dempsey was acted as Fish's defense.

The trial lasted ten days. Fish, standing at five feet five inches, stooped and frail, pleaded insanity. He claimed to have heard voices from God telling him to kill children. Several psychiatrists testified about Fish's sexual fetishes, which included coprophilia, urophilia, pedophilia, and masochism. Dempsey realized that the task of saving his client was other than to suggest that Fish was almost impossible: "a psychiatric phenomenon," and "that nowhere in legal or medical records is there another individual who possessed so many sexual abnormalities."

The star witness for Fish was Dr. Fredric Wertham, a psychiatrist with a focus on child development who conducted psychiatric examinations for the New York courts. Over two days of testimony, Wertham explained Fish's obsession with religion and specifically his preoccupation with the story of Abraham and Isaac (Genesis 22:1–24). Wertham said Fish believed that by similarly "sacrificing" a boy it would be penance for his own sins and that even if the act itself was wrong, angels would prevent it if God did not approve. Fish had already attempted the sacrifice once before but had been thwarted when a car drove past—perhaps with an angel at the wheel. Edward Budd had been the next intended victim, but he turned out to be a larger target than Fish expected, so he settled on Grace.

The jury, in complete ignorance of the other murders committed by the defendant, didn't buy any of this psychobabble, even less of it when it was claimed that while Fish knew that Grace was a girl, he actually perceived her as a boy. Wertham then lost the plot altogether when he detailed Fish's cannibalism, which in the defendant's mind was an act of communion. Now clutching at straws, the last question Dempsey asked Dr. Wertham was 15,000 words long. It detailed Fish's life and ended by asking the doctor how he considered the defendant's mental condition based on his life's history. With the judge nodding off, with the jurors losing the will to live, the court was delighted to receive a very succinct answer: "He is insane."

But all of Wertham's sterling work backfired when another of the defense witnesses—Mary Nicolas, Fish's seventeen-year-old stepdaughter, in answer to the question, "Was Albert a kind and sweet man?" wandered into dangerous antidefense territory by describing how he had taught her brothers and sisters a game involving overtones of masochism and child molestation, before Dempsey eventually shut her up.

It was now the moment for Gallagher to cross-examine Dr. Wertham. Did Fish know the difference between right and wrong? Dr. Wertham responded that he did know the difference, but that it was "a perverted knowledge based on his views of sin, atonement, and religion and thus was an insane knowledge."

Gallagher looked knowingly at the jury and sat down, while the defense called two more shrinks who supported Wertham's findings.

The first of four rebuttal witnesses was Menas Gregory, the former head of the Bellevue Psychiatric Hospital who had treated Fish in 1930. He testified that Fish was "abnormal" but sane. Dempsey asked if coprophilia, urophilia, and pedophilia indicated a sane or insane person. Gregory had the perfect answer. He replied that such a person was not "mentally sick" and further enlightened the court by adding that these were "common perversions" that were "socially perfectly all right."

"Mr. Fish is no different from millions of other people," he added. "Some very prominent and successful suffer from the very same perversions."

The next witness was the Tombs resident psychiatrist, Perry Lichtenstein. Dempsey immediately objected to a doctor with no training in psychiatry testifying on the issue of sanity, but Judge Close overruled on the grounds that the jury could decide what weight to give a prison doctor. When asked if Fish causing himself pain indicated a mental condition, Lichtenstein snappily replied, "That is not masochism. Mr. Fish was punishing himself to get sexual gratification."

The penultimate witness, Charles Lambert, testified that coprophilia was a common practice and that—unaware of the coming pun—"religious cannibalism may be psychopathic, but was a matter of taste."

The last witness, James Vavasour, merely repeated Lambert's opinion.

The jury found Albert Fish sane but guilty, so the judge passed the death sentence.

Albert Fish arrived at Sing Sing Prison in March 1935. Aged sixty-five, he was executed in the electric chair on Thursday, January 16, 1936. Entering the dreaded chamber at 11:06 p.m., he was pronounced dead three minutes later. His body was buried in the Sing Sing Prison Cemetery.

He is recorded as saying that electrocution would be "the supreme thrill of my life." Just before the switch was thrown, he said, "I don't know why I am here." According to one witness present, it required two jolts of "lightning" before Fish died, creating the false rumor that the apparatus was short-circuited by the needles Fish had previously inserted into his body.

# CHAPTER 5

# Peter Kürten— "The Vampire of Düsseldorf"

*After my head has been chopped off, will I still be able to hear, at least for a moment, the sound of my own blood gushing from my neck? That would be the pleasure to end all pleasures.*

—PETER KÜRTEN, AFTER HIS TRIAL

PETER KÜRTEN BEGAN a reign of terror in 1929, and by the time he was caught the following year, he had committed nine murders. He later admitted to a lifetime of crime involving practically every offense and sexual perversion.

AT AROUND FIVE FEET FIVE INCHES, and of slight build, factory worker Peter Kürten was a quiet man whose harmless hobby was bird watching. He has been photographed wearing a pin-striped suit jacket and black trousers at half-mast. There is the indication of oversized feet. His head is large, almost too large for his body. The face is boxy. The wide, flat mouth, weak jaw, and small ears give him a ducklike expression. He was most certainly not a man to stand out on any street.

On the plus side, he was unassuming, neatly groomed, impeccably polite—yet a monster at heart. Behind his gentle mask of normalcy was a seething rage hungry for victims. In both numbers and savagery, his killings easily surpassed those of his idol, England's Jack the Ripper.

Through the summer of 1929, Kürten held the German city of Düsseldorf in the icy grip of fear. Although the citizens did not yet know the name of their tormentor, it was as if a vampire were on the loose. Almost every week a fresh corpse was found, horribly slashed or bludgeoned to death, sometimes sexually assaulted. Most of the victims were young women—it appeared that their killer preferred the texture of fresh, young meat—but older women, men, and children also fell prey, often in clusters of attacks. Indeed, one day in August brought the grim news of the sadistic murders of two foster sisters, ages five and fourteen, and the attempted murder and rape of a twenty-six-year-old domestic worker.

A pitiless chain of days and months stretched to a year as police searched for the killer. They received tips and suspect leads from all over Germany and questioned 9,000 citizens in Düsseldorf alone. Parents forbade their children to play outdoors. Friends, even close neighbors, distrusted one another, and everyone feared to venture out at night.

As for the vampire, he sent happy-go-lucky letters to the authorities, generously notifying the police of the whereabouts of corpses so far undiscovered. Once he even sent a map. Nonetheless, the murders continued unabated and, after fifteen months, his total climbed over thirty.

Then he made a mistake.

An assault charge brought police to Kürten's door in May 1930. What the officers found was a man who, however meek he seemed, had a criminal record spanning three decades. Once in custody, the prisoner confessed freely, not merely to assault, but to serial murder, after warning his shocked interrogators, "You will hear many gruesome things from me."

Kürten said that he liked to kill, "the more people the better. Yes, if I had had the means of doing so," he explained, "I would have killed whole masses of people and brought about catastrophes." Then he said that he did what any sensible vampire would do. He prowled for victims during the hours of darkness and found sexual gratification in the killing.

Born at Mülheim am Rhein in 1883, Peter Kürten was one of thirteen children of a poverty-stricken family steeped in crime and violence. All his brothers spent time in jail. His father and grandfather were brutal alcoholics, the father being cruel and violent to his wife and children. In the one-room apartment, he would take his violent impulses out on his wife by having rough sex with her, and also with the children. He repeatedly raped his thirteen-year-old daughter, and Peter soon followed his father's example and raped his sister, too. The father would serve three years in prison for incest.

Around the age of nine, Peter was apprenticed to the local council's dog- and rat-catcher, who enjoyed torturing animals. This sordid man got further kicks when he allowed Kürten to watch him. The boy found the sight of suffering animals stimulating, more so as the council worker had a predilection for committing sexual acts on the helpless creatures. Thereafter, Peter developed a taste for tormenting animals and for watching houses burn. He stabbed sheep, goats, and other docile farm animals. He tore the heads off swans, drank their blood, and masturbated over the corpses.

Then the young Kürten went a step further. He pushed a playmate off a raft into the Rhine and, when a third child went to the rescue, kept them both submerged until they drowned.

The terrible pattern of his life was forming. It only needed one more depraved influence to transfer his sadistic urges from animals to human beings. He found it in a prostitute twice his age, a masochist who enjoyed being ill-treated and abused. Kürten's sadistic education was complete, and they lived together for some time. During sex, she enjoyed being half-strangled and beaten. She even enticed her sixteen-year-old daughter into their sexual acts. But despite their apparent carnal compatibility, the relationship failed.

After splitting up with the prostitute, Kürten attacked a girl walking in woods. He left her for dead, but she survived. Then he was caught stealing and was jailed for the first of seventeen sentences that would add up to nearly twenty years in prison for arson and theft. Far from straightening him out, the two-year prison sentence left him bitter and angry at the inhuman penal conditions— particularly for adolescents—and introduced him to yet another sadistic refinement, a fantasy world where he could achieve orgasm by imagining brutal sexual acts. He became so obsessed with his fantasies that he deliberately broke minor prison rules so that he could be sentenced to solitary confinement. It was the ideal atmosphere for sadistic daydreaming:

> I imagined myself using schools or orphanages for
> the purpose, where I could carry out murders by
> giving away chocolate samples containing arsenic
> which I could have obtained through housebreaking.
> I derived the sort of pleasure from these visions
> that other people would get from thinking about a
> naked woman.

Shortly after being released from prison, Kürten made his second murderous attack on a girl during sexual intercourse, leaving her for dead in the Gräfenberg Woods. No body was ever found. The girl probably crawled away, keeping her terrible secret to herself. More prison sentences for assault and theft followed. After each jail term, Kürten's feelings of injustice were strengthened.

His sexual and sadistic fantasies now involved revenge on society. This time he was sentenced to a derisory four years penal servitude, and while behind bars he took to poring over the exploits of Jack the Ripper. "I thought what pleasure it would give me to do things of that kind once I got out again," he reported later.

Out of prison in 1913, at age thirty, Kürten started robbing the homes of beer-hall owners on busy Saturday nights while they were serving their patrons. During one such foray, he later confessed, he committed his first murder since childhood, and it seemed to him to avenge his brutal past. Finding the bar owner's ten-year-old daughter asleep, he strangled Christine and then cut her throat:

> I discovered the child asleep. Her head was facing the window. I seized it with my left hand and strangled her for about a minute and a half. The child woke up and struggled but lost consciousness…I had a small but sharp pocketknife with me and I held the child's head and cut her throat. I heard the blood spurt and drip on the mat beside the bed…the whole thing lasted about three minutes.

The next day he lounged in a café opposite the beer hall and overhead outraged discussions of his crime. He found the indignation quite satisfying.

Called up for the army, Kürten deserted twenty-four hours later. He was convicted of arson and sent to prison, where he talked his way into the morgue, enabling him to lay out prisoners who had died.

Although we do not know the exact year, in 1921 or 1922 Kürten married in Altenburg, and he seemed to have calmed down. He found a job in a factory and took an interest in his trade union. He continued to have affairs, leaving the women beaten and half-strangled as his sexual perversions came to a boil again.

A few years later he moved to Düsseldorf, where he had found a new job. "The sunset was bloodred on my return to Düsseldorf," he told a psychiatrist many years later. "I considered it to be an omen symbolic of my destiny.'

In 1925, Kürten was forty-two, and apart from occasional bloodletting, he began to commit more and more crimes of arson and attempted murder, until his final secret rampage of atrocities started in 1929.

In February of that year, Kürten killed an eight-year-old girl, stabbing her thirteen times, dousing her with kerosene, and setting her ablaze. The murders continued unabated. Men, women, and children were stabbed, bludgeoned, and horribly mutilated in frenzied attacks, their corpses sometimes tossed into the river. Kürten cunningly varied the style of his attacks in order to confuse the police who were now certain that most of the crimes had been committed by someone who enjoyed the drinking of blood. On occasions he returned to the graves of those he had killed and dug up the bodies. Once when he did this, he intended to crucify the corpse but then thought better of it. "I caressed the dead body...experiencing the tenderest emotions that as a living woman she failed to arouse in me earlier," he later confessed at his trial.

As the lights went out on the night of Friday, August 23, 1929, the people of Düsseldorf, felt almost inured to horror. Nothing more, they thought, could shock them. As they slept fitfully, they little foresaw that the next few hours would demonstrate the full bestiality of the man they had labeled the Düsseldorf Vampire.

There was one bright, cheerful patch of light that evening. In the suburb of Flehe, hundreds of people were enjoying the annual fair. Old-fashioned merry-go-rounds revolved to the heavy rhythm of German march tunes, stalls dispensed beer and wurst, there was a comforting feeling of safety and warmth in the closely packed crowd.

Around 10:30, two foster sisters, five-year-old Gurtrude Hamacher and fourteen-year-old Louise Lenzen, left the fair and started walking through the adjoining allotments to their home. As they did so, a shadow broke away from among the bean sticks and followed them along a footpath. Louise stopped and turned as a gentle voice said, "Oh dear, I've forgotten to buy some cigarettes. Look, would you be very kind and go to one of the booths and get some for me? I'll look after the little girl."

Louise took the man's money and ran back toward the fairground. Quietly, Kürten picked up Gertrude in his arms and carried her behind the beanpoles. There was no sound as he strangled her and then slowly cut her throat with a Bavarian clasp knife. Louise returned a few moments later and handed over the cigarettes. The man seized her in a stranglehold and started dragging her off the footpath. Louise managed to break away and screamed, "Mama! Mama!" The man grabbed her again, strangled her, and cut her throat. Then he vanished.

Twelve hours later, Gertrude Schulte, a twenty-six-year-old servant girl, was stopped by a man who offered to take her to the fair at the neighboring town of Neuss. Foolishly, she agreed. The man introduced himself as Fritz Baumgart and suggested they take a stroll through the woods. Suddenly, he stopped and roughly attempted sexual intercourse. Terrified, Gertrude Schulte pushed him away and screamed, "I'd rather die!"

The man screamed, "Well, die then!" and began stabbing her frenziedly with a knife. She felt searing pains in her neck and shoulder and a terrific thrust in the back. "Now you can die," said the attacker and hurled her away with such force that the knife broke and the blade was left sticking in her back. But Gertrude Schulte didn't die. A passerby heard her screams and called the police and an ambulance. By then, Kürten had disappeared.

In barely more than half a day, the Düsseldorf maniac had killed two children and attempted to rape and kill another woman. The citizens were stunned as they read their morning papers. Day by day, the attacks continued. Their increasing frequency and ferocity convinced medical experts that the vampire had lost all control of his sadistic impulses.

In one half hour, he attacked and wounded a girl of eighteen, a man of thirty, and a woman of thirty-seven. The Bavarian dagger gave way to a sharper, thinner blade and then to some kind of blunt instrument. It was a bludgeon that hammered to death two more servant girls, Ida Reuter and Elisabeth Dorrier; the thin blade killed five-year-old Gertrude Albermann, her body shredded with thirty-six wounds.

But then Kürten made the mistake that would introduce him to Madame Guillotine—he allowed a victim to go free.

Twenty miles away from Düsseldorf, in the cathedral city of Cologne, a twenty-one-year-old domestic named Maria Budlick read the anguished headlines and said to a friend, "Isn't it shocking? Thank goodness we're not in Düsseldorf." But a few weeks later she found herself unemployed, so on Wednesday, May 14, 1930, she set out to look for work and boarded a train for Düsseldorf...and an unwitting rendezvous with the vampire.

On the platform at Düsseldorf station, she was accosted by a man who offered to show her the way to a girls' hostel. They followed the brightly lit streets for a while, but when he started leading her toward the dark trees of Volksgarten Park, she suddenly remembered the stories of the monster and refused to go any farther. The man insisted and while they were arguing, a second man appeared as if from nowhere, and inquired softly, "Is everything all right?" The man from the railway station slunk away, and Maria Budlick was left alone with her rescuer.

Tired and hungry, she agreed to accompany him to his one-room flat in Mettmannerstrasse, where she had a glass of milk and a ham sandwich. The man offered to take her to the hostel, but after a tram ride to the northeastern edge of the city, she realized they were walking deeper and deeper into the Gräfenberg Woods. Her companion stopped suddenly and said, "Do you know where you are? I can tell you! You are alone with me in the middle of the woods. Now you scream as much as you like, and nobody will hear you."

The man lunged forward, seized her by the throat and tried to have sexual intercourse up against a tree. Maria Budlick struggled violently and was about to lose consciousness when she felt the man's grip relax. "Do you remember where I live?" he asked. "In case you're ever in need and want my help?" "No," gasped Maria, and in one word saved her own life and signed the death warrant of the Düsseldorf Vampire. The man showed her out of the woods, took her to a tram, and let her go.

But Maria Budlick had remembered the address. She vividly recalled the nameplate "Mettmannerstrasse" under the flickering gaslight. In a letter to a friend the next day, she told of her terrifying experience in the Gräfenberg Woods with the quiet, soft-spoken man. The letter never reached her friend. It was misdirected and opened by a Frau Brugman, who took one look at the contents and called the police.

Twenty-four hours later, accompanied by plain-clothes detectives, Maria Budlick was walking up and down Mettmannerstrasse trying to pinpoint the quiet man's house. She stopped at number 71. It looked familiar, and she asked the landlady if "a fair-haired, rather sedate man" lived there. The woman took her up to the fourth floor and unlocked a room. It was the same one in which she had drunk her milk and eaten her sandwich two nights earlier.

Maria turned around to face even more conclusive proof: The quiet man was coming up the stairs toward her. He looked startled but continued to his room and shut the door behind him. A few moments later, he left the house with his hat pulled down over his eyes, passed the two plainclothesmen standing in the street, and disappeared around a corner.

Maria Budlick ran out and told the officers, "That's the man who assaulted me in the woods. His name is Peter Kürten." So far, nothing linked Kürten with the vampire. His only crime was suspected rape. But he knew there was no longer any hope of concealing his identity. Early the following morning, after meeting his wife as usual at the restaurant where she worked late, he confessed, "I am the Monster of Düsseldorf." He said that she should turn him in to claim the reward, which she soon did.

On Saturday, May 24, Frau Kürten told the story to the police, adding that she had arranged to meet her husband outside St. Rochus Church at three o'clock that afternoon. By that time the whole area was surrounded by armed police. The moment Peter Kürten appeared, four officers rushed forward with loaded revolvers. The man smiled and offered no resistance. "There is no need to be afraid," he said.

After exhaustive questioning, during which he admitted sixty-eight crimes, not including convictions for theft and assault, for which he had already spent a total of twenty years in prison. The trial opened on April 13, 1931. He was charged with a total of nine murders and seven attempted murders.

Thousands of people crowded around the converted drill hall of the Düsseldorf police headquarters waiting to catch their first glimpse of the depraved creature that had terrorized the city. A special shoulder-high cage had been built inside the courtroom to prevent his escape and behind it were arranged the grisly exhibits of the Kürten Museum—the prepared skulls of his victims, showing the various injuries, knives, scissors and a hammer, articles of clothing, and a spade he had used to bury a woman. The first shock was the physical appearance of the monster. Despite his appalling crimes, Peter Kürten was far from the maniac of the conventional horror film. He was no Count Dracula with snarling teeth and wild eyes, no lumbering stitched-together Frankenstein's monster. There was no sign of the brutal sadist or the weak-lipped degenerate. With his sleek, meticulously parted hair, immaculate suit, and well-polished shoes, he looked like a prim shopkeeper or civil servant. It was when he started talking that a chill settled over the court. In a quiet, matter-of-fact voice, as if listing the stock of a haberdasher's shop, he described his life of perversion and bloodlust in such clinical detail that even the most hardened courtroom officials paled.

His crimes were more monstrous than anyone had imagined. The man wasn't merely a psychopath but a walking textbook of perverted crime: sex maniac, sadist, rapist, vampire, strangler, stabber, hammer-killer, arsonist, a man who committed bestiality with animals and derived sexual satisfaction from witnessing street accidents and planning disasters involving the deaths of hundreds of people. Yet he was quite sane. The most brilliant doctors in Germany testified that Kürten had been fully responsible for his actions at all times. Further proof of his awareness was provided by the premeditated manner of his crimes, his ability to leave off in the middle of an attack if disturbed, and his astonishing memory for every detail.

To a packed court, Kürten explained:

I thought of myself causing accidents affecting thousands of people and invented a number of crazy fantasies such as smashing bridges and boring through bridge piers. Then I spun a number of fantasies with regard to bacilli which I might be able to introduce into the drinking water and so cause a great calamity. I imagined myself using schools or orphanages for the purpose, where I could carry out murders by giving away chocolate samples containing arsenic which I could have obtained through housebreaking. I derived the sort of pleasure from these visions that other people would get from thinking about a naked woman.

The court was hypnotized by these shocking revelations. To them, Kürten's narrative sounded like the voice of Satan. It was almost impossible to associate it with the mild figure in the wooden cage. While hysteria and demands for lynching and worse reigned outside the court, the trial itself was a model of decorum and humanity, mainly due to the courteous and civilized manner of the presiding judge, Dr. Rose. Quietly, he prompted Kürten to describe his bouts of arson and fire-raising.

"Yes, when my desire for injuring people awoke, the love of setting fire to things awoke as well," said Kürten, speaking in a hushed voice. "The sight of the flames delighted me, but above all it was the excitement of the attempts to extinguish the fire and the agitation of those who saw their property being destroyed."

The court was deathly quiet, sensing that the almost unspeakable had at last arrived. Gently, Dr. Rose asked, "Now tell us about Christine Klein..." Kürten pursed his lips for a second as if mentally organizing the details and then, in the unemotional tones of a man recalling a minor business transaction, described the horrible circumstance of his first sex-killing.

In the courtroom, the horrors were piling up like bodies in a charnel house. Describing his sexual aberrations, Kürten admitted that the sight of his victim's blood was enough to bring on an orgasm. On several occasions, he drank the blood—once gulping so much that he vomited.

He admitted drinking blood from the throat of one victim and from the wound on the temple of another. In another attack, he licked the blood from a victim's hands. He also had an ejaculation after decapitating a swan in a park and placing his mouth over the severed neck.

Everyone in the courtroom realized they were not just attending a sensational trial, but experiencing a unique legal precedent. The prosecution hardly bothered to present any evidence. Kürten's detailed, almost fussy confession was the most damning evidence of all. Never before had a prisoner convicted himself so utterly; and never before had a courtroom audience been given the opportunity to gaze so deeply into the mind of a maniac.

Every tiny detail built up a picture of a soul twisted beyond all recognition. Kürten described with enthusiasm how he enjoyed reading about Jack the Ripper as a child, how he had visited a waxwork Chamber of Horrors and boasted, "I'll be in there one day!" The whole court shuddered when, in answer to one question, Kürten pointed to his heart and said, "Gentlemen, you must look in here!"

When the long, ghastly recital was over, Kürten's counsel, Dr. Wehner, had the hopeless task of trying to prove insanity in the face of unbreakable evidence by several distinguished psychiatrists. During Professor Sioli's testimony, Dr. Wehner pleaded, "Kürten is the king of sexual delinquents because he unites nearly all perversions in one person. Can that not change your opinion about insanity? Is it possible for the Kürten case to persuade psychiatry to adopt another opinion?"

Professor Sioli: "No!"

Dr. Wehner: "That is the dreadful thing: The man Kürten is a riddle to me. I cannot solve it. The criminal Haarmann only killed men, Landru only women, Grossman only women, but Kürten killed men, women, children, and animals, killed anything he found!"

Professor Sioli: "And was at the same time a clever man and quite a nice one."

Here was the final twist to the conundrum. The face peeping over the wooden cage was recognizably only too human. Witnesses had spoken of his courteousness and mild manner. Neighbors had refused flatly to believe he was the vampire. Employers testified to his honesty and reliability. He could charm women to their deaths, yet indeed he was regarded as a local Casanova. His wife had been completely unaware of his double life and had only betrayed him on his insistence so she could share in the reward for his arrest. Right at the beginning of the Düsseldorf Terror, a former girlfriend who suggested he might be the vampire was fined by the police for making a malicious accusation.

Some of the bourgeois Puritanism which made Kürten so plausible as the monster burst out in his final statement before sentence was passed. Speaking hurriedly and gripping the rail, he said:

> My actions as I see them today are so terrible and so
> horrible that I do not even make an attempt to excuse
> them. But one bitter sting remains in my mind. I think
> of Dr. Wolf and the woman doctor; the two Socialist

doctors accused recently of abortions performed
on working-class mothers who sought their advice.
When I think of the five hundred murders they have
committed, then I cannot help feeling bitter.

The court now went deathly silent while Kürten
paused and looked almost ashamed. Then he rallied.
Speaking more confidently he said:

The real reason for my conviction is that there comes
a time in the life of every criminal when he can
go not further. And this spiritual collapse is what
I experienced. But I do feel that I must make one
statement: Some of my victims made things very easy
for me. Man hunting on the part of women today has
taken on such forms that…

At such self-righteousness, the judge's patience finally
snapped. "Stop these remarks," he ordered, banging on
his desk.

The jury took a mere ninety minutes to reach their
verdict: guilty on all counts. Dr. Rose handed down nine
death sentences. Kürten would serve only one of them.

On the evening of July 1, 1932, Kürten was given the traditional Henkers-Mahlzeit, or condemned man's last meal.
He asked for wienerschnitzel, fried potatoes, and a bottle
of white wine, which he enjoyed so much that he had it all
over again. At six o'clock the following morning, the Vampire of Düsseldorf, a priest on either side, walked briskly
to the guillotine erected in the yard of Klingelputz Prison,
Cologne. "Have you any last wish to express?" asked the

attorney general. Without emotion, almost cheerfully, Kürten replied, "No."

In his last moments, Kürten asked his psychiatrist, curiously, "After my head has been chopped off, will I be able to hear, at least for a moment, the sound of my own blood gushing from my neck...?" He paused before adding, "That would be the pleasure to end all pleasures."

His madness was portrayed by Peter Lorre in Fritz Lang's drama thriller of 1931, *M*.

# CHAPTER 6

# Joachim Kroll—"Uncle Joachim's Stew"

JOACHIM KROLL WAS BORN in Hindenburg (Zabrze) Province of Upper Silesia, the son of a miner, in 1933. The last of eight children, he was the sibling runt and a bedwetter. His education in Hindenburg lasted just three years, with him struggling to reach the third grade. Later, when examined by psychiatrists, his IQ was measured at seventy-six; he was mentally handicapped.

At the end of World War II, the Kroll family moved to North Rhine Westphalia. His mother died in 1955, almost immediately after which Kroll, now age twenty-two, started a killing career that lasted twenty-one years until his arrest on Saturday, July 3, 1976. Kroll admitted murdering a dozen people, but due to his poor memory the figure is likely to have been much higher.

IRMGARD STREHL WAS NINETEEN. Her naked, disemboweled body was found in a barn on Tuesday, February 8,

1955. Kroll had taken a bus or a train to the village of Walstedde, just north of the Ruhr district and seized the young woman as she walked along a main road toward the nearby village of Ludinghausen. A postmortem examination revealed that the abdomen had been ripped open and she had been violently raped. These injuries had been committed after death, which was due to manual strangulation.

Around 1960—the exact date is unknown—Kroll found work as a toilet attendant for Mannesmann. Later he worked for Thyssen Industries and moved into lodgings at 24 Friesen Street, Laar, a district of Duisburg.

On Tuesday, June 16, 1959, Klara Frieda Tesmer, age twenty-four, was murdered in the meadows of the Rhine, near Rheinhausen. The killing was almost identical to that of his first victim, but this time the corpse exhibited signs of cannibalism. Using a long-bladed knife, Kroll hacked pieces of flesh from the buttocks and thighs, wrapped them in greaseproof paper, and took them home for his supper.

A mechanic, Heinrich Ott, was arrested for this and several other murders. Sadly, he hanged himself before he went to trial.

On Sunday, July 26, 1959, sixteen-year-old Manuela was raped, then strangled, in the Essen City Park. Slices of flesh were carved from her buttocks and thighs.

In 1962, Barbara Bruder vanished. Kroll admitted abducting the twelve-year-old girl in Burscheid, but her body has never been found.

On Monday, April 23, 1962, thirteen-year-old Petra Geise was raped, then strangled in Dinkslaken-Bruckhausen. She was on her way home from a carnival when she became separated from her friend. Twelve-year-old Monika Tafel was killed in Walsum. Both children, in addition to the rape and mutilation, had pieces of flesh cut from their buttocks and thighs. Petra's left arm was also missing.

A well-known child molester, fifty-two-year-old Vinzenze Kuehn, was arrested for the murder of Petra. He was found guilty and sent to prison for twelve years with an order that he receive psychiatric treatment. He was released after serving half that time.

Walter Quicker soon became a suspect in the murder of Monika Tafel because he had exhibited a fondness for little girls, but that was all it was. Try as hard as they could, police failed to make any charge stick, so he was released. However, according to that old saying "There is no smoke without fire," the local people persecuted Quicker, and his wife left him, refusing to live with a suspected child molester. Shopkeepers refused to serve Walter, and people spat at him and abused him in the street. Now, his life in ruins, the patently distressed man took himself into the forest where Monika had been found and committed suicide by hanging.

Fourteen years later both Kuehn and Quicker were cleared of any involvement in the murders by Kroll's confession. Sadly, it came far too late to save the unfortunate Quicker.

Three years slipped by, and although Kroll undoubtedly killed during this time, the next documented murder was that of Hermann Schmitz, who was sitting with his fiancée, Marion Veen, in a car they had parked in a lover's lane in Duisburg, Grossenbaum. On Sunday, August 22, 1965, Kroll was stalking a secluded area close to an artificial lake, spying on courting couples and working himself into a sexual frenzy. He spotted the couple making out in the front seat.

Taking on a vulnerable woman was one thing, but tackling the boyfriend before attacking Marion Veen was something else entirely. Kroll designed a ruse to get Hermann out of the car: He stabbed one of the front tires with a knife. However, things didn't go entirely to plan, for Hermann immediately drove off and into a dead end. When he turned his car around, there was Kroll standing in the middle of the track trying to flag the lovers down.

Schmitz, now thinking that the man was in trouble, pulled over and got out, whereupon Kroll repeatedly stabbed him with his long-bladed folding knife.

For her part in this terrifying incident, Marion Veen showed great presence of mind. She leaped into the driver's seat, slammed the car into gear, and drove straight at Kroll who managed to jump out of the way, and he vanished into nearby bushes and trees. Jamming a hair clip into the vehicle's horn, which made it sound continuously as a sort of Mayday signal, Marion climbed out of the car only to find her lover dying in a spreading pool of his own blood.

Tuesday, September 13, 1966 found the body of Ursula Rohling, twenty-six, strangled in Foetsterbusch Park near Marl, about forty miles north of Duisburg. Her body was found sprawled among some bushes, and there was no physical evidence to show that she had resisted the rape. Ursula's fiancé, Adolf Schickle, was suspected, for he had been the last person aside from her killer to see her alive. They had met for tea to discuss plans about their wedding, after which she set off home alone. Adolf was questioned for three weeks, and like Walter Quicker he was driven out of town. Four months after Ursula's murder, the heartbroken Schickle drowned himself.

Ilona Harke was just five years old when Joachim Kroll happened upon her on Thursday, December 22, 1966. He raped and drowned the child in a ditch in Wuppertal. Ilona lived in Bredeney—the same location as Kroll's murder of Manuela Knodt. The beast persuaded Ilona to travel on a train with him. Twenty miles away, after killing the little girl, he sliced large quantities of flesh from her buttocks and shoulders, wrapped them up in greaseproof paper, and took them home to eat.

A sixty-one-year-old woman from Huckeswagen, Maria Hettgen was raped and strangled as soon as she opened her front door to Kroll's deadly visitation on Saturday, July 12, 1969. Her body was found in the hallway.

Thirteen-year-old Jutta Rahn was accosted by Kroll while walking home in a town close to Grossenbaum on Sunday, May 19, 1970. One Peter Schay was wrongfully suspected, and while his blood type matched that of Jutta's murderer, there was insufficient evidence to bring charges against him. Notwithstanding, he was taunted with "murderer" by local people for more than six years before Kroll confessed the crime.

Joachim Kroll's penultimate murder was that of ten-year-old Karin Toepfer, whom he raped and strangled in Voerde.

On Saturday, July 3, 1976, Oscar Muller decided he needed to use the shared lavatory on the top floor of 24 Friesen Street in Laar. One of the other tenants was a dirty-looking, brown-eyed, balding little man whom the local children called "Uncle Joachim." As Muller ascended the stairway, he bumped into Joachim Kroll coming down.

"I wouldn't use the toilet if I were you," advised Kroll. "It is all stopped up."

"What with?" asked Muller.

"Guts," mumbled Kroll before opening the door to his own apartment and going inside.

Muller smiled at the mild-mannered man's joke. He knew that Kroll was a secretive character, but he did have a dry sense of humor, and Muller appreciated that. However, when Muller went to see what was blocking the toilet, the smile was quickly wiped from his face. The water was red with blood, and there appeared to be human tissue of some sort floating in the bowl.

The elderly man's stomach heaved. He ran down the stairs as fast as his legs could carry him, into the street, which was teeming with policemen. Four-year-old Marion Ketter had been reported as missing, and the police were making door-to-door inquiries.

The little blonde girl, who lived a few doors away from Kroll, had been to a nearby playground earlier in the day; then she had simply vanished. The hue and cry went up. Police flooded into the area, and one of the officers was approached by a white-faced Oscar Muller. Muller was clearly agitated, for he grabbed the policeman's arm, stammering and spluttering that his toilet and drain were blocked with what seemed like human tissue.

Upon this report, the police themselves paid a visit to the lavatory, where they pulled the porcelain bowl from its mountings and tipped the contents into a large bucket. Out slithered a complete set of tiny internal organs—liver, lungs, kidneys, and heart—along with scraps of flesh.

The police then hammered on Kroll's door. They had visited him earlier that day but reported nothing amiss. This time, however, inside they found what was left of Marion cut up on a kitchen table. In the refrigerator were meal-size portions of the girl's flesh on individual plates. In the freezer were more body parts, all neatly wrapped. On the cooker, Uncle Joachim's stew boiled away in a pan: carrots, potatoes, greens, gravy, an onion, along with a little hand cooked almost to perfection. The sink waste pipe was also clogged with entrails.

After a 151-day trial, Joachim Kroll was convicted on all counts and given nine life sentences. He died of a heart attack in 1991 in the Rheinbach Prison, near Bonn.

Kroll told police that he had first become sexually aroused by the sight of blood upon witnessing pigs being slaughtered when he was a teenager. He preferred the company of men, and his only relationship with a woman had failed simply because he couldn't maintain an erection. Among his possessions was a rubber doll over which he would masturbate and practice strangulation holds. He also kept a large collection of children's dolls, which he used to entice his young victims. He also claimed to have masturbated with one hand while strangling a doll in the other.

In his book *Sex-Related Homicide and Death Investigation,* Vernon Geberth, a former New York police officer and one of the world's top experts in the protocol for homicide investigation, discusses the nature of sexual deviance. He states that sexual behaviors are classified according to sociocultural norms as either acceptable or unacceptable, which makes the label "deviant," essentially a subjective judgment. Some cultures, for example, consider the act of rubbing against a stranger for gratification marginally acceptable, while others view this behavior as sexual abuse. Human beings develop a wide variety of sexual needs and thus they also develop a variety of sexual behaviors. No matter what a culture might dictate about what's acceptable, the sex drive will often override these sanctions, although deviant behavior is largely performed in secret.

During a criminal investigation that involves deviant behavior, the police often rely on such acts as biting, stabbing patterns, binding, and sexual abuse of a corpse to link crimes to a single offender. Perverse behavior is considered a signal to the type of psychopathology an offender may suffer, and because it fulfils a need for that individual, it often becomes ritualistic, repetitive, and unchanging.

"The seeds of sexual perversion are planted early in the psyche of a sex offender," according to Geberth. "However, the sexual perversions do not manifest until the offender reaches puberty. The seed is nurtured through fantasy, masturbatory activities that reinforce and nourish the particular paraphiliac imagery, as well as situational 'acting out' of these perversions with a willing partner." By the time the offender actually commits a crime, its thematic orientation may have been rehearsed mentally, and sometimes physically, many times. "The sexual event is the culmination of an offender's psychosocial and psychosexual conditioning and development."

During his confession, Kroll admitted that on a whim, he had tasted the flesh from one of his early victims and had found that he liked it. Thereafter, he'd stalked women or girls that he thought would yield tender meat, and sometimes indulged his lust, leaving their bodies sans pieces of flesh. He accepted that he had some kind of sickness and asked for a cure so that he could return home. Naively, he believed that now that he was caught, it would be a simple matter of changing him. He expected nothing less and nothing more.

Eleven years after Kroll was arrested, Gabriele Puettmann came forward to describe how she had almost become one of Kroll's victims. It was 1967, and the then ten-year-old had been sitting on a park bench with Uncle Joachim when he produced a book of pornographic pictures. The young girl was shocked and covered her eyes. The she felt Kroll's hand on her shoulder. She leapt up and rushed home, too embarrassed to tell her parents, and like Marion Veen, the lucky lass got away.

# CHAPTER 7

# Karl Denke— "No Such Thing as a Free Lunch"

ONE OF THE BEST KNOWN CANNIBALISTIC serial killers in Germany in the 1920s, ranking alongside Fritz Haarmann, Karl Grossmann, Peter Kürten, and Friedrich Schumann, Karl Denke was born on Friday, August 12, 1870, in Münsterberg/Silesia, in the German Weimar Republik (today's Ziębice in Poland). There is not a great deal of information about his early life, but in adulthood he was an affable man; known as "Papa," he was well liked in his community, devout, and an accomplished organist at the local church. His own tenants could not say a word against him.

The Denke family was relatively well off; they were farmers. Karl, however, was a difficult child to raise, and he ran away from home at age twelve. When he graduated from elementary school, he was apprenticed to a gardener. He started his own life at the age of twenty-five, when his father died. Karl's older brother took over the business, while Karl bought a piece of land with some of his inheritance. Farming didn't suit Karl Denke at all, so he sold the land and bought himself a small house on what is now Stawowa Street in Ziębice. He rented rooms, offering free accommodation for the many homeless people who passed through the city between 1918 and 1924.

At that time, there was uncontrollable inflation. Thousands of investors' savings were devoured, including those of Karl Denke, who was forced to sell his house to make ends meet. But he didn't move out. He still lived in a small ground-floor apartment on the right side of the property, and he still occupied the shop next door.

On Sunday, December 21, 1924, a man living above Denke heard terrible human screams coming from below. He rushed down to find a young man bleeding profusely from a large gash on the back of his neck, caused by a hatchet. Before Vincenz Oliver fell unconscious, he swore by all things holy that he had been attacked by Denke. A passerby rushed off to the local police station to blurt out the almost unbelievable account that one of town's most respected citizens had tried to kill a wretch of a beggar.

Denke was arrested that same night. Later, when a guard peered into his cell, he saw that the prisoner had hanged himself by his braces.

Apart from a sore head, Vincenz Oliver would have considered himself a very lucky man had he known what his landlord had been up to for a number of years, for Herr Denke had been killing and eating tenant after tenant.

After Denke's corpse had been returned to his family, police went to his house and the shop. Hanging in a closet were many bloodstained clothes, including a skirt. On the windowsill lay various documents in the names of people released from prisons or hospitals. They learned that between 1921 and 1924 he had killed at least thirty strangers, male and female, to eat them up bit by bit. Jars of pickled meat proved to human in origin. Tools for the making of belts made from skin were found. Denke had also processed human hair, using it to make shoelaces. He would sell these goods door-to-door. The meat, with the permission of Wroclaw butchers, he sold through their shops. It was a time of economic slump, so every gram of meat would find a hungry buyer.

As a chilling postscript to the murders, Denke methodically entered each victim's name, weight, date of arrival at the boarding house, and date of death in a ledger before pickling pieces of them in brine to snack on later.

# CHAPTER 8

# Carl Friedrich Wilhelm Grossman—"The Butcher of Berlin"

LITTLE IS KNOWN of Grossman's early life except that he possessed sadistic sexual tastes and frequently got in trouble with the police for child molestation.

Grossman's murderous modus operandi was simplicity itself, based upon a get-rich-quick scheme after World War I, when times were austere and meat in short supply. Running his own hot dog stand, he loitered around Berlin's railway station, carefully weighing up destitute-looking women who were particularly rotund and plump. With generous offers of free accommodation, a great number of these vulnerable females willingly accepted Grossman's hospitality and, upon entering his apartment in a nearby rooming house, they were never seen again. Indeed, neighbors had watched with more than a little curiosity as time after time he escorted female companions through his front door. They never seemed to leave. In fact, most did not, for he quickly murdered them and chopped up their bodies into cuts of juicy meat.

He also appeared to be doing quite well for himself, for he sold a lot of this human meat on the black market. With inflation running so high that a loaf of bread cost a week's pay, Grossman's cut-price joints proved hugely popular. He dumped the inedible parts into the river.

In August 1921, neighbors heard screams and banging noises coming from Grossman's Berlin flat. When police burst in, they found the trussed-up corpse of a woman on the bed, waiting to be butchered.

How many women were "processed" by Karl Grossman is unknown. Figures as high as fifty have been suggested, yet only the body of his final victim was found, along with bloodstains and clothes suggesting that three other women had been butchered in recent weeks.

Convicted of murder, Grossman was sentenced to death. Before his sentence could be carried out, he hanged himself in his cell.

# CHAPTER 9

# Friedrich "Fritz" Heinrich Karl Haarmann—"The Vampire of Hanover"

FRITZ HARRMANN WAS BORN in Hanover, on Saturday, October 25, 1879, the youngest of six children—three boys and three girls—of poor parents. His mother, Johanna Claudius, forty-one at the time of his birth, spoiled and pampered him, encouraging him to play with dolls instead of more masculine toys.

"Old Haarmann," otherwise known as "Sulky Ollie," was seven years younger than his wife. He was a morose, cantankerous locomotive stoker who was to be found at night staggering around the local bars of the Old Town, squandering a dowry his wife had provided him with, including several houses and a small fortune. To all intents, the patriarch was a wealthy citizen in this time of rapid economic expansion. Johanna, a simpleminded, slightly stupid woman, ignored her husband's drinking and whoring, and the birth of Fritz left her sick. She spent much of her remaining twelve years as an invalid in her bed.

A quiet child and a poor scholar, Fritz grew up to detest his father—a loathing that would remain with him throughout his life. He and his father argued constantly, often threatening each other with clenched fists. Herr Haarmann said that he would put his effeminate son into a lunatic asylum, while Fritz wanted his father put in jail for the supposed murder of a train driver. But much of it seems to have been no more than hot air, for on occasion the two men would team up to carry out a swindle or to appear in court as alibi witnesses for each other. It was a time after World War I when anarchy reigned, law and order had collapsed, and thieves and confidence tricksters abounded, while the rest of the population got along as well as they could. Herr Haarmann grabbed what pickings were to be had.

But what of the other siblings? The record shows that the eldest son, Alfred, became a lower-middle class factory foreman with solid Philistine and family values. This could not be said of the second son, Wilhelm, who was sentenced at an early age for a sexual offense. The three sisters, all of whom divorced their husbands early in married life, proved to be particularly obsessive and compulsive women who were overly codependent on their spouses, and probably they drove them away. Frau Rudiger was to meet a premature death in World War I;

Frau Erfurdt, Fritz hardly spoke to. It was therefore the youngest, Emma, who provided young Fritz with any family connection.

After failing as an apprentice locksmith, Fritz was packed off to a military academy at New Briesach in April 1895. He was now 16. Initially, he adapted to military life and is reported as performing well as a soldier. According to the record, he was a good gymnast, but after just one year in the academy he began to suffer seizures. Diagnosed with epilepsy, he was discharged in November 1895 on medical grounds and took work in a cigar factory.

In 1898, Fritz Haarmann was arrested for molesting children, but a psychologist declared he was mentally unfit to stand trial, so he was sent to a mental institution indefinitely. Six months later he escaped and fled to Switzerland, where he worked for two years before he returned to Germany.

It seems that during this period Fritz Haarmann lived a sexually unremarkable life. He seduced and married a large, pretty girl by the name of Erna Loewert. His parents, Herr and Frau Haarmann, hoped the union would mend their son's ways. But Haarmann soon deserted the girl and again enlisted in the military, this time under an alias. Nonetheless, in 1902, he was again discharged under medical terms as being "unsuitable for use in community service." Awarded a full military pension, he returned to live with his parents in Hanover.

Soon arguments between father and son recommenced. Fritz was a lazy good-for-nothing in his father's eyes, and acrimony led to a violent fight. Fritz was charged with assault and again sent for psychiatric evaluation. This time, a doctor diagnosed him as mentally unstable, but the court, with more pressing work in hand, discharged him. An attempt by Fritz to open up a small shop foundered almost as soon as the doors opened, and he was declared bankrupt.

*Hang me, do anything you like to me, but don't take me back to the loony bin.*
—FRITZ HAARMANN

For the next decade, this fleshy man with superficial charm coupled with a low IQ survived as a petty burglar and con artist. He was frequently arrested and served several short prison sentences. Although he was blatantly homosexual, among the criminal underworld he was well liked. He also became a police informer.

In 1914, Haarmann was convicted of a series of thefts and frauds and was locked up just as World War I started. Four years later, a newly liberated thirty-nine-year-old Fritz heard the prison gates slam behind him and breathed the free fresh air one more.

With Germany now insolvent, Fritz Haarmann saw great possibilities opening up before his very eyes, and he immediately reverted to type, this time realizing that it paid better to become a police informer than a full-time crook. Besides, he thought, he could still do a bit of thieving on the side while enjoying police protection. The Hanover authorities were, to say the least, delighted with their undercover recruit, who constantly fed them information on any crimes and scams that were afoot. They nicknamed him "the Detective," provided him with a small income based on results, and issued him a badge, which would provide excellent cover for his later terrible crimes.

Between 1918 and 1924, "Detective" Haarmann committed at least twenty-four murders, although he is suspected of murdering twenty-seven or more. Moving among the swindlers at the market in Hanover, Haarmann gravitated to the nearby railway station, where wretched people arrived from all over Germany to sit close to the warm stoves and beg from people passing by. Among this human flotsam were scores of homeless people, some not even in their teens, most of whom had run away from home. They were nameless and untraceable, and Haarmann picked up on the opportunities straightaway. Ever-smiling, he would flash his police badge and invite them to his home. As Moira Martingale writes, "the promise of a good meal tempted these lost and hungry youngsters to return with him to his apartment as easily as the witch persuaded Hansel and Gretel to enter her gingerbread cottage."

Haarmann's first confirmed kill was that of Friedal Rothe, who disappeared on Wednesday, September 25, 1918, at age seventeen. Haarmann claimed to have buried Rothe in Stöckener Cemetery. The boy had run away from home after an argument with his mother, to whom he had written that he would not return home until she was nice to him again.

In late 1919, Haarmann met twenty-five-year-old Hans Grans at the Hanover railway station. A petty thief, Grans had run away from home and now earned his living selling old clothes. The young boy approached the blatantly camp Haarmann with the purpose of prostituting himself for money. Remarkably, a friendship soon developed between the older man and Grans, and they shared Haarmann's flat on the third floor of a crumbling block overlooking the River Leine.

Meanwhile, various friends of the missing Rothe were forthcoming with information, which led to police to Haarmann's home at 27 Cellerstrasse. Here they found Fritz in bed with a young boy, and he was sentenced to nine months' imprisonment for seducing a minor. Incredibly, the rooms were not searched, so Rothe's head, wrapped in newspaper and stuffed behind the stove, was not discovered.

Haarmann managed to avoid going to prison throughout 1919, but eventually he was locked up from March until December 1920. Throughout this period, Grans thieved his way around Germany until the couple were reunited in August 1921. Together, the two men appeared as well-dressed, decent gentlemen, but an odd pair they were, indeed.

Haarmann was certainly sympathetic in appearance, a simple man with a friendly, open expression and a courteous nature. Of average height, broad and well built, he was described as having a rough "full-moon" face and neat, cheerful eyes. His features were generally small and as "unprepossessing as the rest of his appearance, the only notability was a well-groomed, light brown moustache." In speech, however, his voice "was like the querulous voice of an old woman."

For his part, Grans was quite the sociopath. Although a slim, elegant youth, the son of a librarian, he was certainly his lover's superior and tormented Haarmann with his sarcastic remarks and insults. Nonetheless, they got on well, especially when it came down to selecting they prey, killing them, and cleaning up the mess that inevitable followed.

In early 1922, the two men moved to 8 Neuestrasse, situated in the heart of the so-called haunted area. Haarmann's fortunes had improved, and he was earning a good income from his police informer handouts combined with Social Security payments and a good deal of thieving. The civic-minded Haarmann earned himself a reputation as a solid citizen and benefactor of the homeless, but he would double-cross anyone he met.

On Monday, February 8, 1923, Fritz Franke, age seventeen, and originally from Berlin, was murdered.

Wilhelm Schultze, an apprentice writer age seventeen, fell foul of the murderous duo on Tuesday, March 20, 1923.

Wednesday, May 23, 1923, saw the murder of student Roland Huch. He vanished from Hanover railway station, never to be seen again.

A few days later, nineteen-year-old Hans Sonnenfeld, a runaway from the town of Limmer, was murdered and chopped up.

In short order followed the killing of thirteen-year-old Ernst Ehrenberg. On Monday, June 16, 1923, he disappeared while running an errand for his parents.

Eighteen-year-old Heinrich Struss vanished on Friday, August 24. Haarmann was in possession of the youth's violin case when he was arrested.

September brought with it two more homicides: Seventeen-year-old Paul Bronischewski disappeared en route to visit with his uncle on Monday, September 24, while Richard Graff, age seventeen, went missing after telling his friends that a detective from Hanover had found him a job.

In October, the number of murders escalated. Sixteen-year-old Wilhelm Erdner was killed on October 12. Haarmann sold the youth's bicycle. The next day, Heinz Brinkman, age thirteen, missed his train to Clausthal and was last seen walking away from Hanover Railway Station with two men. On either October 24 or 25, 1923, Hermann Wolf was killed and butchered. The fifteen-year-old's clothing was later traced back to Haarmann and his sidekick.

On Sunday, November 11, an apprentice saw Haarmann approach seventeen-year-old Adolf Hannappel, who ended up in various pieces. December 1923 brought some relief from the murders. Only a single killing and dismemberment took place—that of Adolf Hennies, who disappeared while seeking employment in Hanover on December 19.

The murders continued unabated throughout 1924. Haarmann later confessed that he killed most of his victims by biting through their windpipes, then gorged on the spurting blood before engaging in necrophiliac activities. Always with a view to his commercial instincts, the body would then be dismembered and the clothes and meat sold through the usual channels for smuggled goods. Any useless portions would be tossed into the River Leine.

Due to the nature of the victims, angry or estranged parents and friends often took a while to even report a disappearance. By then, the clothing and the meat of the victims had been speedily distributed around Hanover, to all intents and purposes untraceable. The missing boys were even less than dead. Without any sort of hard evidence, the police were at a dead end, although there were some particularly close calls. On one such occasion, a portion of the trader's meat was taken to the police because the buyer rightly thought it was from a Homo sapiens. The police thought otherwise. Their analyst pronounced, "It's pork!"

On Saturday, January 5, 1924, seventeen-year-old Ernst Spiecker disappeared on his way to appear as a witness at a trial.

On Tuesday, January 15, twenty-year-old Heinrich Koch, a known associate of Haarmann's—vanished without a trace.

February 2 saw the abduction and killing of Willi Senger, age nineteen. His clothes were found in Haarmann's apartment after his arrest.

Electrical apprentice Hermann Speicher, sixteen, met his premature fate six days later on February 8.

During April of that year, things really warmed up. The first murder was that of an apprentice mechanic named Alfred Hogrefe, on Sunday, April 6. The sixteen-year-old's clothing was traced to both Haarmann and Grans.

Hermann Bock, twenty-two, was last seen walking toward Haarmann's apartment a few days later.

On Thursday, April 17, Wilhelm Apel, age sixteen, left for work and didn't arrive.

The month's slaughter ended on April 26 with the death of eighteen-year-old Robert Witzel. Haarmann later admitted dumping the remains in the River Leine.

May came and went, leaving three terrible murders in its wake. Heinrich Martin, fourteen, was an apprentice locksmith who met Haarmann and Grans outside Hanover's railway station.

Fritz Wittig, age seventeen, went the same way on Monday, May 26. Haarmann later told police that Grans had ordered him to commit the murder, and the same day ten-year-old Friedrich Abeling was killed and his remains thrown into the river close to Haarmann's rooms.

Despite the enormous manhunt now in operation, the killer or killers still had not been apprehended, and Hanover was at the point of public outcry. Sheer terror had gripped the city, and the media-dubbed "Werewolf" was still on the loose. Police and the authorities dismissed such suggestions as hysteria. Then a skull washed ashore beside the River Leine. It was May 1924, and the terrified public began harassing the police and demanding action. A second human skull, a smaller one, was discovered a few days later, and more would follow in the months to come, together with sackfuls of bleached white bones and other gory human remains. Dredgers were brought in to dig into the riverbed. More than five hundred human bones were found in all.

Yet remarkably, throughout the panic that engulfed Hanover in 1924, Fritz Haarmann remained a suspect. Along with every other local sex offender, he was investigated repeatedly during May and June, yet no conclusive evidence could be found. Time after time, to the point of tedium, parents in search of their lost sons found that the trail of clues led straight to Haarmann, the last person with whom their sons had been seen. Time and again the police declared themselves satisfied that Haarmann was innocent, despite the fact that the interior of his apartment resembled a blood-drenched charnel house.

June 1924 would bring undoing upon both Haarmann and Grans, for their penultimate victim died on the fifth.

Sixteen-year-old Friedrich Koch vanished on his way to college, and the lad was last seen in the company of "Detective" Haarmann.

It was the disappearance of seventeen-year-old Erich de Vries on Saturday, June 14, that signaled the end of the killers' reign. In classic fashion, it was an offer of cigarettes at Hanover Station that tempted the youth to join the friendly stranger in his rooms.

With pressure mounting, the police finally agreed on a course of action that might end with the arrest of the killer. As Haarmann already knew most of the local police, two young cops would arrive at Hanover station from Berlin. They would pretend to be homeless and looking for a place to stay. They would then focus on the suspect's activities and hope to catch him in the act. However, once again the killer's incredible luck conspired against them as Fritz was seen arguing with Karl Fromm, a fifteen-year-old who had spent several days in Haarmann's rooms.

Fromm was being particularly cheeky and supercilious on this June evening, and amazingly Haarmann had the audacity to report him to the railway police, claiming that the boy was traveling on false papers. Once at the police station, Fromm turned the tables on the older man by accusing him of sexual harassment during his stay. Coincidentally, a member of the vice squad was standing nearby and, knowing that his colleagues were hoping to arrest Haarmann, now armed with reasonable cause, the officer decided to apprehend the suspect immediately. Haarmann was taken into custody on the morning of June 23.

When police searched Haarmann's apartment, they found the bloodstained room, together with piles of clothes, but when confronted with this, the cunning killer protested. He was a butcher, he said, and a clothes trader. What did they expect to find? "So what?" argued Haarmann. There was not a shred of evidence to declare he had been responsible for even one of the deaths. He did, however, admit to having sexual relations with some of the children, yet he denied any knowledge of their whereabouts and went on to give plausible explanations for the traces of blood present on the garments.

Haarmann, with his knowledge of police interrogation tactics, would not give himself up without a fight. He displayed considerable skill at avoiding taxing questions and prolonging the inquisition. He also understood the delicate, rather secretive nature of homosexuality prevalent at the time; subsequently, he knew it would be difficult for the police to obtain incriminating evidence from his victims and their families.

Even more pressure was applied on Haarmann when the parents of Robert Witzel turned up at the police station. Their son had vanished on April 26 after visiting a local circus with his best friend, Fritz Kahlmeyer. During gentle questioning, the shy, somewhat girlish Kahlmeyer remained silent and would only confirm that the two boys had traveled to the circus with a police official from the railway station. The reason for the boy's secretive nature was understandable; he too had been approached and sexually abused by Haarmann. When Herr Witzel identified some of his son's clothes that had been found in Haarmann's apartment, still the suspect remained aloof and unshaken. "Well, this does not prove murder," he sniffed.

As in so many high-profile cases, quite often it all comes down to a bit of luck—even call it ordained fate. The breakthrough came when a couple walked into the police station and passed the Witzel family, who were waiting patiently outside the chief commissioner's office. Frau Witzel could not believe her eyes, for she immediately recognized the man's jacket and asked him as to where he had obtained the garment. The visitor admitted that he had bought the coat from Haarmann and even provided an identification card bearing the name "Witzel" that had been left in a pocket. The woman accompanying him was Frau Engel, Haarmann's landlady, who happened to be in the police station on an entirely different matter—she was making inquiries about her companion's military pension.

Haarmann was now given the full treatment by his interrogators, who kept at him for seven days, during which time the suspect ranted and raved like a maniac. Eventually, he broke and asked for the superintendent and examining magistrate. He would make a full and frank confession, starting by implicating Grans from the outset.

Fritz Haarmann's trial began at Hanover Assizes on Thursday, December 4, 1924. It would last fourteen days. He was charged with the murders of twenty-seven boys and young men, and the trial was spectacular. It would become one of the first major media-covered events in Germany's history. The newspapers variously named him as a werewolf and a vampire; one imaginative journalist conjured up "Wolf Man." Apart from the cruelty of Haarmann's crimes, even more scandalous—shaking German society to the core—was the involvement of the police in the case: Haarman, as a police informant, frequently gave up other criminals to investigators. Until his arrest, it had never occurred to the police that the serial killer they were looking for was well-known to them and right under their noses, even though some of the victims were last seen in his company.

*I never intended to hurt those youngsters, but I knew that if I got going, something would happen and that made me cry...I would throw myself on top of those boys and bite through the Adam's apple, throttling them at the same time.*

—FRITZ HAARMANN, AT HIS TRIAL

At one point in the proceedings, Haarmann took court officials on a guided murder tour of Hanover. They were shown parts of as yet undiscovered corpses hidden in bushes, more bones dredged from a lake and skeletons concealed around the city. Inevitably, more and more people, ever anxious to have a piece of the action, stepped forward claiming that they had also obtained meat and clothing from either Haarmann or Grans.

As the result of the information secured, Hans Grans had been arrested on July 8, He would remain silent throughout, while Haarmann behaved like a callous showman, admitting his guilt, showing no remorse but instead making vulgar asides to Grans.

Despite there being heartbroken relatives of his victims in court, Haarmann interrupted proceedings at will, often making quite the most distasteful remarks in a jocular fashion and claiming he was a selective killer, choosing only to kill good-looking boys and denying three of the charges. One parent whose son was missing showed a picture to the court, and Haarmann objected indignantly, saying: "I have my tastes, after all. Such an ugly creature as, according to his photographs, your son must have been, I would never have taken to... poor stuff like him there's plenty...Such a youngster was much beneath my notice." One completely distraught mother broke down weeping while testifying, and Haarmann, finding this tiresome, interrupted to ask the judges if he could smoke a cigar. Amazingly, permission was immediately granted.

*Hans Grans has been sentenced unjustly and that's the fault of the police and also because I wanted revenge. Put yourself in Gran's position: he will question the existence of the Lord and justice just because of me. May Hans Grans forgive me for my revenge and humanity.*

—FRITZ HAARMANN, LETTER CLEARING GRANS OF ANY INVOLVEMENT IN SERIAL HOMICIDE

With some 200 witnesses paraded before Haarmann, he grew more and more nonchalant throughout the trial. At one point he complained that there were too many women in the courtroom. To the journalists he once said reproachfully, "You are not to lie. We all know you are liars," and to the jury, "Keep it short. I want to spend Christmas in heaven with Mother."

Haarmann became livid when it seemed to him that Hans Grans might be found innocent. "Grans should tell you how shabbily he has treated me," he whined. "I did the murders—for that work he is too young." But he told how Grans had knocked on his door while he was dismembering a victim, and asked, "Where is the suit?"

On the last day of the trial, Haarmann shouted:

I want to be executed in the marketplace. And on my tombstone must be put this inscription: "Here lies Mass Murderer Haarmann." On my birthday, Hans Grans must put a wreath on it. Do you think I enjoy killing people? I was ill for eight days after the first time. Condemn me to death…I am not mad. It is true I often get into a state when I do not know what I am doing, but that is not madness…I will not petition for mercy, nor will I appeal. I just want one more merry evening in my cell, with coffee, hard cheese, and cigars, after which I will curse my father and go to my execution as if it were a wedding.

Often after I killed, I pleaded to be put away in a military asylum, but not a madhouse. If Grans had really loved me, he would have been able to save me. Believe me, I'm not ill—it's only that I occasionally have funny turns. I want to be beheaded. It'll only take a moment, then I'll be at peace.

Fritz Haarmann got his wish. He was beheaded by guillotine on Tuesday, April 15, 1925. His last words as he placed his head on the lunette were, "I repent, but I do not fear death."

Hans Grans was initially found guilty of enticement to murder in the case of Adolf Hannappel, the seventeen-year-old apprentice carpenter who vanished from Hanover's railway station on November 11, 1923. Witnesses had seen Grans in the company of Haarmann, pointing to the youth. Haarmann claimed that this was one of two murders committed on the insistence of Grans, and for this reason, Grans was sentenced to death. However, the discovery of a letter from Haarmann declaring Grans's innocence later led to a second trial and a twelve-year prison term for Grans. After serving his time, Hans Grans continued to live in Hanover until his death in 1975.

*I'd make two cuts in the abdomen and out the intestines in a bucket, then soak up the blood and crush the bones until the shoulders broke. Now I could get the heart, lungs and kidneys and chop them and put them in my bucket. I'd take the flesh off the bones and put it in my wax-cloth bag. It would take me five or six trips to take everything and throw it down the toilet or into the river. I always hated doing this, but I couldn't help it—my passion was so much stronger than the horror of the cutting and chopping.*
—FRITZ HAARMANN, AT TRIAL

The remains of Haarmann's victims were buried together in a communal grave in Stöckener Cemetery in February 1925. In April 1928, a large granite memorial in the form of a triptych inscribed with the names and ages of the victims was erected over the grave.

After his execution, Haarmann's head was preserved in a jar by scientists to examine the structure of his brain. His head is now kept at the Göttingen Medical School.

# CHAPTER 10

# Edmund Emil "Big Ed" Kemper III– "The Co-ed Killer"

*If I kiss her, I would have to kill her first.*
—ED KEMPER AT AGE SEVEN

IT IS SOMETIMES CLAIMED that serial killers want to be caught. Increasing sloppiness, risk-taking and taunting yet revealing letters sent to the authorities are often cited as proof of this conscious or subconscious need. Ultimately, this is nothing more than speculation; we cannot really know. However, it can be said with certainty that Ed Kemper, the "Co-Ed Killer," wanted to be caught. He actually turned himself in.

EDMUND EMIL KEMPER III was born on Saturday, December 18, 1948, in Burbank, California, home of the Disney Corporation and Warner Bros. He was the middle child and only son (his older sister was then six; his younger sister came into the world in 1951) born to Edmund "E.E." Emil Kemper Jr. aged twenty-nine, and Clarnell E. Strandberg, twenty-seven, who, it is claimed, suffered a borderline personality disorder.

Ed enjoyed a close relationship with his father, so he was devastated when his parents divorced in 1957. Clarnell took her kids nearly 1,200 miles away to Helena, Montana. Here, young Kemper suffered his mother's physical and emotional abuse. She would constantly belittle and humiliate him, often locking him in the basement, thinking he would molest his sisters. The cellar was a dark, damp place where, Ed believed, goblins and demons lurked. "There was only one way out," he remembers. "Someone had to move the kitchen table and lift a trapdoor." When the patriarch learned of this of some months later, he was furious and put a stop to it, threatening his ex-wife with legal action.

Ed was an extremely bright lad, but he did exhibit sociopathic behavior from a young age. He began to torture and kill animals, and he used his sisters' dolls in acting out aberrant sexual fantasies and situations. On more than one occasion, his younger sister found that her dolls had been decapitated, with their hands cut off—something Kemper would later do to his victims. He enjoyed setting small fires and at one time showed signs of necrophilia. In a favorite childhood game Kemper would dream of his own execution, enlisting one of his sisters to lead him blindfolded to a pretend electric chair, where she would pull an imaginary lever and he would writhe around as if dying. His sister also remembered teasing Ed about a teacher he had a crush on. "Why don't you go and kiss her?" she joked. "If I kiss her, I would have to kill her first," replied the seven-year-old boy. If that was a strange remark from a small child, even more bizarre were the fantasies he nursed before adolescence. Apart from an occasion when he stood outside his teacher's house one night and envisaged what it would be like to kill her and have sex with the corpse, he also imagined killing his neighbors, having sex with dead bodies, and killing his mother.

> When I was at school, I was a chronic daydreamer, and I saw a counsellor twice during junior and high school, and that was very routine. They didn't ask me a lot of questions about myself, and that was probably the most violent fantasy time I was off into.
>
> —ED KEMPER

When he was thirteen, Ed slaughtered his pet cat with a machete and stuffed some of the remains into his closet, while the rest was found by his mother in a trash can. She did not know that her son had been killing neighborhood cats for a long time previously, sometimes burying them alive, then putting their heads on poles and muttering incarnations over his "trophies." The same year, Kemper was suspected of shooting a neighbor's pet dog, and he was ostracized by other boys his age. Ed was an awkward and oversized child, much bigger than his peers, which only served to increase his isolation.

The only person who took to Ed was one of his step-fathers who went fishing and shooting with him—the sort of masculine role modeling of which he had been deprived. Yet the stepfather's kindness was not rewarded. Eventually Ed, armed with an iron bar, tried but failed to muster the courage to attack the man, after which, he planned, he would steal his car and drive to California to see his father.

In the summer of 1963, Ed ran away from home with the intention of living with his father, who by now had remarried and was somewhat less than pleased to see him. It was during that trip that Ed learned he had a stepbrother. The boy had replaced him in his father's affections.

E.E. initially welcomed Ed but soon returned him to the assertive Clarnell, who was busy with her own life and her own marital relationships, which were legion. Her solution was to pack fourteen-year-old Ed off to live with his parental grandparents, children's book writer Maude Kemper and her husband Edmund, on their seventeen-acre ranch in North Fork, California. It was there with Maude and Edmund Sr. that Ed began his murderous career. He had been to the ranch the previous Christmas holidays and remained for the rest of that school year before returning to his mother. Now he was back, and he wasn't happy about that at all.

Already considerably more than six feet tall, Ed was an awkward boy both physically and socially. Despite his height he was easily bullied, and according to Ed, his grandmother was included in his list of tormentors.

During the afternoon of Thursday, August 12, 1964, an argument erupted between sixty-six-year-old Maude and Ed as she sat at the kitchen table writing one of her children's books. Enraged, Ed Kemper took up the .22-caliber rifle his grandfather had given him the previous Christmas, and when she warned him not to shoot the birds he turned and shot her instead, once in the front of the head and twice in the back of the head, before stabbing her repeatedly. He did not have much trouble dragging his grandmother's corpse into the bedroom. But then his seventy-two-year-old grandfather drove up, so Ed decided the finish the job he had begun. As Edmund Sr. got out of his car, Ed raised his rifle and shot him as well.

After telephoning his mother to tell her what he had done, he called the police the waited calmly on the porch for them to take him into custody.

At age fifteen, Ed Kemper was committed to the Atascadero State Hospital, where he befriended his psychologist and even became his assistant. As a result of tests conducted on him, he was revealed to possess an IQ of 136.

On his twenty-first birthday, Thursday, December 18, 1969, against the wishes of several psychologists, he was released into his mother's care. Divorced for the third time, she had moved back to California during her son's incarceration and was now living in a duplex on Ord Drive in Aptos, near Santa Cruz, a rapidly growing beach town to the south of San Francisco, and working at local Merrill College as an administrator.

Ed attended community college and received high marks. He became friendly with various members of the Santa Cruz Police Department. For a time he planned on becoming an officer, a dream that ended when he learned he was too tall. Now standing six feet nine inches, and weighing nearly 300 pounds, Kemper was an imposing figure—the human equivalent of the Sears Tower.

Ed worked at a number of jobs before settling into a position as a laborer with the California Division of Highways, an occupation that had some relationship to his subsequent crimes. Kemper wasn't good with money, but he managed to save enough to move out of his mother's home and share an apartment with a roommate. He also purchased a motorcycle, which played a part in two separate accidents. As the result of one of these, Kemper received a settlement of $15,000. He used this money to buy a yellow Ford Galaxy and began to cruise the area along the Pacific coast in search of female hitchhikers. By his own estimation, he generously provided rides to approximately 150 young women and girls, all the while slowly gathering items of sinister purpose in his trunk: knives, handcuffs, a blanket, and plastic bags. Finally, he felt the urgent inner drive of what he called his "little zapples," and he acted.

Santa Cruz is surrounded by mountains, ocean, and towering redwoods. It is a tourist mecca and an upscale place to own a home or rent an apartment. During the early 1970s, when the murders began, townspeople were already torn over the hippies moving in, thanks in part to the University of California opening a new campus there. Young people flooded in, and not all of them were what residents called "desirable."

On Sunday, May 7, 1972, the eighteen-year-old Mary Anne Pesce and Anita Luchessa hitchhiked from Fresno State College to meet friends at Stanford University.

This was to be a double homicide which should, by rights, have failed. When things didn't go as smoothly as Ed had hoped, he panicked and found himself locked out- side the car with the two girls inside. Amazingly, Mary Anne

*When a girl puts her hand on my car door handle, she was giving me her life.*

—ED KEMPER

Pesce opened the doors to him. Kemper said that he had picked them up and driven to an isolated spot, where he drew a 9mm Browning automatic that he had borrowed from a friend. As if to intensify his own "game," he told them that he intended to rape them and that he was going to take them to his apartment, although he had learned from listening to stories of rapists in Atascadero that it was better to leave no witnesses.

He took out a pair of handcuffs, secured Mary Anne's hands behind her, and locked Anita in the trunk at gun- point. Producing a plastic bag, Kemper thrust it over Mary's head and wound a cord around her neck. As she fought for her life, he stabbed her many times. One jab hit her backbone and would not enter. Finally he cut her throat. Opening the trunk, he stabbed Anita to death when she tried to climb out, threw the knife inside with her body, and drove home. And he was nearly caught.

As Kemper drove to Alameda, he was stopped for a broken taillight. He maintained a calm, polite attitude and got off with a mere warning. During the entire encounter, Kemper later said he was excited. Had the officer decided to do a routine check and look in the trunk, Kemper would have killed him on the spot.

The friend with whom Kemper shared an apartment in Alameda was away, so he carried the bodies, wrapped in blankets, to his room, where he dismembered them, taking Polaroid photographs as he worked. He stuffed the remains in garbage bags and drove off to the nearby mountains. But he kept the heads for some time; committing oral sex with them before tossing them into an isolated ravine.

When the girls failed to arrive at their destination, their families contacted the police. But runaways were all too frequent in those days, and the girls had left behind no clues as to where they had gone. So there was little the authorities could do. Then, on Tuesday, August 15, what remained of a female head was recovered from an area in the mountains and identified as that of Pesce. No other remains were found, but it was assumed that both girls had met with foul play and both were dead.

On the night of Thursday, September 14, 1972, Kemper picked up fifteen-year-old Aiko Koo, who had decided to hitchhike home from a Berkeley dance class instead of waiting for a bus. While keeping the petite girl at gunpoint, he stopped his car at the side of the road and taped up her mouth. Then he suffocated her by blocking her nostrils with his fingers before raping her. He placed the body in the trunk of his car and drove back to his mother's house, stopping for a few beers on the way. In his room, he proceeded to rape and dissect the body, and conducted several experiments on her corpse. He later dismembered her body and buried the remains—except the head—in his mother's backyard.

The day after Kemper killed Aiko Koo, he went before a panel of psychiatrists as a follow-up requirement for parole. He had done well in school, he had found a job, and as far as anyone knew, he had stayed out of trouble. He knew what the shrinks wanted to hear and he put on his best act. The first doctor talked with him for a while and indicated that he saw no reason to consider Kemper a danger to anyone. The second doctor actually used the words "normal" and "safe," and both doctors recommended the sealing of his juvenile records as a way of helping him to become a better citizen. Yet even as the two psychiatrists congratulated themselves on being part of a system that had rehabilitated a killer child, Kemper delighted in his secret. Not only had he killed Aiko Koo the day before this examination, but her head was in the trunk of his car right out front.

As he drove away with a clean bill of mental health, he felt pleased. Now he was free to continue with his experiments. He found a place to bury Koo's head and hands above Boulder Creek, and there they remained undiscovered until the following May.

Short of money and unable to keep up the rent on his Alameda apartment, Kemper returned to his mother's home in Aptos. On the one hand, she tried to make her son's life as comfortable as possible, even going so far as to give him a university bumper sticker so he could park his car on the campus; on the other hand she remained as critical and domineering as ever. He spent some of his time in a saloon called the Jury Room, chatting with off-duty policemen. Although he had been rejected by the police for being too big, he picked up much of their professional approach and was able to follow the progress of the investigation of his crimes from the conversations he had with them. Somehow, he managed to obtain a police training-school badge from an officer he had befriended, and with his car, which was similar in appearance to a patrol cruiser and fitted with a CB radio and whip aerial, he was able to fantasize that he was a police officer—and also set the minds of the hitchhikers he picked up at ease.

The sealing of Kemper's record was confirmed in November. With an apparently clean slate, he was able to buy himself a .22-caliber Smith & Wesson Model 41 on Monday, January 8, 1973. The following day he killed again.

On Tuesday, January 9, on the Cabrillo College campus, Kemper picked up a pretty nineteen-year-old trainee teacher, Cindy Schall. He stopped his car in a secluded area by woods, where he fatally shot her with his new pistol. He placed the body in the trunk of his car and drove back to his mother's house, where he dissected her in a bathtub. He kept the body in his room overnight. Then he removed the bullet from her head and beheaded her. He buried her severed head in his mother's garden as a joke. His mother would often tell him, "I always want people to look up to me." Later, he dismembered the remainder of the body and discarded the pieces over a cliff.

Less than two days later, dismembered arms and legs were found at the foot of a cliff overlooking the Pacific Ocean. Then an upper torso washed ashore. It was identified via x-rays as Schall's. Eventually a lower torso came in. A surfer also found her left hand, which offered fingerprints, but her head and right hand remained missing until they were found in Kemper's mother's garden.

On Monday, February 5, 1973, after an argument with his mother, Kemper left the house in search of possible victims. He later encountered twenty-four-year-old Rosalind Thorpe and twenty-three-year-old Allison Liu, who were on the UC Santa Cruz campus, where his mother worked. According to Kemper, it was a wet night, and Thorpe entered his car first, which apparently reassured Liu to follow. Before leaving the university grounds, Kemper turned to Rosalind sitting in the front passenger seat and shot her in the head. He then turned to the terrified Alice sitting in the rear and shot her several times:

> Miss Thorpe got into the front passenger seat, then
> Miss Liu got in the back seat right behind her. Went

through the main gate. I went down a ways and slowed down. I remarked on the beautiful view. I hesitated for several seconds. I had been moving my pistol from down below my legs in my lap. I picked up the gun and fired. As I fired, she [Rosalind Thorpe] fell against the window. Miss Liu panicked. I had to fire through her hands. She was moving around and I missed twice.

He wrapped the bodies in blankets and placed them both on the backseat of his car. Two young men were at the university security gate, but when they saw a university sticker, given to Ed by his mother, they waved him through. He told the guard that both girls were drunk, and he was trying to get them back to their dorms. The guard accepted the story, and Kemper decided that he was as good as invisible. "It was getting easier to do," he later claimed. "I was getting better at it."

He drove to his mother's house, where he beheaded them while his mother was in the backyard. He then sexually abused their bodies. The following morning, he dismembered the bodies and drove north to the Bay Area, where he dumped them in a canyon and threw the girls' heads and hands into a ravine.

On Sunday, March 4, a couple of hikers came across a human skull and jawbone not far from Highway 1 in San Mateo County. They were not from the same person. Police searched the area and found another skull that went with the jawbone, so they knew they had a pair of victims killed close together. They compared what they had to a number of missing female hitchhikers, subsequently identifying the remains of Rosalind Thorpe and Alice Liu. Thorpe had been shot once in the head and Liu twice.

Things came to a head on Good Friday, 1973, when Kemper battered his sleeping mother, Clarnell Strandberg, to death with a claw hammer. He then beheaded her with his favorite knife, "the General," and used the head for oral sex before propping it against a hat box on the mantle and using it as a dart board. He also cut out her vocal cords and put them in the garbage disposal, but the machine could not break down the tough tissue and regurgitated it back into the sink. "That seemed appropriate," he said after his arrest. "As much as she'd bitched and screamed and yelled at me over so many years. Even when she was dead, she was still bitching at me. I could never get her to shut the fuck up."

Yet his murderous urges were not yet satiated. He invited over his mother's best friend, fifty-nine-year-old Sally Hallett, for "a surprise dinner." When she entered the house, Sally said, "Let's sit down. I'm dead." He took her at his word and punched and strangled her to death, after which he went for a drink at the Jury Room. Upon his return home, he cut off Sally's head and laid her body on his bed. Ed spent the night with the two corpses in the house and blood everywhere. One account indicates that he tried to have sex with Hallett's corpse.

At dawn the next morning, Easter Sunday, without an idea of what to do, Kemper set off in Sally's car, driving aimlessly eastward for many hours, having left a note for the police beside his mother's corpse:

Appx 5:15 A.M. Saturday. No need for her to suffer any more at the hands of this "Murderous Butcher." It was quick—asleep—the way I wanted it. Not sloppy and incomplete, gents. Just a "lack of time." I got things to do!!!!

Keeping himself awake with No-Doz caffeine tablets, Kemper dropped off Hallett's car and rented a green Chevy Impala, finally arriving a thousand miles away in Pueblo, Colorado, where he pulled over to a roadside telephone booth and called the Santa Cruz police to confess that he was the Co-ed Killer. He said he had two hundred rounds of ammo and three guns in the car and this scared him, but at first they did not believe him.

After placing several calls he was able to persuade an officer to go check out his mother's house. He explained that a Sergeant Aluffi had been there not long before to confiscate the .44-caliber revolver he had purchased. Aluffi would know the place.

Sergeant Aluffi did indeed know and went to the home himself. As he entered, he smelled the putrid odor of decomposition. When he opened a closet and saw blood and hair, he secured the scene and called in the coroner and homicide detectives. A call was made to Pueblo police and Kemper was picked up.

District Attorney Peter Chang and a party of detectives traveled across three states to pick Kemper up from detention at a local jail, and they found him waiting calmly for him. He seemed to know that he was dangerous and unable to control himself and understood that he needed to be locked away.

Now back in Santa Cruz, Kemper admitted all his crimes to shocked investigators. He said that he had taken flesh from the legs of women and had frozen the meat, later making a casserole with it. He also admitted having other "keepsakes" of his victims—teeth or pieces of skin. Kemper said, "I wanted them to be part of me, and now they are":

> Alive, they were distant, not sharing with me. I was trying to establish a relationship. When they were being killed, there wasn't anything going on in my mind except that they were going to be mine…that was the only way they could be mine. I had their spirits. I still have them.

While awaiting trial, Edmund Kemper tried twice to commit suicide by slashing his wrists. He failed both times. He was indicted on eight counts of first-degree murder, and the chief public defender of Santa Cruz County, attorney Jim Jackson, was assigned to the case; Jackson immediately offered an insanity plea. He had his hands full, especially because Kemper's detailed confession without an attorney had robbed him of any strategy except an insanity defense. But even this would not be easy, since Kemper was so articulate and clear in the way he had planned and prepared for his fatal encounters. Nevertheless, he had once been diagnosed as psychotic, and despite the psychiatric records, now unsealed for the trial, that pronounced him safe, he clearly had not been cured. For Jackson, there was a glimmer of hope that this defense could work.

Three prosecution psychiatrists found him to be sane. Dr. Joel Fort looked at Kemper's juvenile records to examine the diagnosis that he was then psychotic. He interviewed Kemper at length, including under truth serum and told the court that Kemper had probably engaged in acts of cannibalism. He apparently cooked and ate parts of the girls' flesh after dismembering them. Needless to say, Fort decided that Kemper had known what he was doing in each incident, was thrilled by the notoriety of being a serial murderer, and had been entirely aware that it was wrong. That was good enough to find Kemper sane.

On Thursday, November 8, 1973, the six-man, six-woman jury deliberated for five hours before finding Kemper sane and guilty on all eight counts of first-degree murder. Although he hoped to receive the death penalty, he was convicted dur-

> *Death by torture.*
>
> —ED KEMPER,
> ASKED WHAT HE CONSIDERED
> SUITABLE PUNISHMENT

ing a time when the Supreme Court had placed a moratorium on capital punishment, and all death sentences were commuted to life imprisonment. The death penalty became applicable only to crimes committed after January 1, 1974.

Kemper was sentenced to life imprisonment. Sent first to the California Medical State Prison, at Vacaville, north of San Francisco, for observation, he ended up at the Super-Max facility at Folsom. At one point, he requested psychosurgery, which involved inserting a probe into his brain to kill brain tissue and potentially cure him of his compulsive sexual aggression. His request was denied, possibly because authorities feared that he might then petition for release. After all, he had given doctors the run-around before. Since then he has become a model inmate, helping to read books on tape for the blind, but when he went before the parole board, he told them he was not fit to go back into society. In prison, he was reportedly cooperative and kind and wished to forget his past. While he readily participated in requests for interviews and self-examination, hoping he would help others to learn about offenders like him, he often disliked what some of his interviewers said about him.

Today, Kemper is back among the general prison population at the California Medical Facility in Vacaville. He could qualify for release as early as 2012.

# CHAPTER 11

# David Harker—"The Darlington Cannibal"

*Harker was the nicest bloke I'd ever met
at the time, and the first thing you I noticed
were his eyes; big blue eyes, and he was always
the center of attention with his bottle of
white stuff, his booze.*
—JANET FAREY, FRIEND OF HARKER'S

IN A MOST UNUSUAL CASE of British cannibalism, in February 1999, David Harker admitted to manslaughter in the death of thirty-two-year-old Julie Paterson, on the grounds of diminished responsibility. Prosecutor Paul Worsley told Teesside Crown Court in northeast England that Harker confided to a psychiatrist that he chopped up his victim and ate part of her body with pasta and cheese. Harker, then twenty-four, who has the words "subhuman" and "disorder" tattooed on his scalp, claimed that he had strangled mother-of-four Julie with her tights after he "got bored" during a sex session. He told psychiatrists that he then had sex with her before chopping off her head and limbs, slicing flesh from her thigh, skinning and cooking it.

The six-foot-five-inch, unemployed killer bragged about his cannibal feast and claimed to be a serial killer who had killed two other people, one a tramp, in the northeast, although there is no evidence to show he committed those two crimes. Nonetheless, the case is of interest because it allows us to take a peek into the social life of a man whom most thought to be a really nice guy.

Most visitors see Darlington (pop. 100,000) in County Durham as a quaint market town with good old-fashioned British values, but scratch the surface and a more sinister side appears: Pockets of hardcore unemployment and chronic alcoholism create an underclass without hope of a future. This seedy underbelly is, indeed, an environment where we would expect bad things to happen, but the story of David Harker and Julie Paterson shocked everyone in town.

We know little to nothing about Harker's formative years, his parents, his childhood, his siblings if any, his schooling, until he appeared on the social radar in February 1995. A wannabe musician, he arrived in Darlington after getting himself into a lot of trouble in his hometown of Chester-le-Street. He wanted a new start.

From then on, he lived on the fringes of Darlington society staggering from the liquor store to the post office to cash his Social Security check. Although quite fit enough to hold down a job, he was a slacker, a layabout, and a chronic alcoholic who wasted away his days, most of the time out of his mind with the drink, and associating with like-minded red-nosed drunks on some park bench. Then one day he bumped into a woman upon whom he would play out his personal fantasy—to become Britain's youngest serial killer.

Matt Farey was sixteen when he fell in with the then twenty-three-year-old Harker. "My family used to have him come round and have dinner and stuff. He got on well with my mother and sisters when he had nowhere to stay, an' we'd let him stay for a bit but often he'd stay longer than expected."

During the times he stayed with the Farey family he did not pay any rent, but, "He paid us with his kindness," says Janet Farey, then age eleven. "My mum didn't mind because he did his bit, you know…cleaning and tidying up…helping me with my homework 'cause he said he didn't want me to turn out like him."

Things started looking up for Harker when he met and fell in love with a local girl. With assistance from Social Security, the couple moved into a flat at 6A Harewood Grove, and Harker hit it off immediately with his neighbor, Stuart Boulton: "When I first met David, he just came across as a nice person," Boulton said, "just a nice person, even intelligent in a kind of way. Polite, charming, you could have a conversation with him." But after a year of domestic bliss, Harker's domestic relationship fell apart, and his girlfriend moved out. He turned to drink a lot more and sat in the park. He thought drinking made him feel better, but in fact it made him worse.

It was at this point that Harker met Julie Paterson, a woman who would change his life forever. Quite an attractive, petite blonde, Julie had had a string of childhood tragedies, and she had recently lost her three children in a custody battle. This trauma had led her to leave Durham and to rely on Social Security handouts, Valium, and alcohol. As her friend June Chamberlin explained, "I got to know Julie three years before she died; first as a lodger, then as a friend. She was bubbly and happy, she liked her drink, but when she was depressed she went from extrovert to introvert in the flick of a switch."

Within weeks of arriving in Darlington, Julie met Alan Taylor, with whom she would have a three-year relationship. He was a bit of a loner who had not been with a woman for ages. And he, too, spent more time than was wise in drink and sitting with his boozed-up cronies, eyes-glazed with hard liquor. Alan Taylor remembers, "Me and Julie had our ways of pulling out of difficult times, just making each other laugh. We've had a tough life, some obstacles to go through. It was difficult for us both. I think she'd had a bad life and that's why she ended up in Darlington from Durham."

From time to time the "Darlington Park Bench Fraternity" would depart to Hastings on the south coast. Alan and Julie could not wait to move to the seaside. Then she fell pregnant with Alan's child, so they took off to Hastings for a new life with a new baby, planning to do everything differently.

For reasons we are not sure of, they gave the baby up for adoption—whether it was their decision or that of the authorities we may never know—but they soon returned to Darlington, with Julie more depressed and withdrawn than ever before and her circumstances deteriorating by the day. As Taylor explains, "It was difficult for us both, actually, but I didn't show it as much as Julie did. She seemed lost and gave up."

Throughout Julie's relationship with Taylor, she would disappear for days with no explanation as to where she was going and why. When she returned to Darlington she was dirty, her hair unkempt, and even more depressed. Then she would eat a meal, take a bath, spruce herself up, and the next day she would be almost as good as new. She would repeat the cycle again and again. Making the excuse to Alan during the night that she was visiting the bathroom, she would vanish into thin air, at one time for a week.

Then, from one such wandering, Julie never returned to pick up her Valium prescription or her Social Security check.

On April 29, 1998, Alan Taylor reported Julie as missing to local police. He explained that she had now been absent for some three weeks and he had not heard a word from her. She had left home with nothing more than the clothes she had been wearing, carrying a small bag that contained her essential toiletries.

The police acted quickly, for they knew that Julie was "vulnerable" and in a state of emotional upheaval. They carried out a few checks then launched an appeal for her whereabouts in the *Northern Echo* newspaper, which also showed her photograph. A few days later, the police received a tipoff. A man who had seen the newspaper article recognized Julie. He had recently had a conversation with Mr. David Harker. The man advised police to take a look down Polham Lane, a quiet, secluded road in Darlington. Detective Inspector Ian Phillips went to investigate.

It did not take long for the police to track Harker down, for he had not only boasted to some twenty people about killing and cannibalizing Julie Paterson, but he was living at a bail hostel after being charged with committing a robbery using violence. Detective constables Ian Watson and David Ripley were to interview him. Detective Watson described their prisoner as having "penetrating blue eyes, a shaved head with the tattoos *subhuman* and *disorder* on his forehead. He was a big guy…a bit of a handful."

For the first two interviews, Harker talked freely about this life and the murder of Julie, whom he called "Roxanne." Toward the end of the second interview, he became agitated and started complaining that he had heard voices inside his head telling him what to do.

Meanwhile, investigators and crime scene technicians went to Harker's home at 6A Harewood Grove. They went into a cluttered backyard. Their mood of grim trepidation, and their worst fears were confirmed when they opened a basement door and saw a trail of dried blood leading to a cupboard under the stairs. The blood trail indicated that a heavily bleeding corpse had been dragged along the ground. The room was dark, the entire setting one of decay, eerie and macabre. Here, police found items of clothing that corresponded with items Julie was known to have worn, including track-suit bottoms. In a plastic bag they found a serrated kitchen knife covered in blood. On a kitchen shelf were Julie's black and white sneakers. In Harker's squalid bedroom, officers spotted heavy bloodstains in a corner where Julie's blood had soaked through the carpet

> When I arrived at the scene, which would be 2:30, maybe 2:45 in the morning, the lane had been closed off by my colleagues. The nightshift police dog handler, with his German shepherd "Tyler" had located something suspicion in the undergrowth…it turned out to be plastic trash bag containing a human torso.
> —Detective Inspector Ian Phillips

into the floorboards. On the wall was scrawled, "I HAVE LOST THE WILL TO LIVE…NOTHING MORE FOR ME TO GIVE." On another wall, Harker had written, "BORN AGAIN WITH SNAKE'S EYES…BECOMING GOD SIZE."

Harker was charged with murder and remained in custody while the search for the rest of Julie's body continued and the police left no stone unturned.

Harker had refused to reveal where he had dumped Julie's head, arms, and legs. Police looked everywhere, extending their search from Polham Lane to every local drain all over the ninety-one-acre South Park and onto one of the largest dumps in Europe. Here, for three weeks, they turned over 20,000 tons of trash, but came up with nothing.

On July 24, 1998, what was left of Julie Paterson was buried in what a local woman described as "a funeral with a difference, for there just isn't enough of her, so she'll never be at rest."

Before his trial, David Harker was sent to Ashworth Hospital for psychiatric evaluation by forensic psychologist Dr. David Nais, who determined that Harker suffered from a sexual disorder combined with a psychopathic disorder, to the degree that it placed him in the top 4 percent of psychopaths in the United Kingdom—making him a very dangerous individual indeed.

During his interviews with Dr. Nais, Harker claimed it was he who was the victim, and he showed no remorse for the killing of Julie Paterson. He told a pack of lies about his childhood, claiming that he had been beaten by his father since the age of two; that at age six he had tried to hang himself with a skipping rope; and that at age ten his father forced him to watch a dog fight at the

*I'm not evil, I'm a monster. The detectives who interviewed me were too stupid to see who I was.*
*—DAVID HARKER*

family home and had him clean up the blood and flesh afterward, only to get beaten because he used the wrong type of cloth. "My mother was disabled," he moaned. "I was forced to do the housework to her specification, and if I didn't my father would beat me."

It was also learned that at age sixteen he had been found guilty of two assaults, one charge of criminal damage, and one charge of cruelty to an animal. He had kicked a dog to death.

While at Ashworth Hospital, Harker wrote several self-serving letters to the editor of the *Northern Echo*, in which he further taunted the police. In one case, he sent them the following riddle, which he titled "Churchill," as to where the remains of Julie might be found:

> I own a bank but have no money
> I have falls but keep going
> I have a mouth but do not eat
> I have a bed but do not sleep
> I have a beginning but have no end
> What am I...Do you know where it is?

Church Hill is close to the "banks" of the River Skerne, of which there are "falls," or a stretch of fast-running water a few hundred yards downstream. Of course the river has a "mouth"; it also has a river "bed." Every river starts somewhere, and the River Skerne—a tributary of the River Tees—runs into the sea which has "no end."

Yet no one figured the riddle out.

David Harker lived in a world where lead balls bounce, elephants fly, and fairies reign supreme. He has claimed that his idol was Jeffrey Dahmer. He was an avid reader on Ed Gein, too, for he talked about making domestic items out of human skin. Moreover, not a shred of evidence proves that he cannibalized Julie at all. But this case does pose the question, What is evil? What is bad, mad, or insane?

It is also now known that when not in the company of drunks, he hung around impressionable kids much younger than himself, whom he would regale with stories of evil and Satanism. Standing bare-chested on a park bench, while calling himself Devil Man, this booze-soaked loser tried to terrify the teenagers who actually thought of him as a joke. "He was kind of funny," remembers Janet Farey. "We never took him seriously until we found out what he had done to Julie. It's great to know that he's locked up."

Harker was a wannabe musician, and it is now believed by psychiatrists and police that he was a wannabe serial killer, too. His psychopathic personality disorder enabled him to believe that he actually was a serial killer. He has all the traits commonly associated with an antisocial personality, with a total lack of compassion and remorse for the killing of Julie Paterson, and the grief and loss suffered by her father, Jim, who rightly needs to find the remainder of his daughter's body so he can put her—and his own mind—to rest, thus bringing some form of closure to this tragic affair.

By any legal or medical definition, the attention-seeking Harker is not "mad" or "insane," for he knew that killing Julie was wrong. He transcends "bad," of this there can be no doubt. He is simply evil. My own conclusion is that the cannibalistic scenario Harker has tried to paint for us is nothing more than a pack of lies. While drunk, probably during sex, he strangled his victim and, upon sobering up he was faced with the equally sobering reality of having to dispose of her remains. Without access to a motor vehicle, for he had never passed a driving test, the body was dismembered and placed in garbage sacks to be distributed as he saw fit. The heavy torso could not be disposed of easily, so the isolated Polham Lane was a good option. The head, perhaps, did go out separately with the arms and legs in the trash, and Detective Ian Phillips firmly believes that somewhere, out on that vast, stinking landfill site, they rest today.

David Harker is presently serving a life sentence at Her Majesty's Prison Wakefield, Yorkshire.

# CHAPTER 12

# Issei Sagawa— "Going Dutch"

WHEN THE DIMINUTIVE Issei Sagawa turned cannibal, he literally "went Dutch." Foregoing his usual fare—perhaps a rice bowl, sushi, noodles, or sukiyaki, he dined on a beautiful Dutch student and ate quite a lot of her, too.

ISSEI SAGAWA WAS BORN to wealthy parents in Kobe, Hyōgo Prefecture, Japan, on Saturday, June 11, 1949. Standing just under five feet, he was a weak, ugly man who attended college at the University of Paris. While there, he became besotted with Renée Hartevelt, a petite thirty-two-year-old Dutch beauty with dark hair and beautiful eyes. Renée was also a student of French literature at the illustrious Sorbonne Academy in Paris, and Sagawa was a classmate.

On Tuesday, June 9, 1981, Sagawa invited Renée to his 10 Rue Erlanger apartment. They enjoyed literary conversation, and she readily agreed. Over the course of the evening, Sagawa decided that his desire for the pretty woman went far beyond sexual attraction. As she sat on his bed reading German poetry, Sagawa realized what he truly desired was to eat her. So he took up a rifle and, while she read with her back toward him, he took aim at her head. The gun misfired. The rest of the evening passed uneventfully, leaving a frustrated Sagawa to invite her back again the next evening to celebrate his thirty-second birthday.

Renée returned to Sagawa's apartment the next evening as agreed. In the interim, Sagawa had prepared a tape recorder to capture her words as she read more poetry. While she sat at his desk with her back to him, he picked up a rifle and shot her once in the back of the neck. She slumped forward and died instantly.

*My passion was so great, I wanted to eat her. If I did she would be mine forever.*
—Issei Sagawa, *In the Fog*

Sagawa later said that he fainted with the shock of killing Renée but came to with the realization that he now had to carry out his desire to eat her. He grabbed a heavy knife from the kitchen and started to cut into the dead woman's buttocks. "Suddenly a lot of sallow fat oozes from the wound," Sagawa later wrote in his best-selling book, *In the Fog:*

> It reminds me of Indian corn. It continues to ooze. It
> is strange. Finally I find the red meat under the sallow
> fat. I scoop it out and put in my mouth. I chew. It has
> no smell and no taste. It melts in my mouth like a
> perfect piece of tuna. I look into her eyes and say:
> "You are delicious."

This unsavory little man spent the remainder of the evening cutting off portions of Renée's body and cooking them, trying various parts of the body to see how they tasted. He roasted a hip and ate it at his dinner table with a sprinkle of salt and a spoonful of French mustard, using her underwear as a napkin with an air of fervent authority while declaring it "a very high-quality meat." Sagawa baked Renée's right breast in the oven, but apparently he was displeased with the result, saying that it was too greasy. Then he proceeded to photograph her remains, have sexual intercourse with the body, and eventually fall into a fitful sleep.

The next day, he continued to gorge on Renée, trying out various other parts of her anatomy, eventually saving the parts he did like and placing them in the refrigerator. After rendering Renée Hartevelt into something resembling a butcher's shop display, and taking even more photographs of his necrophiliac handiwork, he placed the leftovers into a series of suitcases and sat down to ponder on what to do next.

Sagawa might have been a bright literature student, but he was certainly unschooled in the art of body disposal. On this occasion, he was out on a limb. Two days later, a couple of people watched somewhat curiously as an Asian man dumped two suitcases in a Paris park. They called the gendarmes, who, upon opening the cases, recoiled in horror, for they found the decaying remains of Renée Hartevelt. The cases were eventually traced to Sagawa's apartment, and a search warrant was obtained.

Officers found Renée's lips, her left breast, and both buttocks in the refrigerator. Sagawa was arrested and carted
off to jail.

Initially, Sagawa was placed under psychiatric care at the
Henri Colin psychiatric ward in Villejuif to be assessed for
his competency to stand trial. Three psychiatrists examined him and determined that Sagawa could never be
cured of his deviant fantasies. However, after two years
in the psychiatric hospital without trial, French judge
Jean-Louis Bruguières amazingly found him "obviously"
legally insane and unfit to stand trial; he ordered Sagawa
to be held indefinitely in a mental institution, never mind
that the cost of maintaining him in a French asylum for
the remainder of his life would be exorbitant.

Following a visit by author Inuhiko Yomota, Sagawa's
account of the murder was published in Japan with the
title *In the Fog*. The subsequent publicity and macabre
celebrity of Sagawa most likely caused the French to back-
pedal. Issei's wealthy industrialist father stepped in and,
supported by a top lawyer, convinced the authorities that
his son should be released without charge.

After much debate, in the interests of Franco/Japanese
relations they decided to extradite him to his home
country, where he was taken immediately to the Tokyo
Metropolitan Matsuzawa Hospital. Examining psychiatrists all found him to be sane but "evil."

With all now said and done, one would have hoped,
even prayed, that this human-flesh eater would have

remained under heavy sedation, preferably wearing a straitjacket, for the remainder of his days, but it was not to be. With one eye focusing on the French sentiment of how much money was being spent to keep Issei incommunicado from the rest of society, and the other on a legal loophole, the Japanese authorities found it "impossible" to hold him because certain important papers from the French court had conveniently gone missing.

As a result, on Tuesday, August 12, 1986, a very happy Sagawa skipped lightly out of the mental institution. He has been a free man ever since.

Like many cannibals—Jeffrey Dahmer being an obvious example—Sagawa quickly became a celebrity. However, rather than being treated as a social outcast, he managed to pull off a rather bizarre form of fame...he was notoriously willing to admit his crime and even took some pride in it. The fact that he had lured a highly respected and much-loved woman to his apartment, shot her dead, and eaten her no longer crossed his twisted mind. His book *In the Fog* fanned the flames of his notoriety higher and higher.

Some years later, Sagawa gave an interview, and he had this to say:

Q: Tell me about the first time you felt cannibalistic urges.

I was physically weak from the moment I was born. My legs were so skinny they looked like pencils. It was in the first grade of elementary school when I saw quivering meat on a male classmate's thighs and I suddenly thought, "Mmm, that looks delicious." But I'm not homosexual, so from around the time I entered junior high school I became obsessed with the actress Grace Kelly—an obsession that lasted right through high school. That was the beginning of my infatuation with Occidental people. Before I knew it, tall, healthy-looking Western women became the trigger for my cannibalistic fantasies. I guess my infatuation with such women stemmed from the fact that I was short, ugly, and had an inferiority complex and therefore sought people who were the exact opposite of myself. Eventually, I began feeling a strong desire to bite into them—not to kill them or eat them per se, but merely gnaw on their flesh. It was purely a form of sexual desire. It wasn't like I felt like eating someone every time I was hungry. But you know how you tend to feel a stronger sexual desire when you've eaten a full meal? That's when I would start feeling the urge to eat a girl? In essence, it's different from the type of hunger that people experience with food. This cannibalistic urge, where I'm going, "I want to eat human meat," is a sort of sexual appetite, so if it doesn't make sure that I ejaculated frequently enough, the desire only gets stronger and stronger.

Q: And this urge of yours got so pent up that it eventually exploded in the form of the…let's say, the "incident" in Paris?

After I went to study in Paris, my cannibalistic urges showed no signs of slowing down. Almost every night

I would bring a prostitute home and then try to shoot them from behind while they washed their vaginas in the bidet. I tried hundreds of times, but for some reason my fingers froze up and I couldn't pull the trigger. From around that time, it became less about wanting to eat them, but more an obsession with the idea that I simply had to carry out this "ritual" of killing a girl no matter what. Yet for some reason, I failed so many times to pull the trigger. Rather than morals and whatnot, it was instinct that stopped my hand from moving. Somewhere in my mind I knew that I, and the world I lived in, would shatter to pieces the moment I pulled that trigger.

Some time after that, I spotted the girl who would later become my victim in one of my classes at university. All of the French women I had before then were beautiful, but were stuck-up and totally out of my league. In contrast, this girl was so friendly and warm. I found out after the murder that she was Jewish, which is probably why a Japanese guy like me felt an affinity with her. In any case, we became friends. Then one day, we decided to have an "asukiyaki" [hot pot] party—just the two of us—at my house. The moment I saw her wash her hands in the bathroom, the image overlapped with the prostitutes washing themselves at the bidet in my mind, and inevitably she became another candidate for my ritual. From that point on, every time I invited her up to my room, I found myself pointing a gun at her from behind. Still, I just couldn't shoot. Then one day, one of the employees from my father's company came to Paris and took me to a Japanese restaurant. I had a bit of a fever that day, which might have made me delusional, because the whole time I was thinking about how she was coming over the next day, and how if I got food poisoning from the raw fish I ate there, I wouldn't be able to finally realize the fantasy that I'd been obsessing about for 32 years.

Q: And that made you feel even more that you just had to do this...?

Yes. So the next day, I finally pulled the trigger on her—and it misfired. This made me even more hysterical and I knew that I simply had to kill her. I invited her to my house again two days later, and as usual I slowly crept up from behind, took a deep breath, held it in and when my lungs were half-full I pulled the trigger. This time, the gun went off. The girl died instantly without feeling pain. The autopsy showed that the gun wasn't powerful enough to send a bullet through her skull, so it just kept spinning round and round in her head. For a split second I thought about calling an ambulance, but then I thought, "Hang on, don't be stupid. You've been dreaming about this for 32 years and now it's actually happened."

This may sound rich coming from me, but the moment the girl became a corpse, I realized that I had lost an important friend and even regretted killing her for a moment. What I truly wished was to eat her living flesh. Nobody believes me, but my ultimate intention was to eat her, not necessarily to kill her. To this day, I still think, "If only she had let me taste her, just a little bit..." If we had spent another evening having dinner and chatting about our families, I never would have been able to kill her. In other words, I can't project my fantasies onto somebody who is already personified in my mind. That's why my first candidates were all prostitutes. I had a lot of other female friends as well, but I would never have dreamed of eating them since I considered them human beings with their own individual personalities. People tell me that I killed her because I loved her, but why would I kill and someone I truly loved?

Issei Sagawa later found himself speaking gigs on various Japanese television shows, mainly guest spots on talk shows wanting to speak with the famed cannibal who "got away with murder." His fame didn't stop at killing and eating a woman, either. At the time of writing, Sagawa is sixty-two, and he has taken up painting female rear ends. And, for a modest fee, he will invite you to his Tokyo apartment for dinner.

# CHAPTER 13

# Tracey Avril Wigginton and Lisa M. Ptaschinski— "The Vampire Killers"

*I can't eat solid foods. I need blood to survive on.*
—TRACEY WIGGINTON

WHEN THESE TWO WOMEN, both lesbians, turned to murder, they seized on a man—any man. Tracey Wigginton, the 240-pound "vampire," picked up and brutally stabbed a complete stranger, killed him, and drank his blood.

IN 1989, SUMMER was approaching the warm, subtropical city of Brisbane, capital of the Australian state of Queensland. Not all the city was sedate, however, for the area called Fortitude Valley (generally known as "the Valley") was a busy red-light district, a lively strip of massage parlors, gambling dens, Chinese restaurants, and gay nightclubs tucked away on the fringe of the city.

In one of these nightclubs—the lilac-fronted "Club Lewmors—a group of four women in their early twenties were enjoying themselves on the night of Friday the Thirteenth. There was a full moon that night, and as they drank, they commented on the eerie conjunction of the lunar cycle with the ominous date. An interest in the occult was one of the things that brought the four of them together.

The dominant member of the group was Tracey Wigginton, a technical student on a sheet-metal course. She had met Tracey Waugh and Kim Jervis in the Valley a few weeks earlier, at another gay nightspot called The Set. The three women agreed to meet again at Club Lewmors, and Jervis decided to bring along a fourth woman, Lisa Ptaschinski, whom she had known for eight years, and introduce her to Wigginton.

Wigginton had a personality to match her frame—big. She was deeply committed to her causes: lesbianism, occultism, and devil-worship. Her tattoos reflected the then-fashionable attraction of occult symbolism: the Egyptian Eye of Horus on the back of one hand, her zodiac sign of Leo on the other, Merlin the Magician on her left arm, and a black rose on her right.

Jervis's feeling that Ptaschinski and Wigginton would hit it off was correct. Indeed, these two women fell in love after sharing the buzz from an asthma inhaler. Ms. Wigginton, once a devout Catholic schoolgirl, now a committed lesbian obsessed with the occult. Ptaschinski, then age twenty-four, was an erratic personality with a history of drug overdoses and suicide attempts. After a brief, unsatisfactory heterosexual marriage, the dark-haired girl had been admitted to Brisbane Hospital no fewer than eighty-two times in five years—on one occasion to empty her stomach full of razor blades.

The relationship was fueled by Wigginton's aggressive personality and Ptaschinksi's vulnerable infatuation. "She has a strange attraction," Ptaschinski said later, "I don't know what. She dominated me more than anyone has in my life. She had some form of inner power."

There is nothing particularly unusual in this kind of dominant-submissive relationship, but Ptaschinski claimed that Wigginton made a bizarre demand. As they lay in their jumbo-size bed one day, Wigginton mentioned that she was hungry. She said that she never ate food, but drank blood she collected from butchers' shops. This was, of course, a bit of a white lie, as her substantial figure testified. Nonetheless, on what was to become the first of four occasions, Ptaschinski, who had been a heroin user, wrapped a tourniquet around her arm, pumped up a vein and nicked her wrist to allow her new lover to suck her blood.

When she was later asked why she had submitted to this strange ritual, Ptaschinski replied, "I wanted to keep the relationship going. If you're going out with someone, you do what you can to please them."

The impressionable Ptaschinski later claimed, as did Tracey Waugh and Kim Jervis, that Wigginton lived out the vampire role in other ways. They said that, like the mythical vampires of countless horror films, she avoided sunlight and mirrors at all costs and went out only at night. Even though she was nearly six feet, they never saw her eat real food. Wigginton, as far as they knew, lived on nothing but pig and goat blood.

If this whole business sounds like an adolescent fantasy, it is because in some ways it was. The women moved among a trendy group who called themselves "swampies." Their world was awash with Gothic imagery of black magic and death. It was a scene Tracey Wigginton found irresistible as a hunting ground for homosexual women who liked to flirt with the occult.

Kim Jervis, who worked as a photo processor, was also a swampie, and Wigginton described how attractive she immediately found her: "Kimmie was wearing a black satin vest with purple bats on the back. She had a purple bandanna on her head and she was really into acid house music."

Wigginton was less than excited by Kim's lover, Tracey Waugh, an unemployed secretary: "Tracey always bemused me. She was very quiet, very introverted. I'd never seen her drink or take drugs. She's almost a recluse in a relationship," which probably made Waugh the best of bad bunch.

Waugh was said to be the brightest of the four women, but even she was quickly overwhelmed by Wigginton's forceful personality: "Tracey has a mind power. She has a hold on you. She is like a magnet. You can't stop yourself doing what she tells you to do." And, with echoes of Charles Manson, Wigginton claimed to be "the chosen one" and "the devil's wife" and said the devil wanted her to become a "destroyer."

She soon had an iron grip on the other three members of the group. On Wednesday, October 18, 1989, only five days after the quartet had come together, the four met in Jervis's flat in the suburb of Clayfield to plan how to stalk, trap, and kill a human victim to satisfy Wigginton's thirst for blood. "I can't eat solid foods," she said. "I need blood to survive on."

The contents of the flat formed strange contrasts. Jervis had a collection of dolls and Garfield cats. But on the walls hung pictures of cemeteries. A headstone she had pilfered from a cemetery stood gravely in her living room.

The women drank the Italian anise-flavored aperitif sambuca as they formulated the details of their plot. It sounded simple. Waugh and Ptaschinski would pose as prostitutes to lure a man or woman chosen at random from one of the inner-city parks. The victim would then be taken to a secluded spot, where Wigginton and Jervis would commit murder and drink the blood.

The women would then take the body to a cemetery and dump it in a freshly dug grave. They thought that if they covered the body with earth, a coffin would be lowered on top of it and the victim would be buried without anyone realizing it. There would be no witnesses, no clues, and no corpse. The plan seemed foolproof.

Tracey Wigginton was born in 1965 in Rockhampton, a large cattle town that straddles the Tropic of Capricorn about 600 miles north of Brisbane. Early photographs of Tracey portray a sweet girl with dark eyes and an almost cherubic face framed by a mass of dark, long hair that cascaded down her back almost to her waist. Her mother, Rhonda, was the adopted daughter of self-made millionaire George Wigginton. Tracey's father, Bill Rossborough, was a drifter who soon left his wife and small daughter. Not long after, Rhonda also ran away, leaving Tracey in the care of her maternal grandparents.

The grandparents, George Wigginton and his wife, Avril, already had two other children in their care. One was an adopted daughter, Dorelle, and the other, a foster child, Michelle Wright. Tracey's mother, Rhonda, kept in touch with family, but she never had young Tracey live with her again.

George Wigginton was a genial man and a womanizer. His wife, Avril, was consumed by hatred for her husband and affection for her three Chihuahuas. Toward the children in her care, she was very cruel. Dorelle described Avril as "twisted, warped, and abusive," and said of her and Tracey's childhood, "We seemed sad until adolescence…She changed…She became a loser…"

When Tracey was interviewed by psychiatrists after the murder, she said that she loved her grandfather dearly, but that he had started to demand sex with her after she turned eight. Tracey was expelled from school for molesting the other pupils and was sent to the nearby Sisters of Mercy Range Catholic College. She soon became notorious there, too, for her lesbianism and strange behavior. A former classmate claimed, "I'd always stay clear of her. She had that strange evil look."

When Tracey left school in 1982 at age seventeen, she started to call herself "Bobby" and began to reveal violent tendencies. She vandalized her grandmother's property and punched her mother. "Bobby" had a lesbian "marriage," the formal ceremony conducted by a member of the Hare Krishna sect. In 1986, after both her grandparents had died, Tracey inherited over £35,000 from their estate, and she moved to a seaside resort, Cairns, far from her family and old friends.

She spent money quickly and foolishly, as most people do when it is freely given to them without dint of hard work, and found employment as a bouncer in a gay nightclub. Here, lonely after the breakup of her "marriage," she asked the man who ran the club, John O'Hara, to help her have a baby. They had intercourse in front of "six close friends," and she fell pregnant, but then Tracey lost the baby in a miscarriage.

In 1987, she moved away from Cairns to Brisbane and began a stormy love affair with a woman named Donna Staib. They lived together, although both girls continued to lead promiscuous lesbian lives, which Tracey claimed made her unhappy. Around this time, Tracey Wigginton dyed her hair midnight blue and tattooed her body. She was still living with Staib when she planned and carried out murder.

On Friday evening, October 20, 1989, just seven days after their first meeting, the four women were back, once again, at Club Lewmors.

At the same time, three miles away across Brisbane River, Edward Clyde Baldock, age forty-seven, was drinking with his friends at a club. The father of five children, he had recently celebrated his twenty-fifth wedding anniversary.

The two groups could not have been more different. The lesbians were champagne-sipping girls plotting a killing, while the beer-swilling Baldock and his friends were getting drunk over a game of darts. Their locations also presented sharp contrasts. Club Lewmors was a dingy hangout frequented by lesbians. The Caledonian Club was a proudly Scottish and clannish drinking hole enjoyed by men.

Two nights earlier, the women had planned this meeting for 10 p.m. at their club. Now they sat at a back table near the jukebox and ordered two bottles of champagne. "I found that unusual...I had never served them champagne before," said the club's owner and manager, Bettina Lewis, who knew Jervis and Waugh because they had been regulars since early 1987.

But, as yet, there was little to celebrate. The murderous deed had been planned, but few details had been worked out. Wigginton and Jervis were armed with knives, but Wigginton told her conspirators she would kill with her bare hands if necessary. The women finished their drinks and left at 11:30.

Baldock was still in his club. As a road paver for the city, he worked on a flexible schedule, and today had been his day off. He had spent most of it drinking. Just after midnight, he staggered out of his club and clung to a lamppost for support.

Meanwhile, the women were driving around in Wigginton's green Holden Commodore sedan. They had roamed through the Botanic Gardens and New Farm Park for over twenty minutes, searching for a likely murder victim. They were playing Prince's song "Batdance" on the car stereo as they crossed the Storey Bridge and turned up River Terrace toward Kangaroo Point, when they spied a lone man, clinging drunkenly to a lamp post. He was pot-bellied and middle-aged, so the women stopped the car.

Wigginton and Jervis got out to ask Baldock if he would like a lift home. He just climbed into the backseat with Wigginton and held her hand. She instructed Ptaschinski to drive the four miles to Orleigh Park, an isolated part of the river, not far from Baldock's home. The journey passed in silence.

Ptaschinski parked the car beneath a spreading fig tree near the deserted South Brisbane Sailing Club. "I told him I'd like to have a good time. He said he was all for it," Wigginton was to report later. With the drunken man, she walked down to the riverbank, where they both undressed. Wigginton returned to the car a few minutes later and said, "I need help, the bastard's too strong."

When they returned, Baldock was sitting down, naked except for his socks. Ptaschinski crept up behind him in the darkness. Wigginton told her to stick the knife in, but the girl couldn't bring herself to use the knife to kill the poor old drunk. Instead, she collapsed in the sand in front of him and began to rant at him.

Later, Wigginton described what she did then:

> I walked around him. I took my knife out of my back pocket. He asked me what I was doing. I said nothing and stabbed him…I withdrew the knife and stabbed him on the side of the neck. I stabbed him on the other side of the neck and I continuously stabbed him. I then grabbed him by the hair…and pulled him back, stabbing him in the front of the throat and, at that stage, he was still alive…
>
> I stabbed in the back of the neck again, trying to get into the bones, I presume, and cut the nerves. I then sat in front of the tilt-a-doors and watched him die.

Wigginton almost cut Baldock's head off, and the two knives were used to stab him fifteen times.

Wigginton then told Ptaschinski to go back to the car and wait while she gorged herself on the dead man's blood. "She cut his throat," explained Ptaschinski, "to drink his blood."

After she had washed herself in the river, Wigginton returned to the car. Asked if she had fed, she answered that she had. Wigginton, however, never admitted this to the police. The other women were adamant that she had drunk the man's blood. Waugh claimed that she smelled blood on Wigginton's breath as they drove back to Jervis's flat, and Jervis said that after the killing Wigginton was looking "almost satisfied, like a person would look if they had just sat down to a three-course dinner—which is a gross thing to say," she added hastily.

The four women felt they had committed the perfect murder. There were no witnesses, and no one could ever link the victim with them, the killers. But close to the body of Edward Baldock lay a clue so damning it would put the women in custody within hours.

On that fateful night, Baldock may have been too drunk to drive, or even to perform sexually, but alcohol did not drive away the habits of a lifetime. He was a fastidious man, and, even on the beach, he folded his clothes fussily, checking that nothing had fallen out of his pockets.

When Wigginton went to call Ptaschinski from the car, he took the opportunity to tuck his blue Velcro wallet behind one of the garage doors of the sailing club. Obviously he feared being robbed by one of these strange women whose offer of sex seemed too good to be true. He was suspicious, but only of theft.

Baldock also stooped to pick up a yellow Commonwealth Bank bank card from the ground, then tucked it into one of his shoes. He banked with the Commonwealth, but this card did not belong to him. It bore the name T. A. Wigginton.

Kim Jervis's flat in Clayfield was six miles away, and the four women drove off from the murder scene in a weird state of exhilaration. They stumbled into the apartment with some relief. But their sense of security was short-lived when Wigginton realized that she had lost her Commonwealth bank card. She admitted that she might have dropped it near Baldock's body.

They decided it was safer to risk returning to the scene of the crime to look for the card than to leave such a vital clue for the police to find. Wigginton and Ptaschinski drove back to Orleigh Park and were glad to see the victim still lying there, apparently unnoticed by anyone.

The two women scoured the area in the dark but found nothing. After a while, Wigginton convinced herself she must have lost the card someplace else. They started to drive back to Clayfield along a riverside road frequented by lovers in cars and the occasional peeping tom. But they were not interested in either activity. They were fearful now and simply longed to return home. But just then, their worst fears were realized. They were stopped by a police patrol car.

It was a routine inquiry, checking for drunk drivers and illegal vehicles. In their panic, because their thoughts were so completely involved with the murder, the women had rushed from the flat without the required car documents.

Ptaschinski, at the wheel, was unable to produce her driver's license. Consequently, the young officers took down details of the car and the driver. They also gave her a breath test that proved that she was sober. Ptaschinski was instructed to take her driver's license to a police station as soon as possible, and the two were allowed to proceed on their way.

They returned to Jervis's apartment in total panic. Now, the four accomplices were very frightened. Their perfect crime was flawed. They were convinced that the police would connect their car to the murder scene beside the river. Huddled together, they concocted alibis that would throw the police off their trail.

Fear kept someone else awake during the gray, early hours of that Saturday morning. Mrs. Elaine Mable Baldock had woken with a start and felt for her husband beside her. He was not there. At 5 a.m. she could bear her worry no longer and called the police. But they knew nothing about Edward Baldock and did not share her concern over her drunken spouse. It was their experience that, sooner or later, errant husbands did roll home to their worried and angry wives, usually to receive a tongue-lashing.

But Mrs. Baldock knew her husband's habits. She had been married to him for twenty-five years. She knew that something was dreadfully wrong, for he never stayed out this late, and at 8 a.m. she called the police again. This time they sent three detectives to interview her, because now the police had received reports of the murder of a middle-aged man. His body had been discovered at 6:20 a.m. by a man on an early morning row along the river and two women out walking.

Police sealed off the death scene. One of the first officers to arrive was Detective Senior Sergeant Pat Glancy. Within minutes, he had found Wigginton's bank card in Baldock's left shoe. Television crews, too, had rushed to the riverside beach to film the grisly scene. Tracey Wigginton was also there, back at the crime scene. As she had sat through the dawn hours, the woman knew that she had ruined the "perfect murder." She knew she must have lost her card at the very spot where she had killed Baldock. She did not take any of the other women with her when she went out once more. She determined she would look again in the light of early morning, but she was not early enough. When she saw the crowd around the body, she slunk off and returned to the apartment. Tracey knew she must warn the other girls that the police had found the old man's corpse.

Not long after the crime had been reported to them, the police established that a green Holden that had been stopped during the night by their patrol unit was registered to the person whose bank card was in the victim's shoe. They thought that, perhaps, they had an easy solution to this particular murder. The card owner might prove to be Baldock's mistress, who could have killed him during an argument.

So by 1 p.m. Wigginton was back at the sailing club for the fourth and last time during those twelve dreadful hours. This time she was with detectives who took a videotaped recording of this final visit. When asked if she had been with anyone else in the vicinity of the body, Wigginton's answer was vague: "Well, I can't remember exactly, but Kimmie and I were sort of racing all round this area here…"

She told them the story the four girls had agreed to give the police. Wigginton said that she and Jervis had been at Orleigh Park the day before—but not at night. She mentioned, too, a suspicious-looking couple loitering in the area. But she began to waver under interrogation and changed her story. She admitted that she had gone to the park early the previous evening and she had stumbled over a body in the dark, but, she added, she had been "too frightened to report it to the police."

But Tracey Wigginton was not the only member of the gang who could not maintain a false alibi. About the same time as Tracey changed her story, Ptaschinski lost her nerve. She had left the flat to wander about in a state of fear and confusion, until she could not bear her guilt or the suspense of being on the run. Lisa Ptaschinski turned herself in at the Ipswich police station, about thirty miles from the flat.

By 7 p.m. that day, the police had charged both Wigginton and Ptaschinski with the murder of Edward Baldock. Soon after, Jervis was arrested on the same charge. Waugh, who had been picked up, then released, was arrested the next day. Tracey Wigginton was charged separately from her three lesbian accomplices, and only Tracey Waugh was allowed bail.

While the distraught Mrs. Baldock had to come to terms with the loss of her husband, the Australian press was going to town with sensational headlines about "Tracey the Vampire," murderer. The trial of her three female accomplices was a reporter's dream, combining the copy-selling issues of murder and lesbianism and the horrific aspect of vampirism. The trial took place fifteen months after the murder. It aroused the interest of Brisbane residents, feminist groups, and psychologists alike. Many found the headlines incredible or absurd, and they were curious to learn if the extraordinary facts were true.

In late January 1991, Tracey Avril Wigginton, a student, of Wardell Street, Enoggera, Brisbane, pleaded guilty to murder and received a life sentence, to be served in Brisbane's County Jail.

On Thursday, January 31, 1991, the trial of Ptaschinski, Jervis, and Waugh started in Brisbane's Supreme Court. The accused showed little emotion during the trial and rarely spoke to each other. Their main contact was in passing cups of water to each other. They refused to give evidence, but their videotaped interviews with the police were presented in court by the prosecution.

Ptaschinski had no family in court. She sat with her arms folded, her face fixed in a frightening glare. She dressed in black, and displayed a tattoo of the female sex organs on her right forearm. Her hair, cropped short at the time of the killing, had grown out to shoulder-length curls.

Jervis had been sadly changed by her stay in prison while awaiting trial. Her hair was slack and greasy, her eyes lost in dark circles. She had an open-mouthed expression and seemed dumfounded by what was happening to her. Toward the end of the trial she began to share the occasional smile with her former lover, Tracey Waugh, the only one of the three to have been granted bail.

Waugh was supported every day in court by her parents. She looked the picture of innocence, which prompted the prosecutor, Mr. Gundelach, to comment that she looked "like a sixteen-year-old schoolgirl."

The defense lawyers painted a picture of Wigginton as a dangerous and manipulative woman who controlled the others through fear. Miss Julie Dick, who represented Ptaschinski, said her client had been under the woman's "spell." She said that while Ptaschinski had been fascinated by the "thrilling and chilling" plan to drink blood, she never believed it would happen. A psychiatrist called by the defense said Ptaschinski suffered from a mental illness known as borderline personality disorder, which impaired her ability to understand her actions.

After fourteen days of hearing evidence the jury retired to consider its verdict. Ptaschinski, twenty-four, of Tongarra Street, Leichhardt, stood motionless in the dock as she was found guilty of murder. Mr. Justice MacKenzie sentenced her to life in prison. Jervis, twenty-three, of

Montpelier Street, Clayfield, sobbed quietly when she was found guilty of the lesser charge of manslaughter. She was given eighteen years. The jury acquitted Waugh, aged twenty-three, unemployed from Miles Street, Clayfield. She ran from the court, a free woman, accompanied by her parents.

Tracey Wigginton fell into a profound depression when she first entered prison but has since adapted to life at Brisbane's Woman's Prison at Boggo Road Jail. She has been the prison librarian and is learning computing. Reports that she is to be released have been hotly denied by Queensland Corrective Services.

Kim Jervis's sentenced was reduced to twelve years on appeal.

Presently, Ptaschinski is at the Numinbah Prison Farm on the Gold Coast. She is in the resettlement program, which permits twelve hours leave every two months for six months.

# CHAPTER 14

# Andrei Romanovich Chikatilo— "The Rostov Ripper"

JUST AFTER MIDNIGHT on a bitterly cold Monday, February 14, 1994, fifty-seven-year-old Andrei Romanovich Chikatilo heard the boot steps he had been dreading since January 4, when Russian President Boris Yeltsin had refused a last ditch appeal for clemency. From that day onward, the "Rostov Ripper" had waited in his cell in the bleak Novocherkassk Prison for his execution. He had no idea when it would come. When all appeals fail, death may visit within hours, days, weeks, or months, for this was the Russian way.

There are varying accounts published concerning Chikatilo's execution, most of which are false—namely that he was taken to a soundproofed room where he was dispatched with a single pistol shot to the head; the latter part is true, but the soundproofed chamber is not. I visited the prison many years ago while filming a TV documentary about the Russian penal system and specifically the Novocherkassk facility deep within the Rostov Oblast (region), and I was granted access to this room.

In the United States, we take for granted the clinical environment of the chamber where lethal injections take place. Perhaps more archaic are the rooms where electrocutions occur. The gallows at, say, the Washington State Penitentiary, Walla Walla, are functional yet spotless, while the occasional shooting by firing squad usually takes place in an old warehouse or storage area outfitted for such purpose. But in Russia, before the abolishment of capital punishment, the death room was something else.

With its gray stone-slab floor and faded yellow paint-peeling walls, the room at Novocherkassk is a place where the prison guards wash off their muddy boots as they come in from the bitter cold following a long duty tramping around in the crisp snow outside. It is a place where the dogs are rubbed down and fed. There is a single, dripping tap on one wall, several buckets and mops, a long wooden bench, numerous coat hooks, and a cracked window looking out on a yard and allowing the frigid blast of Russian winter air to chill the place like a grave. From the ceiling, a single bare light bulb hangs from a brown braided cord, its yellowish light barely illuminating the grim interior, which is perennially damp. But most ominous of all is the hole in the center of the room, which is functionally designed to drain away the detritus washed into it when the place is hosed down.

It was to this room that Chikatilo was escorted without shackles, frog-marched by a group of large men dressed from head to toe in black combat coveralls, wearing balaclavas, with one restraining a vicious dog on a tight leash. Chikatilo stumbled on the steel stairs as he was half pushed toward his death. He was a diminutive, pathetic figure, his eyes wide in the knowledge of what awaited him. Long gone was the cursing creature that had snarled and sneered throughout his trial. Chikatilo was now stooped and scared to death.

Along a narrow dead-end passage, the steel door to the room is on the left. Chikatilo briefly paused before being pushed roughly inside. Instantly, an officer stepped up behind him and fired at point-blank range. The single bullet entered his head directly behind the left ear. He was stone dead before he hit the floor, his blood draining away before the room was hosed down again.

No bells and whistles, no final last meal, no last-minute visitation with lawyers or family and no final words. He was simply put down like the rabid dog that he was, and the world was a better place without him in it. That is the Russian way.

ANDREI CHIKATILO WAS BORN on Friday, October 16, 1936, in the village of Yablochnoye, Sumy Oblast, Ukraine SSR. His parents, peasant farm laborers, had struggled through the famine caused by Joseph Stalin's forced collectivization of agriculture. Mass starvation ran rampant, and cannibalism was rife. The family lived in a one-room hut. Andrei slept with his parents, he was a chronic bed-wetter, and his mother, Anna, was a brutal woman who beat him frequently.

There are claims that Andrei's older brother, Stephan, had been kidnapped and cannibalized by neighbors. While there is no evidence to support this, considering the austere times, it is entirely possible. So, despite living in fear of his mother, he always stayed close to her. She had told him what could happen to small boys if they wandered too far from home, and there were starving wolves out there, too. He had heard other tales of monsters: dragons with fierce teeth that ached to tear into tender flesh of little children; witches who would entice children into their houses and, hurling them into cages, would keep and fatten the boys, then would cut them into little pieces and eat them. The child shivered at such stories, but they excited him, too.

When the Soviet Union entered World War II, Andrei's father was drafted into the Red Army and subsequently taken prisoner after being wounded in combat. Then the Nazis raided the area, and Andrei and his mother were forced to watch as their hut was burned to the ground. Anna fell pregnant by another man and gave birth to a baby girl, Tatyana, in 1943. To cap it all, when Andrei's father, who had been liberated by the Americans, returned home, he was not honored as a hero but derided as a traitor for surrendering to the Germans. He was arrested and thrown into a work camp—the last that history has heard of him.

Andrei was a shy child, but studious. He was an avid reader of Communist literature. As Ukraine had among the highest junior literacy rates in the world, he took to schooling like a duck takes to water. In fact, even today, when heavy snow falls make routes to school impassable, the Army turns out to clear the way.

During adolescence, Andrei discovered that he suffered from chronic impotence, which worsened his social awkwardness and self-hatred of having come from peasant stock. He was shy in the company of females. His only sexual experience as a teenager arrived at the age of seventeen, when he jumped on an eleven-year-old friend of his younger sister and wrestled her to the ground, ejaculating as the girl struggled from his grasp.

Chikatilo finished school in 1953 at age seventeen. He applied for a scholarship at the Moscow State University, passing the entrance exam; however, his grades were not good enough for acceptance. Then, between 1957 and 1960, he completed his compulsory military service.

In 1963, Tatyana introduced Chikatilo to an attractive young woman named Fayina. Tatyana had told her friend that Andrei was quite a catch. He was twenty-seven years old, tall, shy, gentle, and well educated. This was an attraction for Fayina, who was on the large size herself. Suitable men were in short supply during this time, since millions of them had being killed during the war.

She liked Chikatilo. He was good-looking in a soft sort of way, and although his shoulders sloped in a manner perhaps unmasculine, giving the impression that his neck was elongated, he was the complete gentleman, and he treated her very well indeed. They married that same year. Despite the fact that Chikatilo's lovemaking left a lot to be desired, they eventually had a daughter, Ludmila, in 1965, and then a son, Yuri, in 1969. Thereafter their sex life was minimal. Unable to penetrate his wife, he had to ejaculate over her and push the semen inside her vagina with his fingers, and he could only manage this with the manual dexterity of his everpatient wife.

There is no doubt that Andrei wanted to make something of himself and become an achiever. To this end, in 1971, he completed a correspondence course in Russian literature and obtained degrees in the subjects of Russian literature, engineering, and Marxist–Leninism from Rostov University. He began his career as a teacher of Russian language and literature in Novoshakhtinsk, but it ended in March 1981 following several complaints of child molestation of pupils of both sexes. He had discovered he liked the fear he instilled in the children after grabbing one girl who screamed and pushed him away. It caused him to ejaculate almost immediately.

Keeping this secret from Fayina, Chikatilo soon took up another job, an inferior one at a mining school and moved into a school-owned house in Shakhty, a small coal-mining town near Rostov-on-Don. Fayina also got a job at the school. Then, unknown to his wife, Chikatilo bought a run-down three-room shack in the shabbiest part of town. There he would bring a succession of prostitutes in an effort to overcome his impotence. He also brought small girls to the filthy hut, where he could sexually assault them, but in a community where secretiveness was second nature, never so seriously as to bring the law down upon him. There amid the squalor, he killed for the first time.

On Friday, December 22, 1978, Chikatilo noticed nine-year-old Yelena Zakotnova at a tram stop in Shakhty. Wearing a red coat and brown fur hat, she was returning home from an afterschool skating trip. He started chatting with her. Chikatilo's shack was just around the corner, and maybe he suggested that she use the toilet there.

Once inside, the vulnerable child stood no chance. He threw her to the ground and ripped off her clothes, silencing her screams with an arm on her throat. He blindfolded her with her own scarf and tried to rape her, but he could not sustain his initial erection. Taking out his knife, one used for "personal protection," he stabbed into the child's lower abdomen. When he had achieved that everevasive ejaculation, he cleaned up the mess and dumped Lena's body into the nearby Grushevka River. Her school satchel went in after her.

Lena's body did not get swept far from Shakhty, certainly as far as Chikatilo might have hoped, for it was soon recovered, and many fingers started pointing the police in the direction of the tall, bespectacled man with sloping shoulders who had been seen at the tram stop talking to Lena. Door-to-door inquiries revealed this man had frequently taken women and children back to his shack, and further information revealed that he had been the subject of child molestation complaints in the past. One woman gave a police artist an excellent description of the man seen leaving the tram stop with Lena, and spots of the girl's blood were found in the snow close to Chikatilo's hut.

Surely the police had their man. Accompanied by his wife, Chikatilo was hauled in for questioning. His head hung in shame as he admitted his past problems, explaining that little girls no longer interested him. His sexual interests had declined, and Fayina was quick to confirm that. But she went farther. She told police that Andrei had been with her during the times in question. He could not have been in two places at once, she argued, while gently patting her cowering husband on his knee. It was a false alibi, but with little else to go on, the police had to let him go, keeping his file open.

Only yards from the place where Lena's corpse was found lived twenty-three-year-old Alexsandr Kravchenko, who, as a teenager, had served a jail sentence for the rape and murder of a teenage girl. He was now making a new life for himself with his wife and family, but with majestically self-destructive misjudgment, a month after Lena's death he was involved in some kind of petty theft, caught red-handed with the stolen goods, and hauled into the police station. Having discovered that Kravchenko had the same semen type as that found on Lena's body, the police used all the means at their disposal—which included beating him up—to extract a "confession." They succeeded. He was tried in 1979 and immediately retracted his confession, claiming that it been made under duress. Nevertheless, he was convicted and sentenced to fifteen years' imprisonment—the maximum possible length of incarceration at that time. No one bothered asking the eyewitness who had been the last to see Lena alive to identify Kravchenko. If they had, the police would have realized they had the wrong man, because Kravchenko looked completely different from the description give to the police artist, and no one visited Chikatilo again.

Under pressure from Lena's family and relatives, Kravchenko was retried and eventually executed for Lena's murder in July, 1983.

Following the murder of Lena Zakotnova, Chikatilo changed jobs once again. He became a supply clerk for an industrial company, which, conveniently for him, involved traveling all over the region to collect and deliver goods. This often entailed an overnight stay. When he was required to stay on somewhere he invented a reason, "business," and this business started with Larisa Tkachenko.

On Thursday, September 3, 1981, Chikatilo approached seventeen-year-old boarding school student Larisa Tkachenko at a bus stop. She, like his previous victim, was wearing a red jacket—the color of his fantasies. According to most sources, they chatted, and Larisa indicated that she was prepared to have sex with Chikatilo in return for a little supper. Together they set off across the River Don to a forested area frequented by young lovers.

As soon as they were out of sight, the monster boiling inside Chikatilo was unleashed. He ripped off her red jacket and her other clothes, yet still he could not get an erection. She screamed and fought, while he strangled her to near unconsciousness. He tore into her with his teeth, biting her neck like an animal deranged by the smell of blood. His face was covered in it. He bit off part of her breast and swallowed it, then mutilated her genitalia. After reaching sexual climax, he cleaned himself up and dumped the corpse like so much trash. He covered the body with pages from *Pravda* and the *Young Communist*, which, being a loyal party member, he just happened to have with him.

*They [his victims] followed me like dogs. Vagrants... they beg, demand and seize things...They crawl into your very soul, demanding money, food, vodka and offering themselves for sex...I saw scenes of these vagrants' sex lives and I remembered my humiliation, that I could prove myself as a real man.*

—CHIKATILO, AFTER HIS ARREST

Lyubov Biryuk, age thirteen, was abducted while returning home from a shopping trip in the village of Donskoi, on Saturday, June 12, 1982. The girl was waiting at a bus stop when Chikatilo approached her and started idle chat. She agreed to abandon waiting for the bus and allow Chikatilo to accompany her along a path, close to woods, to her home. From that moment on, her fate was sealed.

On Friday June 25, 1982, Lyubov Volobuyeva was killed and mutilated in an orchard near Krasnodar Airport. Her body was found Saturday, August 7.

Chikatilo's first male victim, nine-year-old Oleg Pozhidayev was killed in Adygea on Friday, August 13, 1982. His body has never been found.

Killed Monday, August 16, in Kazachi Lagerya, Olga Kuprina's badly mutilated body, minus her lips and nipples, was found Wednesday, October 27.

Irina Karabelnikova, age nineteen, became Chikatilo's first September 1982 victim. On Wednesday, September 8, he lured her away from Shakhty Railway Station. Her body was found on Thursday, September 20. She had been raped, her body crisscrossed with knife slashes, and her throat cut, causing death.

Fifteen-year-old Sergey Kuzmin was a runaway from a boarding school. He bumped into the affable Chikatilo on Wednesday, September 15, 1982. His body was found in dense woodland close the station in January 1983. Chikatilo had cut off his penis and testicles and mutilated the body to such a degree that seasoned police officers broke down and cried.

Chikatilo lured ten-year-old Olga Stalmachenok off a bus while she rode home from her piano lessons in Novoshakhtinsk on Saturday, December 11, 1982.

On Saturday, June 18, 1983, Laura Sarkisyan, a fifteen-year-old Armenian girl, vanished without trace. Her body has never been found.

Thirteen-year-old Irina Dunenkova's body was found in Aviator's Park, Rostov, on Wednesday, August 13, 1983.

Lyudmila Kushuba was murdered and mutilated in the woodland near the Shakhty bus station on Sunday, July 24, 1983. Her body was discovered on Monday, March 12, 1984.

A seven-year-old boy from Bataisk, just off the M-4 highway, Igor Gudkov was to become Chikatilo's youngest victim. Murdered on Tuesday, August 9, 1983, he was the first male victim linked to the manhunt.

The accumulation of bodies and the similarities between the patterns of wounds inflicted on the victims forced the Soviet authorities to acknowledge that a serial killer was on the loose. On September 6, 1983, the public prosecutor of the USSR formally linked six of the murders thus far committed to the same killer. A Moscow police team headed by Major Mikhail Fetisov was sent to Rostov-on-Don to direct the investigation. Fetisov centered the investigations on and around Shakhty and assigned a specialist forensic analyst, Victor Burakov, to head the investigation. Due to the sheer savagery of the murders, much of the police effort concentrated on mentally ill citizens, homosexuals, and known sex offenders, slowly working through all that were known and eliminating them from the inquiry.

A number of young men confessed to the murders, though most were mentally handicapped youths who had admitted to the crimes only under prolonged and often brutal interrogation. Three known homosexuals and a convicted sex offender committed suicide as a result of the investigators' heavy-handed tactics, but as police obtained confessions from suspects, bodies continued to be discovered, proving that the suspects who previously confessed could not be the killer the police were seeking.

Valentina Chuchulina, age twenty-two, was murdered by Chikatilo on Monday, September 19, 1983. Her body was found in the woodland near Kirpichnaya station on Sunday, November 27, that year. In the same period, Chikatilo later admitted killing an unknown prostitute after she offered him sex.

Nineteen-year-old Vera Shevkun, another prostitute, was killed in a mining village near Shakhty on Thursday, October 27, 1983. Her body was found three days later.

Age fourteen, Sergey Markov disappeared while returning home from his work-experience job on Tuesday, December 27. His body was found Wednesday, January 4, 1984.

The year 1984 heralded continual slaughter—seventeen killings in total. The first victim of the new year was Natalya Shalapinina, aged seventeen, who had been a close friend of Chikatilo's sixth victim, Olga Kuprina Natalya. She died on Monday, January 9.

Chikatilo's oldest victim at forty-five years old, Marta Ryabenko was murdered in Aviator's Park on Friday, February 21.

Dmitriy Ptashnikov was buying old stamps at a kiosk when the ten year old was lured away on Saturday, March 24, by Chikatilo, who pretended to be a collector. The pair were seen together by several witnesses who were later able to give police a detailed description of the killer. When Dmitry's body was found three days later, police also found a footprint of the murderer and semen and saliva samples on the boy's clothing.

Tatyana Petrosyan, thirty-two, had known Chikatilo since 1978. Svetlana Petrosyan saw Chikatilo murder her mother before he chased her and killed her with a hammer outside Shakhty on Friday, May 25.

Yelena Bakulina, twenty-two, was murdered on Friday, June 22. Her body was found Monday, August 27, in the Bagasenki Oblast of Rostov.

Vanishing in Rostov while on his way to get a health certificate for summer camp, 13-year-old Dmitriy Illarionov was killed on Tuesday, July 10.

A nineteen-year-old student, Anna Leemesheva, disappeared on her way to a dental appointment in Shakhty on Thursday, July 19.

Killed on an unknown date in July 1984, the corpse of Svetlana Tsana, aged sixteen, originally from Riga, was found by walkers on Sunday, September 9, in Aviator's Park, Rostov.

Sixteen-year-old Natalya Golosovskaya was on her way to visit her sister in Novoshakhtinsk when she vanished without trace on Thursday, August 2. She was also killed in Aviator's Park.

Lyudmila Alekseyeva, a seventeen-year-old student, was lured from a bus stop by Chikatilo, who offered to direct her to Rostov's bus terminal, on Tuesday, August 7, 1984.

Several days later, sometime between August 8 and 11, Chikatilo murdered an unknown woman around twenty-three years of age in Tashkent while he was on a business trip to Uzbek SSR.

Akamaral Seydaliyeva, a 12-year-old runaway from Alma-Ata, Kazakhstan, fell easy prey to Chikatilo when he picked her up, in Tashkent, on Monday, August 13, 1984.

Tuesday, August 28, saw the murder and dismemberment of eleven-year-old Alexander Chepel on the banks of the Don River, near where Lyudmila Alekseyeva (victim number 28) had been killed.

By now, Aviator's Park had become a favorite killing zone for Chikatilo. Irina Luchinskaya, a 24-year-old Rostov librarian, was killed there on Thursday, September 6, 1984. It would prove to be the last murder of the year.

On Thursday, September 13, exactly one week after his fifteenth murder of the year, Chikatilo was spotted by an undercover detective attempting to lure a young woman away from a Rostov bus station. He was arrested and held. A search of his belongings revealed a knife and rope. He was also discovered to be under investigation for minor theft from one of his former employers, which gave the investigators the legal right to hold him for a prolonged period of time. The master criminal had stolen a roll of linoleum and a car battery—a crime which cost him his membership of the Communist Party, causing him enormous shame and increasing his sense of society's injustice.

Chikatilo's dubious background was uncovered, and his physical description matched the description of the man seen with Dmitriy Ptashnikov at the stamp kiosk in

March. These factors, however, provided insufficient evidence to convict him of the murders. He was found guilty of the theft of property from his previous employer and sentenced to one year in prison. He was freed on Wednesday, December 12, 1984, after serving three months.

Nonetheless, following the September 6 murder of Irina Luchinskaya, no further bodies were found bearing the trademark mutilation of Chikatilo's murders, so investigators—completely unaware that they actually had their killer in custody—theorized that the man they were hunting down might have moved to another part of the Soviet Union and continued killing there. The Rostov Police sent bulletins to all forces throughout the country, describing the types of wounds their unknown killer had inflicted upon his victims and requesting feedback from any force that had discovered murder victims with wounds matching those upon the Rostov Oblast victims. The response was negative.

Chikatilo did not commit another atrocity until Wednesday, July 31, 1985, when he lured Natalya Pokhlistova, eighteen, off a train near Domodedovo Airport, Moscow. Her body was discovered on Saturday, August 3.

Chikatilo was back in Shakhty on Tuesday, August 27, 1985, when he murdered eighteen-year-old Irina Gulyayeva in a grove of trees near the bus station. Her body was found the following day.

By the time of Chikatilo's arrest, the investigation was so wide that it solved 1062 unrelated crimes, including ninety-five murders. In November 1985, the Soviet Union's Department for Crimes of Special Importance joined the manhunt. A special procurator, Chief Inspector Issa Kostoyev, was appointed to supervise the investigation. The known murders around Rostov were carefully reinvestigated, and police began another round of questioning known sex offenders. The following month, the *militsiya* (civilian police) and Voluntary People's Druzhina (voluntary groups for maintaining public order, similar to Neighborhood Watch) renewed the patrolling of railway stations around Rostov. The police also took the step of consulting psychiatrist Dr. Aleksandr Bukhanovsky—the first such consultation in a serial killer investigation in Soviet Union history.

Bukhanovsky produced a sixty-five-page psychological profile of the unknown killer for the investigators, describing him as a man between forty-five and fifty years old, of average intelligence. He was likely to be married, or had been previously married, but was also a sadist who could only achieve sexual arousal by seeing his victims suffer.

Bukhanovsky also argued that because many of the killings had occurred on weekdays near mass transportation areas and across the entire Rostov Oblast, the killer's work required him to travel regularly, and based upon the actual days of the week when the murders had occurred, the killer was most like tied to a work schedule.

For his part, Chikatilo read the newspaper reports about the manhunt and followed the investigation carefully. Realizing that the heat had been turned up, he kept his homicidal urges under control. Throughout 1986 he is not known to have committed any murders.

Aged 13, Oleg Makarenkov was murdered and mutilated in Sverdlovsk, Ukraine, on Saturday, May 16, 1987. The killer led police to Oleg's remains after his arrest.

Chikatilo was on one of his business trips to Zaporizhya, Ukraine, when he spotted twelve-year-old Ivan Bilovetskiy on Wednesday, July 29, 1987. The boy's body was found the next day.

Sixteen-year-old Yuri Tereshonok was lured off a train in Leningrad (now St. Petersburg) Oblast on Tuesday, September 15, 1987; the carnivorous beast that was Chikatilo gave up the boy's remains after his arrest.

Between April 1 and 4, 1988, using a slab of concrete, Chikatilo murdered an unknown woman between eighteen and twenty-five years of age near Krasny Sulin train station. Her remains were discovered on Wednesday, April 6.

Alexey Voronko, age nine, was murdered near a train station in Illovaisk, Ukraine, on Sunday, May 15, 1988.

Fifteen-year-old Yevgeniy Muratov became the first victim killed near Rostov since 1985 when he was killed on Thursday, July 14, 1988. His remains were found on Monday, April 10, 1989.

Another runaway, Tatyana Ryzhova, aged 16, from Krasny Sulin, was murdered in Chikatilo's own daughter's apartment on Wednesday, March 8, 1989. He hid the body in a sewer.

The day after his eighth birthday, Alex Dyakonov was killed in Rostov's city center on Thursday, May 11, 1989. His body was found on Friday, July 14.

Ten-year-old Alexey Moiseyev was murdered in the Vladimir region east of Moscow on Wednesday, June 20, 1989. Chikatilo confessed to this murder after his arrest.

Helen Varga, a nineteen-year-old student from Hungary who had a child, was lured off a bus and killed in a village near Rostov, on Saturday, August 19, 1989.

Ten-year-old Alexey Khobotov vanished from outside a theater in Shakhty on August 28, 1989. Chikatilo took police to the boy's remains after his arrest.

Andrei Kravchenko, eleven, was lured from a movie theater on Sunday, January 14, 1990. He was killed in Shakhty, and his body was found on Monday, February 19.

Lured from a Rostov train station by Chikatilo, ten-year-old Yaroslav Makarov was killed in Rostov Botanical Gardens on Wednesday, March 7, 1990. The eviscerated body was found the following day.

On March 11, the leaders of the investigation, still headed by Mikhail Fetisov, held a meeting to discuss progress made in the hunt for the killer. Fetisov was under intense pressure from the public, the press, and the Ministry of the Interior in Moscow, to solve the case. The intensity of the manhunt in the years up to 1984 had between 1985 and 1987, when Chikatilo had murdered only two victims conclusively linked to the serial killer—both of them in 1985. By March 1990, six more victims had been added to the list. Fetisov had noted laxity in some areas of the investigation, and with his own neck on the block, he warned many of his colleagues that they would be fired if the killer was not caught soon.

With Fetisov crawling all over his investigators, the discovery of more victims sparked a massive operation by the police. Several victims had been found at railway stations on one rail route through the Rostov Oblast. Viktor Burakov, who had been involved in the manhunt since 1982, suggested a plan to saturate all larger stations in the region with a uniformed police presence so obvious that the killer could not fail to notice, discouraging the killer from attempting to strike at any of these locations. Smaller and less busy stations would be patrolled by undercover agents, where his activities would be more likely noticed.

The plan was approved, and both the uniformed and undercover officers were instructed to question any man in the company of a young woman or child and note their name and identity documents. Police deployed 360 (some reports claim 600) men at all stations and riding trains. Only undercover officers were assigned to the three smallest stations—Kirpichnaya, Donleskhoz, and Lesostep—where the killer had struck most frequently, in an effort to force the killer to return to one of these three stations. However, red tape and Russian bureaucracy stalled implementation until on Saturday, October 27, 1990. In the interim, while the bosses were running around with rubber stamps, four more victims fell foul of Chikatilo.

Lyubov Zuyeva, age thirty-one, was lured off a train near the Donleskhoz station near Shakhty on Wednesday, April 4, 1990. Her body was found Friday, August 24.

Thirteen-year-old Viktor Petrov was murdered in Rostov Botanical Gardens on Saturday, July 28, 1990, a few yards from where Makarov (victim number 47) had been killed.

Killed at Novocherkassk Municipal Beach on August 14, 1990, the body of eleven-year-old Ivan Fomin was found three days later.

Vadim Gromov, a Shakhty student age sixteen, vanished into thin air while riding on a train to Taganrog on Tuesday, October 30.

Chikatilo's penultimate victim, sixteen-year-old Viktor Tishenko, was also lured from a train and killed the same day as Gromov. Like Gromov, he had been abducted from right under the noses of surveillance officers. During his struggle for his life, Viktor, a physically strong lad, had sunk his teeth into one of Chikatilo's fingers, and this would prove part of the killer's undoing. Viktor's body was found in a nearby forest, and it was self-evident that a ferocious struggle had taken place between the victim and his murderer.

On Monday, November 6, 1990 (but some reports claim that it was November 7), Chikatilo killed and mutilated twenty-two-year-old Svetlana Korostik in the woods near Donleskhoz Station.

At 4 o'clock, a police sergeant saw a middle-aged man wearing a gray suit and carrying a shoulder bag emerging from the woods. The man walked toward a nearby hydrant, where he washed his hands, face, and shoes. When he approached the station, the undercover officer noted that the man's coat had grass and soil stains on the elbows. He also had a small red smear that looked like blood on his cheek and a bandaged finger. To the detective, he looked suspicious. The only reason people entered the woods near the station at that time of year was to gather wild mushrooms, a popular pastime in Russia. Chikatilo, however, was not dressed like a typical forest hiker; he was wearing more formal attire. The bag was not something one would put mushrooms in, either.

The sergeant stopped the man and checked his papers, which were in order. With no formal reason for arrest, Chikatilo was not held. When the policeman returned to his office, he filed a routine report indicating the name of the person he had questioned at the station. It was Andrei Chikatilo.

On Tuesday, November 13, 1990, Svetlana's body was found by police in the woods near Donleskhoz Station. She had been stabbed multiple times, and her tongue and nipples had been cut off and were missing. The mutilation was clearly the work of the "Forest Strip Murderer," as Chikatilo was becoming known. The sergeant in charge of surveillance at Donleskhoz Station was summoned by his boss, who examined the reports of all men stopped and questioned the previous week. Chikatilo's name was among those questioned in 1984 and placed on the suspect list. Upon checking with Chikatilo's present and past employers, investigators were able to place him in various towns and cities at times when several victims had been killed. Former colleagues from Chikatilo's teaching days informed investigators that Chikatilo had been forced to resign from his teaching position due to complaints of sexual assault from several pupils.

The day after Svetlana Korostik's decomposing remains were found, police placed Chikatilo under close surveillance. In several instances, particularly on trains or buses, he was observed to approach lone women or children and engage them in conversation. If the subject broke off the conversation or gave him the brush-off, he would wait a few minutes before selecting someone else to talk to.

Tuesday, November 20, 1990, proved to be Chikatilo's last day of freedom. He had now been under surveillance round-the-clock for six days, not suspecting a thing, although the impression the police had was that, because he kept glancing over his shoulder in a shifty manner, he was possibly looking to see if he was being watched. That morning, he left his house wearing a leather jacket, a somewhat gaudy shirt, gray trousers, and cheap black shoes. Carrying a gallon flask of beer and a briefcase, he wandered around Novocherkassk, attempting to make contact with any child he met on his way.

A team of four undercover officers, including Inspector Aleksandr Zanasovski and Detective Akmatkhanov, stalked Chikatilo for nine hours. Chikatilo's determination to find a victim almost paid off when a young girl performed an indecent act on him. He returned to his hunt for prey, but the sex act was enough excuse for the policemen to arrest Chikatilo for licentious behavior.

Exiting a café, the cops pushed him against a wall. Chikatilo protested that any suspicion the police officers had was a mistake. He complained that he had been arrested in 1984 for murder and had been allowed to go free. There had been some "confusion" over a DNA match, he said. However, a strip search of the suspect now revealed a further piece of evidence: One of Chikatilo's fingers had a flesh wound. A doctor concluded the wound was, in fact, from a human bite—Tishchenko's bite—and a finger bone was broken and his fingernail had been bitten off, Chikatilo had never sought medical attention for the injury. In his briefcase police found a kitchen knife with an eight-inch blade together some lengths of rope and a jar of petroleum jelly.

Police knew their case against Chikatilo was largely circumstantial. The strategy chosen by the police force to make him confess included one of the chief interrogators telling Chikatilo that they all believed he was a very sick man and needed psychiatric help. The strategy was to give Chikatilo hope that if he confessed, he would escape prosecution by reason of insanity.

Nine days passed without a true confession of his crimes, only vague hints and evasions. Finally, at the request of Burakov and Fetisov, the psychiatrist who had written the 1985 psychological profile of the then-unknown killer for the investigators, Dr. Aleksandr Bukhanovsky, was invited to assist with the questioning of the suspect. Bukhanovsky read extracts from his sixty-five-page psychological profile to Chikatilo. Within two hours, he confessed to thirty-six murders police had linked to the killer. On November 30, 1990, he was formerly charged with all of them.

Because he had been duped by police into thinking that he would escape execution because he was mentally ill, the garrulous Chikatilo confessed to twenty more murders that had not been connected to the case, either because the crimes had been committed outside the Rostov Oblast or because the bodies had not yet been found.

In December 1990, Chikatilo led police to the body of Alexey Khobotov, a boy he confessed to killing in 1989, whom he had buried in woodland near a Shakhty cemetery, proving unequivocally that he was the killer. Later, he took investigators to the bodies of two other victims he confessed to having murdered. Three of the fifty-six victims could not be found or identified, but, in total, he was charged with fifty-three killings of women and children between 1978 and 1990.

By this time his blood and semen had been tested. Twenty-one lives would have been saved if only this had been done in 1984.

Chikatilo was segregated from the general prison population for fears about his safety. Like everywhere else in the world, sexual crimes against children are taboo, and child sex molesters and child killers become "untouchables" and "cast down" by other prisoners. There was every chance that he could be murdered by another inmate.

While in his cell, Chikatilo was placed under twenty-four-hour CCTV surveillance. He often acted bizarrely in front of his interrogators or prison staff—still playing the "I am nuts" game to convince them that he was insane—but inside his cell he acted normally, unable to maintain the façade around the clock. He ate well and slept like a log. He exercised every morning and spent a lot of time writing letters and making complaints to his family, government officials, and the mass media.

The Soviet Union collapsed on Sunday, August 18, 1991, when Boris Yeltsin seized power in the aftermath of a failed coup that had intended to topple reform-minded Mikhail Gorbachev. On August 20, after completing the interrogation of Chikatilo and having carried out a re-enactment of all the murders at each crime scene, he was transferred to the Serbsky Institute in Moscow for a six-day psychiatric evaluation to determine whether he was mentally competent to stand trial.

On October 18, Chikatilo was analyzed by a senior psychiatrist, Dr. Andrei Tkachenko, who declared that although he was a sado-sexual psychopath, Chikatilo was legally competent.

Then, the day before his trial started, Chikatilo threw a wrench in the works; he started to play even crazier. He became Mr. Hyde, withdrawing his confessions to six of the murders, now claiming seventy victims.

The trial of Chikatilo was the first major event of post-Soviet Russia. Chikatilo stood trial in Rostov-on-Don Regional Court beginning on Tuesday, April 14, 1992, during which time he was kept in a specially designed iron cage in a corner of the courtroom to protect him from attack by the many hysterical relatives of his victims. His head had been shaven—a standard prison precaution against lice—which had the effect of making him look even more evil than he already did. Relatives frequently shouted threats and insults at him throughout the case, demanding the authorities to release him so they could kill him themselves. Each murder was discussed indi-vidually, and on several occasions, relatives broke down in tears when details of their relatives' gruesome murders were revealed.

They heard that he would bite off his victims' tongues and breasts and eat them, cut off the noses and lips, slice off boys' genitals—or remove the testes, leaving the empty scrotal sac—and excise the girls' internal reproductive organs, then devour them on the spot, sometimes cooking them over a rough fire scrambled together in the forest. Family members retched, while others hastily left the court to vomit. At one point during the proceedings, the female clerk of the court fainted and had to be replaced. Even hardened soldiers keeping guard collapsed.

So vicious was his butchery, the court learned, that a number of Russian policemen—who are as hard as cops can get—broke down and requested to be removed from the case. Most chilling of all, sometimes forensic evidence suggested that the savage-

*The uteruses were so beautiful and elastic.*

—ANDREI CHIKATILO, DURING HIS TRIAL

ry had taken place while the victim still lived, that it was the pain and torture, more than death, that gave Chikatilo his horrible pleasure. He had carved slits in some corpses to use for his own brand of necrophiliac sex.

Through it all, the crowds keened, wailed and shouted. An elderly woman denounced Chikatilo as "a damned soul and an evil sadist." The aunt of one murdered boy shouted at one point, "This trial is rubbing salt into the wounds of the relatives of the victims." Voicing a popular opinion, she demanded, "Liquidate the criminal. Too much money is being spent on supporting his life."

Many others concurred. Chikatilo had confessed, they said. "What's the point of even having a trial...What's the use of announcing the verdict? It would have been a better idea to shoot him here at once," said a student from a nearby college.

The grief of parents who had lost sons and daughters was pitiable. Nina Beletskaya, whose twelve-year-old son, Ivan, disappeared and was murdered in Zaporozhe, Ukraine, in 1987 after going to pick apricots in the forest near their home, broke down completely while talking to a journalist: "The day I buried my son, I gave him my word I would try long enough to see this killer with my own eyes," she said. "I wanted to see this man who could rip open my son's stomach and then stuff mud in his mouth so that he would not cry out. I wanted to know what he looked like, to know which mothers could bear such an animal. And now I see him...look he is still smiling. He's taken part of my life...He's an animal. He doesn't deserve a human trial."

Lida Khovata, whose ten-year-old son was murdered in August 1989, said, "It's so painful I can't even describe it. I have no wish other than to kill him. I just want this to end."

Fayina Chikatilo also had good reason to feel sick. When she was first told her husband had been arrested, she thought it was because he had been making a nuisance of himself with the authorities, protesting in numerous letters about some garages being built close to his son's house. She could not believe that Andrei was really capable of the terrible things they were saying he had done. After all, hadn't he always been a devoted father who loved his own children? How could he perpetrate such abominably evil acts upon other small children? As for these crimes being sexually motivated, she found this hard to understand because of his lack of interest in sex with her. When she accepted the truth, she also began to fit pieces of the jigsaw puzzle into place: the business trips and the nights away; the blood he sometimes had on his clothes, which he claimed was from cuts he had suffered when unloading goods. Unreasonably, Fayina felt a huge burden of guilt that she was to blame for trusting him and not inquiring too deeply into his activities. If she had, she said, she would have done something to stop him, but "I could never imagine him being able to murder one person, let alone fifty-three...he could never hurt anyone."

Overcoming her revulsion, she visited her husband just once to get his authorization for her to have access to the couple's savings. Hanging his head like a naughty child, Chikatilo could not meet his wife's penetrating gaze but used his pet name for her. "If only I had listened to you, Fenechka...If only I had listened to your advice and got treatment," he whined. Fayina was too appalled to have anything more to do with her husband. The two children, Ludmila and Yuri, found it equally hard to come to terms with the fact that they had been fathered by such a heinous monster. The family were later forced to change their name and move away after receiving death threats.

Chikatilo regularly interrupted the proceedings by rattling the bars of his cage, dropping his trousers or tearing off his clothes to wave his penis in court, screaming, "Look at this useless thing. What do you think I could do with that?" before loudly singing the Russian anthem "Internationale," only then to produce pornographic magazines.

*I crossed him out of my mind as if he never existed.*

—Fayina Chikatilo, to writer Peter Conradi

He refused to answer questions put to him. He was regularly removed from the court when he persisted in trying to make a nuisance of himself.

Another time-wasting strategy was to declare that he wanted the trial conducted in his native Ukrainian language and demand an interpreter. Yet another was to claim hallucinations and offer the belief that the KGB was firing invisible rays at him—standard schizophrenic symptoms suddenly harnessed by a killer playing a madman to Oscar-winning standards. Once again he was dragged back to his cell and given a beating by the guards.

During the trial, Judge Leonid Akhobzyanov remarked, "He was constantly on the lookout for victims. On holidays, on business trips, visiting relatives. This defendant was already ready to kill." In July, Chikatilo, dressed in gray trousers and an old shirt decorated with the five-ring symbol of the 1980 Moscow Olympics, countered the judge's remark by cooling stating, "I did not need to look for them. Every step they were there. I am a mistake of nature, a mad beast. I have led a wretched life, constantly having to travel to work and stay in dirty railway stations and miserable hotels and put up with the rudeness of my bosses." Chikatilo began lolling his head, rolling his eyes, gnashing his teeth, and drooling.

Then Chikatilo demanded that Judge Akhobzyanov be replaced for making too many rash remarks about his guilt. His defense counsel backed his claim. The judge looked to the prosecutor, and even the prosecutor backed the defense's judgement, stating the judge had made too many such remarks. Not to be outdone, the judge replaced the prosecutor instead.

On Sunday, August 9, 1992, after an almost five-month hearing, both prosecution and defense, led by Marat Khabibulin, delivered their final arguments before the judge. Chikatilo yet again attempted to interrupt proceedings and had to be removed from the courtroom. Final sentencing was postponed until October 14, and, as the final deliberations began, the brother of Lyudmila Alekseyeva threw a metal ball at Chikatilo, missing him by inches. When security tried to arrest the young man, other victims' relatives shielded him, preventing him from being taken into custody.

When the court reconvened on October 14, the judge read the list of murders again, not finishing until the following day when Chikatilo was found guilty of fifty-two of the fifty-three murders and sentenced to death for each offense. He kicked his bench across his cage when he heard the news and started hurling abuse. "Swindlers!" he screamed. Guards around the metal cage tried to grab the spitting, biting man as the angry crowed bayed for his blood. "You gave him nothing! Give this murderer to us!" cried one woman. Others screamed, "Give him to us so that we can tear him to pieces, as he did to our children!"

When offered a final chance to make a speech in response to the verdict, he clammed up.

Upon passing final sentence, amid shouts of fury and applause, the judge said:

> Taking into consideration the monstrous crimes he committed, this court has no alternative but to impose the only sentence he deserves. I, therefore, sentence him to death.

# Other Ulysses Press Books

Online Killers: Portraits of Murderers, Cannibals and
Sex Predators Who Stalked the Web for Their Victims
*Christopher Berry-Dee and Steven Morris, $14.95*

It starts as a harmless online date but can quickly turn to kidnap,
torture, and death. More than just tales of sinister criminals,
this collection of true horror store chronicles the stories of men,
women, and children whose Internet adventures led them into
disastrous circumstances.

Serial Killers: Up Close and Personal: Inside the World of
Torturers, Psychopaths, and Mass Murderers
*Christopher Berry-Dee, $15.95*

The headline-grabbing crime. The grizzly facts in the coroner's
report. The shocking revelations from the trial. Going deep into
the bowels of the world's toughest prisons to face these monsters
and hear their stories, this book provides all these details plus one
more: the murderer's first-person perspective.

How to Make a Serial Killer: The Twisted Development of
Innocent Children into the World's Most Sadistic Murderers
*Christopher Berry-Dee and Steven Morris, $13.95*

They were born into this world as innocent children. They ended
up as merciless killing machines. This book leads the reader on
an insightful, scary, and often disturbing investigation into what
made these infamous murderers go bad.

Serial Killers and Mass Murderers: Profiles of the World's
Most Barbaric Criminals
*Nigel Cawthorne, $14.95*

In one chilling chapter after another, this book profiles a terrifying
succession of homicidal maniacs. It takes readers inside the
minds of the people who committed the world's most notorious
and horrendous crimes.

Serial Killer Timelines: Illustrated Day-by-Day Accounts
of the World's Most Gruesome Murders
*Dr. Chris McNab, $16.95*

By examining the depraved, deceptive, very deliberate actions
of famed serial killers as a series of specific events, this fully
illustrated book offers a unique perspective on the working of
the criminal mind and breaks down step by step how they did
it, how they got away with it for so long, and how they finally
got caught.

To order any of our titles directly call 800-377-2542 or 510-601-8301; fax 510-601-8307; e-mail ulysses@ulyssespress.com; or write to Ulysses Press, P.O. Box 3440, Berkeley, CA 94703. All retail orders are shipped free of charge. California residents must include sales tax. Allow two to three weeks for delivery.

# About the Author

**Christopher Berry-Dee** is an investigative criminologist who has published several papers and books, including *Online Killers, Serial Killers: Up Close and Personal,* and *How to Make a Serial Killer.* He is the director of The Criminology Research Institute and owner of *The New Criminologist,* the world's most respected professional journal on all matters criminology. He consults with law enforcement world-wide, lectures on serial murder, and is responsible for solving a number of U.S. murder cases. Chris has homes in the UK and Samara, Russia.